Rebecca Springer

Within Heaven's Gates

D0972524

Originally entitled: INTRA MUROS

All Scripture quotations are from the King James Version (KJV) of the Bible.

Editor's note: This book has been edited for the modern reader. Words, expressions, and sentence structure have been updated for clarity and readability.

WITHIN HEAVEN'S GATES
(originally published as *Intra Muros*)

ISBN: 0-88368-125-0
Printed in the United States of America
© 1984 by Whitaker House
Cover Photo: Fred Sieb

Whitaker House
30 Hunt Valley Circle
New Kensington, PA 15068
Visit our web site at: www.whitakerhouse.com

No part of this book may be reproduced or transmitted in any form or by any means, electronic or mechanical, including photocopying, recording, or by any information storage and retrieval system, without permission in writing from the publisher.

12 13 14 15 16 17 18 / 09 08 07 06 05 04 03

CONTENTS

Author's Preface   5
1. The Journey Begins   7
2. My Celestial Home   16
3. The Paradise Life   25
4. Meeting Loved Ones   30
5. Meeting The Master   40
6. A Child's Homecoming   49
7. A Divine Speech   55
8. Rebecca Meets Her Sister   61
9. A Visit With A Special Friend   69
10. A Visit To The Heavenly City   74
11. The Temple   82
12. Meeting Special Friends   89
13. A Reunion Of Mother And Son   93
14. The Best Reunion Of All   98
15. The Celestial Sea   106
16. The Vision Ends   111
17. Reflections   113

AUTHOR'S PREFACE

This volume is not a fancy sketch, written to while away the hours. Rather, it is the true, though greatly condensed, record of an experience when my life hung in the balance between time and eternity, with the scales leaning toward the eternity side.

I am painfully aware of the fact that I can never paint the scenes as they appeared to me during those wonderful days. If I can only dimly show the close link between the two lives—the mortal and the divine—as they appeared to me then, I may be able to partially tear the veil from the death we so dread. Thus I can show it to be an open door into a new and beautiful phase of the life we now live.

I must state that this glorious vision of heaven is not necessarily a definitive or exact revelation of what heaven will be like. As I learned, heaven partially consists of those things which make us happiest on earth—wonderfully glorified by the presence of the Master. In this respect, my vision is not everyone's vision.

If any of the scenes depicted seem irreverent in view of our Christian training here, I can only say, "I give it as it came to me." In those strange, happy hours, the close blending of the two lives, so wrapped about with the Father's watchful care and tender love, filled me with unspeakable joy. The reunion of friends, the satisfied desires, and the glad surprises—all intensified and illuminated by the reverence, love, and adoration that all hearts gave to the blessed Trinity—appeared to me as a most perfect glimpse of that "blessed life" of which we so fondly dream. I submit this imperfect sketch of a most perfect vision with the hope that it may comfort and uplift those who read it.

R.R.S.

Chapter 1

THE JOURNEY BEGINS

Several hundred miles away from home and friends, I had been very ill for many weeks. I was entirely among strangers, and my only attendant, though a kind person, knew nothing about caring for the ill. As a result, I had none of the many delicate attentions which maintain an invalid's failing strength. I had received no nourishment of any kind for nearly three weeks, scarcely even water, and was greatly reduced in both flesh and strength. Consciousness seemed to wholly desert me at times.

I had an unutterable longing for the presence of my distant loved ones. I needed the gentle touch of their beloved hands and their whispered words of love and courage. But, they never came—they could not. Responsible duties, that I felt must not be neglected, kept these loved ones away, and I would not recall them.

I lay in a large, comfortable room, on the second floor of a house in Kentville, Canada. The bed stood in an alcove at one end of the apartment and faced a large, stained-glass window which opened upon a veranda overlooking the street. During much of my illness I lay with my face to this window and my back to the room. I remember thinking how easy it would be to pass through the window to the veranda, if one so desired.

When the longing for the loved faces and voices became more than I could bear, I prayed that the dear Christ would help me to realize His blessed presence. Since the beloved ones of earth could not minister to me, I longed to be comforted by other dear ones who are "all ministering spirits."

A Vision

I especially asked to be sustained should I indeed be called to pass through the dark waters alone. It was no idle prayer, and the response came swiftly, speedily. All anxieties and cares slipped away from me, as a worn-out garment, and peace, Christ's peace, enfolded me. I was willing to wait God's time for the coming of those so dear to me and often said to myself, "If not here, it will be there. There is no fear of disappointment there."

In those wonderful days of agonized suffering and great peace, I felt that I had truly found, as never before, the refuge of "the Everlasting Arms." They lifted me; they upheld me; they enfolded me. I rested in them as a tired child upon its mother's bosom.

One dark, cold, and stormy morning, after a day and night of intense suffering, I seemed to be standing on the floor by the bed, in front of the stained-glass window. Someone was standing beside me. When I looked up, I saw it was my husband's favorite brother who had "crossed the flood" many years ago.

"My dear brother-in-law Frank!" I cried out joyously, "how good of you to come!"

"It was a great joy to me that I could do so, little sister," he said gently. "Shall we go now?" and he drew me toward the window.

Leaving The Earth-Life

I turned my head and looked back into the room that I felt I was about to leave forever. It was in its usual good order: a cheery, pretty room. The attendant sat by the stove at the farther end, comfortably reading a newspaper. On the bed, turned toward the window, lay a white, still form with the shadow of a smile on the poor, worn face. Frank drew me gently, and I yielded. I went with him through the window, out onto the veranda, and from there, in some unaccountable way, down to the street. There I paused and said earnestly, "I cannot leave Will and our dear boy."

"They are not here, dear, but hundreds of miles away," he answered.

"Yes, I know, but they will be here. Oh, Frank, they will need me—let me stay!"

"Would it not be better if I brought you back a little later—after they come?"

"Would you surely do so?"

"Most certainly, if you desire it. You are worn

out with the long suffering, and a little rest will give you new strength."

I felt that he was right, so we started slowly up the street. He had drawn my hand within his arm and tried to distract me as we walked. But my heart clung to the dear ones whom I felt I was not to see again on earth. Several times I stopped and looked wistfully back the way we had come. He was very patient and gentle with me, always waiting until I was ready to proceed again. At last my hesitation became so great that he said pleasantly, "You are so weak I think I had better carry you."

Without waiting for a reply, he stooped and lifted me in his arms as though I were a little child. And, like a child, I yielded, resting my head on his shoulder and laying my arm around his neck. I felt so safe, so content, to be in his care. It seemed so sweet, after the long, lonely struggle, to have someone assume the responsibility of caring this tenderly for me.

Entering Paradise

He walked on with firm, swift steps. I think I must have slept, for the next I knew, I was sitting in a sheltered nook, made by flowering shrubs. I was resting upon the softest and most beautiful turf of grass, thickly studded with fragrant flowers. Many of them were flowers I had known and loved on earth. I remember noticing heliotrope, violets, lilies of the valley, and mignonette, with many similar species wholly unfamiliar to me.

But, even in that first moment, I observed how

perfect each plant and flower was. For instance, the heliotrope, which on earth often runs into long, ragged sprays, there grew upon short, smooth stems. Each leaf was perfect and smooth and glossy, instead of being rough and coarse-looking. The flowers peeped up from the deep grass, so like velvet, with sweet, happy faces, as though inviting the admiration one could not withhold.

What a scene I beheld as I rested upon this soft, fragrant cushion, secluded and yet not hidden! Away, away—far beyond the limit of my vision— stretched this wonderful field of perfect grass and flowers. Out of it grew equally wonderful trees, whose drooping branches were laden with exqui-site blossoms and fruits of many kinds. I found myself thinking of John's vision in the Isle of Pat-mos and "the tree of life" that grew in the midst of the garden, bearing "twelve manner of fruits. . .and the leaves of the tree were for the healing of the nations" (Revelation 22:2).

Beneath the trees, in many happy groups, little children were laughing and playing. They were running around filled with joy and catching bright-winged birds that flitted in and out among them, as though sharing in their sports. All through the grounds, older people were walking with an air of peacefulness and happiness that made itself felt even by me, a stranger. All were clothed in spot-less white, though many wore or carried clusters of beautiful flowers. As I looked at their happy faces and their spotless robes, again I thought,

"These are they. . .which have washed their robes, and made them white in the blood of the Lamb" (Revelation 7:14).

Everywhere I looked, I saw, half-hidden by the trees, elegant and beautiful houses of strangely attractive architecture. I felt these must be the homes of the happy inhabitants of this enchanted place. I caught glimpses of sparkling fountains in many directions, and close to me a placid River flowed with water clear as crystal. The walks that ran in many directions through the grounds appeared to be made of pearl, spotless and pure, bordered on either side by narrow streams of clear water, running over stones of gold.

The one thought that fastened itself upon me as I looked, breathless and speechless, upon this scene was, "Purity, purity!" There was no shadow of dust, no taint of decay on fruit or flower. Everything was perfect; everything was pure. The grass and flowers looked as though they were freshly washed by summer showers, and not a single blade was any color but the brightest green. The air was soft and balmy, though invigorating. Instead of sunlight there was a golden and rosy glory everywhere. It resembled the afterglow of a southern sunset in midsummer.

As I drew in my breath with a short, quick gasp of delight, I heard my brother-in-law, who was standing beside me, say softly, "Well?" Looking up, I discovered that he was watching me with keen enjoyment. I had, in my great surprise and delight, wholly forgotten his presence.

The River Of Life

Recalled to myself by his question, I faltered, "Oh, Frank, that I—" when such an overpowering sense of God's goodness and my own unworthiness swept over me. I dropped my face into my hands and burst into uncontrollable and very human weeping.

"Ah!" said my brother-in-law, in a tone of self-reproach, "I am inconsiderate." He lifted me gently to my feet. "Come, I want to show you the River."

When we reached the brink of the River, a few steps away, I found that the lovely field ran even to the water's edge. In some places I saw the flowers blooming placidly down in the depths, among the many-colored pebbles with which the entire bed of the River was lined.

"I want you to see these beautiful stones," said Frank, stepping into the water and urging me to do the same.

I drew back timidly, "I fear it is cold."

"Not in the least," he said, with a reassuring smile. "Come."

"Just as I am?" I said, glancing down at my lovely robe, which, to my great joy, I found was similar to those of the dwellers in that happy place.

"Just as you are," with another reassuring smile.

Thus encouraged, I, too, stepped into the gently flowing River. To my great surprise I found the water, in both temperature and density, almost identical to the air. Deeper and deeper grew the stream as we passed on, until I felt the soft, sweet ripples playing about my throat. As I stopped, Frank said, "A little farther still."

"It will be over my head," I reasoned.

"Well, and what then?"

"I cannot breathe under the water—I will suffocate."

An amused twinkle came into his eyes, though he said soberly enough, "We do not do those things here."

I realized the absurdity of my position and with a happy laugh said, "All right." Then I plunged headlong into the bright water, which soon bubbled and rippled several feet above my head. To my surprise and delight, I found I could breathe, laugh, talk, see, and hear as naturally under the water as above it. I sat down in the midst of the many-colored pebbles and filled my hands with them as a child would have done. My brother-in-law lay down upon them, as he would have done on the green field, and laughed and talked joyously with me.

"Do this," he said, rubbing his hands over his face and running his fingers through his dark hair.

I did as he told me, and the sensation was delightful. I threw back my loose sleeves and rubbed my arms, then my throat. Again I thrust my fingers through my long, loose hair, thinking at the time how tangled it would be when I left the water. Then the thought came, as we at last arose to return, "What are we to do for towels?" for the earth-thoughts still clung to me. I also wondered if the lovely robe was entirely spoiled. But, as we neared the shore and emerged from the water, the moment the air struck my face and hair I realized that I would not need a towel or brush. My flesh, my hair, and even my beautiful garments were soft and dry as before the water touched them.

The material out of which my robe was fashioned was unlike anything I had ever seen. It was soft and light and shone with a faint luster, reminding me more of silk crepe than anything I could recall, only infinitely more beautiful. It fell about me in soft, graceful folds, which the water seemed to have rendered even more lustrous than before.

"What marvelous water! What wonderful air!" I said to Frank, as we again stepped upon the flowery field. "Are all the rivers here like this one?"

"Not exactly the same, but similar," he replied.

We walked on a few steps, and then I turned and looked back at the shining River flowing on tranquilly. "Frank, what has that water done for me? I feel as though I could fly."

He looked at me with earnest, tender eyes, as he answered gently, "It has washed away the last of the earth-life and prepared you for the new life upon which you have entered."

"It is divine!" I whispered.

"Yes, it *is* divine," he said.

Chapter 2

MY CELESTIAL HOME

We walked on for some distance in silence, my heart wrestling with the thoughts of the new, strange life, my eyes drinking in fresh beauty at every step. The houses, as we approached and passed them, seemed wondrously beautiful to me. They were built of the finest marbles and were encircled by broad verandas. The roofs or domes were supported by either massive or delicate columns.

Winding steps led down to pearl and golden walks. The style of the architecture was unlike anything I had ever seen. The flowers and vines that luxuriously grew everywhere surpassed in beauty even those of my brightest dreams. Happy faces looked out from these columned walls, and happy voices rang through the clear air from many a celestial home.

"Frank, where are we going?" I asked.

"Home, little sister," he answered tenderly.

"Home? Do we have a home? Is it anything like these?" I asked, with a great desire in my heart to cry out for joy.

Rebecca's Mansion In Heaven

"Come and see," was his only answer, as he turned onto a side path leading toward an exquisitely beautiful house whose columns of very light gray marble shone through the green of the overhanging trees with most inviting beauty. Before I could join him, I heard a familiar voice saying, "I just had to be the first to bid you welcome!" Looking around, I saw the beloved face of my dear friend, Mrs. Wickham.

"Oh! Oh!" I cried, as we met in a warm embrace.

"You will forgive me, Colonel Springer," she said a moment later, giving her hand cordially to my brother-in-law. "It seems unpardonable to intercept you thus, in almost the first hour. But I heard that she was coming, and I could not wait. Now that I have looked upon her face and heard her dear voice, I will be patient until I can have her for a long, long talk."

"You must come in and see her now," said Frank cordially.

"Do, do come!" I urged.

"No, dear friends, not now. You know, dear little Blossom" (the old pet name for me years ago), "we have all eternity before us! But you will bring her to me soon, Colonel Springer?" she said.

"Just as soon as I may, dear madam," he replied, with an expressive look into her eyes.

"Yes, I understand," she said softly. Then with a

warm hand-clasp and the parting injunction, "Come very soon," she passed swiftly out of my sight.

"Blessed woman!" I said, "what a joy to meet her again!"

"Her home is not far away. You can see her often. She is indeed a lovely woman. Now, come, little sister, I long to welcome you to our home." He took my hand and led me up the low steps onto the broad veranda. Its beautiful inlaid floor was of rare and costly marble, and its massive columns were silver-gray. Between the columns were vines covered with rich, glossy leaves of green intermingled with flowers of exquisite color and delicate perfume hanging in heavy garlands. We paused a moment here, that I might see the charming view visible on every side.

"It is heavenly!" I said.

"It is heavenly," he answered. "It could not be otherwise."

I smiled my acknowledgment of this truth—my heart was too full for words.

"The entire house, both below and above, is surrounded by these broad verandas. But, come within."

Divine Artistry

He led me through a doorway, between the marble columns, into a large reception hall whose inlaid floor, mullioned window, and broad, low stairway captivated me at once. Before I could speak, Frank turned to me and, taking both my

18

hands, said, "Welcome, a thousand welcomes, dearest Rebecca, to your heavenly home!"

"Is this beautiful place indeed to be my home?" I asked.

"Yes, dear," he replied. "I built it for you and my brother, and I assure you it has been a labor of love."

"It is your home, and I am to stay with you?" I asked, a little confused.

"No, it is your home, and I am to stay with you until my brother comes."

"Always, dear Frank, always!" I cried, clinging to his arm.

He smiled and said, "We will enjoy the present. We never will be far apart again. Come, I am eager to show you all."

Turning to the left, he led me through the beautiful marble columns that substituted for doorways into a large, oblong room. I stopped in wondering delight upon the threshold. The entire walls and floor of the room were still made of that exquisite light gray marble, polished to the greatest luster. But over the walls and floors were strewn gorgeous, long-stemmed roses, of every variety and color, from the deepest crimson to the most delicate shades of pink and yellow.

"Come inside," said Frank.

"I do not wish to crush those perfect flowers," I answered.

"Well, then, suppose we gather some of them."

I stooped to take one from the floor close to my feet, when I found it was embedded in the marble.

I tried another with the same astonishing result. Then turning to Frank, I said, "What does it mean? You surely do not mean that none of these are natural flowers?"

He nodded his head with a pleased smile, then said, "This room has a history. Come in and sit with me here upon this window-seat, where you can see the whole room, and let me tell you about it." I did as he desired. He continued, "One day as I was busily working on the house, a company of young people, boys and girls, came to the door and asked if they might enter. I gladly consented. Then one of them said: 'Is this house really for Mr. and Mrs. Springer?'

" 'It is,' I answered.

" 'We used to know and love them. They are our friends and the friends of our parents. May we do something to help you make it beautiful?'

" 'Indeed you may,' I said, touched by the request. 'What can you do?'

"At once the girls, all of whom had immense bouquets of roses in their hands, began to toss the flowers over the floor and against the walls. Wherever they struck the walls, they, to even my surprise, remained, as though in some way permanently attached. When the roses had all been scattered, the room looked just as it does now, only then the flowers were fresh-gathered roses.

"Then the boys each produced a small case of delicate tools. In a moment they were all down upon the marble floor, busy at work. How they did it I do not know—it is one of the celestial arts, taught to those of highly artistic tastes—but they embedded each living flower just as it had fallen. They preserved it in the marble as you see before you. They came several times before the work was completed, for the flowers do not wither or fade here, but are always fresh and perfect.

"I never saw such a merry, happy company of young people. They laughed and chatted and sang as they worked. I could not help wishing more than once that the friends whom they had left mourning for them might look in on this happy group and see how little cause they had for sorrow.

"At last, when all was complete, they called me to see their work. And I was not sparse in my praises either for the beauty of the work or for their skill in performing it. Then, saying they would be sure to return when either of you came, they went away together to do similar work."

Happy tears had been streaming down my cheeks during much of this narrative. I asked, overcome with emotion for I was greatly touched, "Who are these lovely people, Frank? Do you know them?"

"Of course, I know them now. But they were all strangers to me until they came here that first morning, except Lulu Springer."

"Who were they?"

"There were three Marys—Mary Green, Mary Bates, Mary Chalmers—Lulu Springer and Mae Camden. These were the girls, each lovely and beautiful. The boys, all manly, fine fellows, were

Carroll Ashland and Stanley and David Chalmers."

Building For Eternity

"Precious children!" I said. "How little I thought my earthly love for them would ever bring me this added happiness here! How little we know of the links binding the two worlds!"

"Ah, yes!" said Frank, "that is just it. How little we know! If only we realized while we are mortals that day by day we are building for eternity. How different our lives in many ways would be! Every gentle word, every generous thought, every unselfish deed will become a pillar of eternal beauty in the life to come. We cannot be selfish and unloving in one life and generous and loving in the next. The two lives are too closely blended—one is but a continuation of the other. But come now to the library."

Rising, we walked through the room that, from this moment on, was to hold for me such tender associations, and then we entered the library. It was a glorious room—the walls lined from ceiling to floor with rare and costly books. A large, stained-glass window opened upon the front veranda. A semicircular row of shelves, supported by very delicate pillars of gray marble, about six feet high, extended some fifteen feet into the spacious main room and cut it into two sections lengthwise. The concave side of the semicircle of shelves was toward the entrance of the room. Close to it stood a beautiful writing desk, with everything ready for use. There was a chaste golden bowl filled with scarlet carnations whose spicy odor I had been dimly conscious of for some time.

"My brother's desk," said Frank.

"And his favorite flowers," I added.

"Yes, that follows. Here we never forget the tastes and preferences of those we love."

I did not notice these details at once, but they unfolded to me gradually as we lingered, talking together. My first sensation upon entering the room was genuine surprise at the sight of the books.

"Why do we have books in heaven?" I asked.

"Why not?" asked my brother-in-law. "What strange ideas we mortals have of the pleasures and duties of this blessed life! We seem to think that death of the body means an entire change to the soul. But that is not the case, by any means. We bring to this life the same tastes, the same desires, and the same knowledge we had before death. If these were not sufficiently pure and good to form a part of this life, then we ourselves may not enter.

"What would be the use of our long lives, given to the pursuit of certain worthy and legitimate knowledge, if at death it all counts as nothing, and we begin this life on a wholly different line of thought and study? No, no.

"If only we all could understand, as I said before, that we are building for eternity during our earthly life! The purer the thoughts, the nobler the ambitions, the loftier the aspirations, the higher the rank we take among the hosts of heaven. The more earnestly we follow the studies and duties in our life of probation, the better prepared we will be to carry them forward, on and on to completion and perfection here."

"But the books—who writes them? Are any of them books we knew and loved below?"

"Undoubtedly, many of them; all, indeed, that in any way helped to elevate the human mind or immortal soul. Many of the rarest minds in the earth-life, upon entering this higher life, gain such elevated and extended views that, pursuing them with zest, they write for the benefit of those less gifted. They express the higher, stronger views they have themselves acquired, thus remaining leaders and teachers in this rarer life, as they were while yet in the world.

"Is it to be expected that the great souls of those who have so recently joined our ranks, and who uplifted so many lives while on earth, should lay aside their pens? Not so. When they have learned their lessons well, they will write them out for the benefit of others, less gifted, who must follow. Leaders there must always be, in this divine life as in the former life, leaders and teachers in many varied lines of thought. But all this knowledge will come to you simply and naturally as you grow into this new life."

Chapter 3

THE PARADISE LIFE

After a short rest in this lovely room among the books, Frank took me through all the remaining rooms of the house. Each was perfect and beautiful in its own way, and each was distinctly and imperishably etched in my memory. I will only speak of one other room at this time. As he drew aside the gauzy, gray draperies, lined with the most delicate shade of amber, which hung before the columned doorway of a lovely room on the second floor of the house, he said: "Your own special place for rest and study."

Rebecca's Special Room

The entire second story of the house indoors, instead of being finished in gray marble like the first floor, was finished with inlaid woods of fine, satiny texture and rare polish. The room we now entered was exquisite both in design and finish. It was oblong in shape, with a large bowed window at one end, similar to those in the library, a portion of which was directly beneath this room.

Within this window, on one side, stood a writing desk of solid ivory, with silver ornaments. Opposite this was a case of well-filled bookshelves of the same material. Among the books I found many of my favorite authors.

Rich rugs, silver-gray in color, lay scattered over the floor, and all the hangings in the room were of the same delicate hue and texture as those at the entrance.

The framework of the furniture was made of ivory. The upholstering of chairs and ottomans was made of silver-gray cloth, with the finish made of finest satin. And the pillows and covering of the dainty couch were made of the same.

A large bowl of wrought silver stood upon the table near the front window, filled with pink and yellow roses. Their fragrance filled the air. There were also several rare, delicate vases filled with roses.

The entire room was beautiful beyond description. I had seen it many times before I fully comprehended its perfect completeness. My whole being was full of adoration and thanksgiving for the great love that had guided me into this haven of rest, this wonderful home of peace and joy.

Divine Fruit

After visiting this delightful place, we passed through the open window onto the marble terrace. A stairway of artistically-finished marble wound gracefully down from this terrace to the lawn beneath the trees. There was no pathway of any kind approaching at its foot—only the flowery turf.

The fruit-laden branches of the trees hung within easy reach from the terrace, and I noticed seven different types of fruit as I stood there that morning. One kind resembled our fine Bartlett pear, only much larger and infinitely more delicious to the taste, as I soon found. Another variety was in clusters. Its fruit was also pear-shaped but smaller than the former and of a consistency and flavor similar to the finest frozen cream. A third, something like a banana in shape, they called bread-fruit. Its taste was similar to our dainty finger-rolls.

It seemed to me, and really proved to be so, that food for the most elegant feast was provided here without labor or care. Frank gathered some of the different varieties and invited me to try them. I did so with much relish and refreshment. Once the rich juice from the pearlike fruit (whose distinctive name I have forgotten, if indeed I ever knew it) ran out profusely over my hands and down the front of my dress. "Oh!" I cried, "I have ruined my dress!"

Frank laughed as he said, "Show me the stains."

To my amazement not a spot could be found.

"Look at your hands," he said.

I found them clean and fresh, as though just from the bath.

"What does it mean? My hands were covered with the thick juice of the fruit."

"Simply," he answered, "that no impurity can

remain for an instant in this air. Nothing decays, nothing tarnishes, or in anyway disfigures or mars the universal purity or beauty of this place. As fast as the fruit ripens and falls, all that is not immediately gathered at once evaporates, not even the seed remaining."

I had noticed that no fruit lay beneath the trees—this, then, was the reason for it.

" 'And there shall in no wise enter into it any thing that defileth,' " I quoted thoughtfully (Revelation 21:27).

"Yes, even so," he answered. "Even so."

Reunited With Her Family

We descended the steps and again entered the "flower-room." As I stood once more admiring the inlaid roses, Frank asked, "Whom, of all the friends you have in heaven, do you most wish to see?"

"My mother and father," I answered quickly.

He smiled so significantly that I hastily turned. There, advancing up the long room to meet me, I saw my dear father and mother and with them my youngest sister. With a cry of joy, I flew into my father's outstretched arms and heard his dear, familiar, "My precious little daughter!"

"At last! at last!" I cried, clinging to him. "At last I have you again!"

"At last!" he echoed, with a deep-drawn breath of joy. Then he resigned me to my dear mother, and we were soon clasped in each other's embrace.

"My precious mother!" "My dear, dear child!" we cried simultaneously. My sister, enfolding us both in her arms, exclaimed with a happy laugh, "I cannot wait! I will not be left out!" Disengaging one arm, I threw it about her into the happy circle of our united love.

Oh, what joy that was! I did not dream that even heaven could hold such joy. Eventually, Frank, who had shared our joy, said, "Now, I will leave you to this blessed reunion, for I have other work before me."

"Yes," said my father, "you must go. We will with joy take charge of our dear child."

"Then, good-bye," said Frank kindly. "Do not forget that rest, especially to one who recently entered this new life, is not only one of the pleasures, but one of the duties of heaven."

"Yes, we will see that she does not forget that," said my father, with a kindly smile and glance.

Chapter 4

MEETING LOVED ONES

As I grew more accustomed to the heavenly life around me, I found its loveliness unfolded to me like the slow opening of a rare flower. Delightful surprises met me at every turn. A dear friend, from whom I had parted years ago in the earth-life, would come upon me unexpectedly, offering a cordial greeting. Another—perhaps greatly admired on earth, but one I had avoided from the fear of unwelcome intrusion—would approach me, showing their lovely soul so full of kindness that I felt a pang of regret for what I had lost.

Then the clear revelation of some truth, only partly understood in life, though eagerly sought for, would stand out clear and strong before me. It would overwhelm me with its luster and perhaps reveal the close tie linking the earth-life with the divine.

But the most wonderful surprise was the occasional meeting with someone whom I had never hoped to meet "over there." Someone who, with eager handclasp and tearful eyes, would pour forth his earnest thanks for some helpful word, solemn warning, or even a stern rebuke that had turned him, all unknown to myself, from the paths of sin into the "life everlasting." Oh, the joy of such a revelation! Oh, the regret that my earth-life had not been more full of such work for eternity!

Another Reunion

My first impulse on arousing from happy, blissful rest was to rush to the "River of Life" and plunge into its wonderful waters, so refreshing, so invigorating, so inspiring. With a heart full of thanksgiving and lips full of joyful praise, I went there. I always returned to our home full of new life and hope and purpose.

Once, as I was on my way to the River, I saw a lovely young girl approaching me swiftly, with outstretched arms.

"Dear, dear Aunt Rebecca!" she called, as she drew near, "do you not know me?"

"My little Mae!" I cried, gathering the dainty creature into my arms. "Where did you spring from so suddenly, dear? Let me look at you again!" Holding her a moment at arm's length, I then drew her tenderly to me.

"You have grown very beautiful, my child. I may say this to you here without fear, I'm sure. You were always lovely. But you are simply radiant now. Is it this divine life?"

"Yes," she said modestly and sweetly. "But most of all it's being near the Savior so much."

"Ah, yes, that is it—being near Him! That will

31

make any being radiant and beautiful," I said.

"He is so good to me—so generous, so tender! He seems to forget how little I have done to deserve His care."

"He knows you love Him, dear heart. That means everything to Him."

"Love Him? Oh, if loving Him deserves reward, I am sure I ought to have every wish of my heart, for I love Him more than anything in earth or heaven!"

The sweet face grew surpassingly radiant and beautiful as she talked, and I began to dimly understand the wonderful power of Christ among the redeemed in heaven. This dear child, so lovely in all mortal graces, so full of earth's keenest enjoyments during the whole of her brief life, now loved Christ more than anything else. Pure and good, as we count goodness below, yet she was seemingly too absorbed in life's gaieties to think deeply of the things she yet in her heart revered and honored. In this blessed life, she now esteemed the privilege of loving Christ, of being near Him, beyond every other joy!

How that love refined and beautified the giver! As a great earthly love always shines through the face and elevates the whole character of the one who loves, so this divine love uplifts and glorifies the giver. Then not only the face but the entire person radiates the glory that fills the heart.

A Trip To The Lake

"Come with me to the River, Mae," I said presently, after we had talked together. "Come with me for a delightful plunge."

"Gladly," she said, "but have you ever been to the lake or the sea?"

"The lake or the sea? No indeed. Are there a lake and sea here?"

"Certainly there are," said Mae, with a little pardonable pride that she should know more of the heavenly surroundings than I. "Shall we go to the lake and leave the sea for another time? Which will it be?"

"Let it be the lake," I said.

So, turning in an entirely different direction from the path that led to the River, we walked joyously on, still talking as we went. So much to ask, so much to recall, so much to look forward to with joy!

Once she turned to me and asked quickly, "When is my Uncle Will coming?"

My hand closed tightly over hers, and a sob almost rose in my throat, though I answered calmly, "That is in God's hands alone. We may not question."

"Yes, I know. His will is always right. But I so long to see my dear uncle again. And to *long* is not to be discontent."

She had grown so womanly, so wise, this child of tender years, since we parted. It was truly a joy to talk with her. I told her of my journey from earth and the sorrow of the dear ones I had left.

"Yes, yes, I know it all!" she whispered, with her soft arms about me. "But it will not be long to wait. They will come soon. It never seems long to wait for anything here. There is always so much to keep one busy; there are so many pleasant duties, so many joys—oh, it will not be long!"

Heaven's Golden Glory

Thus she cheered and comforted me as we walked through the ever-varying and always-perfect landscape. At length she cried, lifting her arm and pointing with her rosy finger, "Behold! Is it not divinely beautiful?"

I caught my breath, then stopped abruptly and covered my face with my hands to shield my eyes from the glorified scene. No wonder Frank had not brought me to this place sooner. I was scarcely yet spiritually strong enough to look upon it. When I again slowly lifted my head, Mae was standing like one entranced. The golden light rested upon her face and, mingling with the radiance from within, almost transfigured her. Even she, so long an inhabitant here, had not yet grown accustomed to its glory.

"Look, darling Auntie! It is God's will that you should see," she softly whispered, not once turning her eyes away from the scene before her. "He let me be the one to show you the glory of this place!"

I turned and looked, like one only half awake. Before us spread a lake as smooth as glass, but flooded with a golden glory caught from the heavens. It was like a sea of molten gold. The blossom and fruit-bearing trees grew down to its very border in many places. Far, far away, across its shining waters, arose the domes and spires of what seemed to be a mighty city.

Many people were resting upon its flowery banks, and on the surface of the water were boats of wonderful structure, filled with happy souls and propelled by an unseen power. Little children, as well as grown persons, were floating upon or swimming in the water. As we looked, a band of singing cherubs, floating high overhead, drifted across the lake, their sweet voices borne to us where we stood, in notes of joyful praise.

"Come," said Mae, seizing my hand, "let us join them." We hastened onward.

"Glory and honor!" sang the child voices. "Dominion and power!" caught up and answered the voices of the vast multitude together. And I found that Mae and I were joining in the refrain. The cherub band floated onward. Away in the distance we caught the faint melody of their sweet voices and the stronger cadence of the response from those waiting below.

We stood upon the bank of the lake. My cheeks were tear-stained and my eyes dim with emotion. I felt weak as a little child. But oh, what rapture, what joy unspeakable filled and overmastered me! Was I dreaming? Or was this indeed but another phase of the immortal life?

Mae slipped her arm about my neck and whispered, "Dearest, come. After the rapture—rest."

I yielded to her passively; I could not do otherwise. She led me into the water, down, down into its crystal depths. When it seemed to me we must be hundreds of feet beneath the surface, she threw herself prostrate and bade me do the same. I did so, and immediately we began to slowly rise. Presently I found that we no longer rose, but were slowly floating in mid-current still many feet beneath the surface.

Then a marvel appeared to me. Wherever I looked, perfect, prismatic rays surrounded me. I seemed to be resting in the heart of a prism. And such vivid yet delicate coloring, mortal eyes never rested upon. Instead of the seven colors, as we see them on earth, the colors blended in such a rare graduation of shades as to make the rays seem almost infinite. Or else they really were infinite. I could not decide which.

Celestial Music

As I lay watching this marvelous panorama, the colors deepened and faded like the lights of the aurora borealis. Although Mae and I no longer clung together, we did not drift apart, as one would naturally suppose we might. Instead, we lay within easy speaking distance of each other, although few words were spoken by either of us, for the silence seemed too sacred to be lightly broken. We lay upon, or rather within, the water, as upon the softest couch. It required no effort whatever to keep ourselves afloat. The gentle undulation of the waves soothed and rested us.

I was also attracted by the sound of distant music. As it arrested my attention, I turned and looked at Mae. She smiled back at me but did not speak. Presently I caught the words, "Glory and honor, dominion and power," and I knew it was still the cherub choir, although they must now be many miles away. Then the soft tones of a bell—a silver bell with silver tongue—fell on my ear. As the last notes died away, I whispered, "Tell me, Mae."

"Yes, dear, I will. The waters of this lake catch the light in a most marvelous manner, as you have seen. A wiser person than I must tell you why. They also transmit musical sounds—only musical sounds—for a great distance. The song was evidently from the distant shore of the lake."

"And the bell?"

"That is the bell which is in the city across the lake. It calls us to certain heavenly duties."

"There never was a sweeter call to duty," I said.

"Yes, its notes are beautiful. Hark! now it rings a chime."

We lay and listened. As we listened, a sweet peace wrapped around me, and I rested as peacefully as a child on its mother's bosom. I awoke with a strange sense of invigoration and strength. It was a feeling wholly dissimilar to that experienced during a bath in the River, yet I could not explain how.

Mae said, "The River takes away the last of the earth-life and prepares us for the life upon which we enter. The lake fills us to overflowing with a shower from the Celestial Life itself."

And I think the child was right.

No Anxiety!

When we emerged from the water we found the banks of the lake almost deserted, everyone having gone to their happy duties. Groups of children still played around in joyous freedom. Some climbed the trees that overhung the water with the agility of squirrels and dropped with happy shouts of laughter into the lake, floating upon its surface like immense and beautiful water-lilies or lotus flowers.

"No fear of harm or danger! No dread of ill or anxiety that a mishap might occur! Security! Security and joy and peace! This is indeed the blessed life," I said, as we stood watching the happy children.

"I often think how we were taught to believe that heaven was where we would wear crowns of gold and stand with harps always in our hands! Our crowns of gold are the halos His blessed presence casts about us. And we do not need harps to accentuate our songs of praise. We do see the crowns, and we do hear the angelic harps, when and as God wills it, but our best worship is to do His blessed will," said Mae as we turned to go.

"You are wise in the life of heaven, my child," I answered. "How happy I am to learn from one so dear! Tell me all about your life here."

So as we walked she told me the history of her time in heaven—her duties, her joys, her friends, her home. I found her home was distant from our own—far beyond the spires of the great city across the lake—but she added, "What is distance in heaven? We come and go at will. We feel no fatigue, no haste, and experience no delays. It is blessed, blessed!"

"When will I behold the Savior? When will I meet, face to face, Him whom my soul so loves?" my hungry heart began to cry out in its depths.

Mae, as though understanding the silent cry, placed both arms about my neck, looked tenderly into my eyes, and whispered, "You, too, dearest, will see Him soon. He never delays when the time is ripe for His coming. It will not be long. You, too, will see Him soon."

So we parted, each to our own duties.

Chapter 5

MEETING THE MASTER

Finally, Frank said to me, "Shall we go for the promised visit to Mrs. Wickham now?"

"Indeed, yes!" I answered eagerly. So we at once were on our way.

We soon reached her lovely home and found her waiting at the entrance as though expecting us. After a cordial greeting to our friend, Frank said, "I will leave you together for that long talk for which I know you are both eager. I must go my way to other duties. I will see you at home, dear sister."

"All right," I answered. "I am familiar with the way now and need no assitance."

A Delightful Visit

After he had gone, my friend took me all over her lovely home, showing me with great pleasure the rooms prepared for each beloved member of her earthly household still to come. One very large room was evidently under her special care. She whispered to me, "Douglass always did like a large room. I am sure he will like this one." And I was also sure.

Returning down the broad stairway, we entered into a very large music room with broad galleries supported by marble columns running across three sides of it. In this gallery there were numerous musical instruments—harps, viols, and instruments unlike any I had ever seen. The room itself was filled with easy-chairs, couches, and window-seats where listeners could rest and hear the sweet harmonies from the galleries.

"My daughter," my friend explained, "who left us in early childhood, has received a fine musical training here. She is fond of gathering in her young friends and giving us quite a musical treat. You know our old home of Springville has furnished some rare voices for the heavenly choirs. Mary Allis, Will Griggs, and many others you will often hear in this room, I trust."

We entered, from this room, the dainty reception hall opening upon the front veranda and outer steps. Here Mrs. Wickham drew me to a seat beside her and said, "Now, tell me everything of the dear home and all its blessed inhabitants."

Holding each other's hands as we talked, she questioning, I answering, things too sacred to be repeated here were dwelt upon and cherished. At last she said, rising hastily, "I will leave you for a little while—no, you must not go," as I would have risen, "there is much yet to be said. Wait here, I will return."

I had already learned not to question the judgment of these wiser friends, so I yielded to her will. As she passed through the doorway to the inner house, I saw a stranger at the front entrance and arose to meet him. He was tall and commanding in form, with a face of ineffable sweetness and beauty. Where had I seen him before? Surely, surely I had met him since I came. "Ah, now I know!" I thought. "It must be John, the beloved disciple." He had been pointed out to me one morning by the Riverside.

"Peace be unto this house," was his salutation as he entered.

How his voice stirred and thrilled me!

"Enter. You are a welcome guest. Enter, and I will call the mistress," I said, as I approached to bid him welcome.

"No, do not call her. She knows that I am here. She will return," he said. "Sit beside me awhile," he continued, as he saw that I still stood after I had seen him seated. He arose and led me to a seat near him. Like a child I did as I was bidden—still watching, always watching, the wonderful face before me.

"You have only recently come?" he said.

"Yes, I have been here but a short time. So short that I do not know how to refer to time as you have it here," I answered.

"Ah, that matters little," he said with a gentle smile. "Many cling to the old earth language. It is a link between the two lives. We would not have it otherwise. How does the change impress you? How do you find life here?"

"Ah," I said, "if they could only know! I never fully understood until now the meaning of that sublime passage, 'Eye hath not seen, nor ear heard, neither have entered into the heart of man, the things which God hath prepared for them that love Him' (1 Corinthians 2:9). It is indeed beyond human conception." I spoke with deep feeling.

" 'For them that love Him'? Do you believe that all Christians truly love Him?" he asked. "Do you think they love the Father for the gift of the Son and the Son because of the Father's love and mercy? Or is their worship often that of duty rather than love?" He spoke reflectively and gently.

"Oh," I said, "you who so well know the beloved Master—who were so loved by Him—how can you doubt the love He inspires in all hearts who seek to know Him?"

In The Master's Presence

A radiant glow overspread the wonderful face, which He lifted, looking directly at me. The mist rolled away from before my eyes, and I knew Him! With a low cry of joy and adoration, I threw myself at His feet, bathing them with happy tears. He gently stroked my bowed head for a moment then, rising, lifted me to His side.

"My Savior—my King!" I whispered, clinging closely to Him.

"Yes, and Elder Brother and Friend," He added, tenderly wiping away the tears stealing from beneath my closed eyelids.

"Yes, yes, the chiefest among ten thousand, and the One altogether lovely!" again I whispered.

"Ah, now you begin to meet the conditions of the new life! Like many others, the changing of faith to sight with you has engendered a little shrinking, a little fear. That is all wrong. Have you forgotten the promise, 'I go to prepare a place for you...that where I am, there ye may be also' (John 14:2-3)? If you loved Me when you could not see Me except by faith, love Me more now when we have really become co-heirs of the Father. Come to Me with all that perplexes or gladdens. Come to the Elder Brother always waiting to receive you with joy."

Then He drew me to a seat and conversed with me long and earnestly, unfolding many of the mysteries of the divine life. I hung upon His words. I drank in every tone of His voice. I watched eagerly every line of the beloved face. And I was exalted, uplifted, upborne, beyond the power of words to express. At length, with a divine smile, He arose.

"We will often meet," He said. And I, bending over, pressed my lips reverently to the hand still clasping my own. Then laying His hands a moment in blessing upon my bowed head, He passed noiselessly and swiftly from the house.

As I stood watching the Savior's fast-receding figure passing beneath the flower-laden trees, I saw two beautiful young girls approaching the way He went. With arms intertwining they came, happily conversing together, sweet Mary Bates and Mae Camden. When they saw the Master, they flew to meet Him with a glad cry. He joyously extended a hand to each. They turned, and, each clinging to His hands, one upon either side, they accompanied Him on His way.

Looking up trustingly into His face as He talked with them, they were apparently conversing with Him with happy freedom. I saw His face from time to time in profile, as He turned and looked down lovingly, first upon one, then the other lovely, upturned face. I thought, "That is the way He would have us be with Him—really as children with a beloved elder brother."

I watched them until the trees hid them from my sight, longing to gather the dear girls to my heart, but knowing His presence was, at that moment, more important than anything else. Then I turned and passed softly through the house to the beautiful entrance at the rear. Just before I reached the door, I met my friend Mrs. Wickham. Before I could speak, she said, "I know all about it. Do not try to speak. I know your heart is full. I will see you very soon—there, go!" She pushed me gently to the door.

How my heart blessed her—for it indeed seemed sacrilege to try to talk about ordinary topics after this blessed experience. I did not follow the walkway, but went across the flowery turf, beneath the trees until I reached home. I found Frank sitting on the veranda, and, as I ascended the steps, he rose to meet me. When he looked into my face, he took both hands into his for an instant and simply said, very gently, "Ah, I see. You have been with the Master!'' and stepped aside almost reverently for me to enter the house.

Glorious Solitude

I hastened to my room, and I threw myself upon the couch. With my eyes closed, I relived every instant I had spent in that hallowed Presence. I recalled every word and tone of the Savior's voice and fastened the instructions He had given me indelibly upon my memory. I seem to have been lifted to a higher plane of existence, to have drunk deeper truths from the fountain of all good, since I had met ''Him whom my soul loveth'' (Song of Solomon 3:1).

It was a long, blessed communion that I held thus with my soul. I wondered why I had not at once recognized Christ. But I concluded that for some wise purpose my ''eyes were clouded'' until it was His pleasure that I should see Him as He is.

When I arose, the soft, golden light was about me. I knelt by my couch to offer my first prayer in heaven. As I knelt, all I could utter over and over was, ''I thank Thee, blessed Father; I thank Thee, I thank Thee!''

When I at last descended the stairs, I found my brother-in-law standing in the great ''flower-room.'' Going to him, I said softly, ''Frank, what do you do in heaven when you want to pray?''

''We praise!'' he answered.

''Then let us praise now,'' I said.

Heavenly Praises

And standing there with clasped hands, we lifted up our hearts and voices in a hymn of praise to God. Frank with his clear, strong voice was leading, I following. As the first notes sounded, I thought the roof echoed them. But I soon found that other voices blended with ours, until the whole house seemed filled with unseen singers. Such a grand hymn of praise, earth never heard. As the hymn went on, I recognized many dear voices from the past—Will Griggs' distinct tenor, Mary Allis' exquisite soprano, and many other voices that wakened memories of long ago. Then as I heard sweet child-voices and looked up, I saw above us such a cloud of radiant cherub faces that my heart was flooded with joy. The room seemed filled with them.

"Oh, what a life—what a divine life!" I whispered as Frank and I returned to the veranda and sat in the golden light.

"You are only in the first pages of its unfolding," he said.

"Its blessedness must be gradually revealed to us, or we could not, even here, bear its dazzling glory."

Then followed hallowed fellowship when Frank led my soul still deeper into the mysteries of the glorious life upon which I had now entered. He taught me; I listened. Sometimes I questioned, but rarely. I was content to take in the heavenly manna as it was given me, with a heart full of gratitude and love.

Chapter 6

A CHILD'S HOMECOMING

Once, when my brother-in-law was away on an important mission, I started out alone to see if I could find my dear, young friends I had seen previously. I knew that all things were ordered aright in that happy world, and that sooner or later I would find them again. Yet, I could not help hoping it might be very soon. I recalled the happy light upon their fresh young faces as they had met the beloved Master, and I longed to talk with them. From thinking of them, I began again to think of my blessed interview with Him. I became so absorbed in these thoughts that I was even oblivious to the beautiful world around me.

Suddenly I heard someone say, "Surely that is Mrs. Springer!" Looking up, I saw sweet, little Mary Bates a few steps away regarding me intently.

I cried joyfully, "My precious Mamie!"

She flew to me and, folding me in her arms, drew my head to her shoulder in the old caressing way almost sobbing in her great joy.

"Dear, dear little muzzer!"—a pet name often

used by her in the happy past—"How glad I am to have you here! I could scarcely wait to find you."

"How did you know I was here, Mamie?"

"The Master told me," she said softly. "Mae had already told me, and we were on the way to find you when we met Him. He told us He had just left you. Then we knew we must wait a little," she said reverently.

How my heart thrilled! He had thought about and had spoken of me after we parted! I longed to ask her what He had said, but dared not.

Seeming to read my thoughts, she continued, "He spoke so tenderly about you and said we must be with you often. Mae had work to do today, and, as she had already seen you once, I came alone. She may be here later on. May I stay a long time with you? There is so much to tell you, so much to ask about!"

"Indeed you may. I had started out to find you, when we met. Come, dear child, let us return home at once."

Comfort For Those Who Mourn

So, clinging to each other, we set out toward my home. "What shall I tell you first?" I asked.

"Everything about the dear ones—every individual member of our beloved household. Begin with my precious, heart-broken mother." Here her voice broke a little, but she soon continued. "If only she could be with me here, could know God's wisdom and love as we know it, how the cloud would lift from her life! How she would see that the two lives, after all, are but one."

"Yes, dear," I answered, "I always urged her to think of it in that light and to trust implicitly in the Father's tender care and never-failing love. But it is difficult for us to see beyond the lonely fireside and the vacant chair."

"Ah, if she only knew that I need just that to complete my happiness," she said. "We cannot sorrow here as we did on earth, because we have learned to know that the will of the Father is always tender and wise. But even heaven can never be complete for me while I know that my precious mother is forgetful of her many rare blessings, simply because I may not be with her in the flesh to share them.

"There are my father and the boys—why, I am as truly hers still as they are! My dear little mother! Why must she see me to recognize this? But this is almost complaining, is it not? Some day she will know all—we must be patient."

The Glory Of His Presence

We walked on slowly and conversed about the earth-life, still in many phases so dear to us, she asking eager questions, I answering as best I could. Then we saw a group of four persons, three women and a man. They were standing under the trees a little to one side of the walkway. The man's back was toward us, but we at once recognized the Master. The women were all strangers, and one of them seemed to have just arrived. The Savior held her hand as He talked with her. All were intently listening to His words.

We regarded the group in silence as we slowly passed, not hoping for recognition from Him at such a time, but, just as we were opposite to them, He turned and looked upon us. He did not speak—but oh, that look! So full of tenderness and encouragement and benediction! It lifted us; it bore us upward; it enthralled and exalted us. And, as we passed onward, the clasp of our hands tightened, and unspeakable rapture flooded our hearts.

We finished our walk in silence and sat down on the marble steps in the shadow of the overhanging trees. The dear child nestled close against my side and laid her head upon my shoulder, while I rested my cheek caressingly upon it. After a time I whispered, half to myself, "Was there ever such a look!"

Instantly she raised her head and said eagerly, "You think so, too? I was sure you would. It is always just so. If He is too engaged to speak to you, He just looks at you, and it is as though He had talked with you for a long time. Is He not wonderful! Why, why could we not know Him on earth as we know Him here?"

"How long were you here before you met Him?" I asked.

His Divine Compassion

"Oh, that is the wonderful part of it! His was the first face I looked upon after I left my body. I felt bewildered when I first realized that I was free, and I stood for a moment feeling uncertain. Then,

I saw Him standing beside me with that same, tender look on His face.

"At first I felt timid and half afraid. Then, He stretched forth His hand to me and said gently, 'My child, I have come to take care of you; trust Me; do not be afraid.' Then, I knew who He was, and instantly all fear left me. I clung to Him as I would have done to either of my brothers. He did not say much to me, but somehow I felt that He understood all of my thoughts.

"What a blessed life this is!"

I can only give this brief outline of our conversation. The remainder of our discussion is too sacred to be scanned by curious eyes.

We watched the little birds nestling in the vines, heard the solemnly joyous notes of the angels' choral song and joined our voices in the hymn of praise. Later, we went to my room and sat down upon my dainty couch for rest. The last words I heard before sinking into heaven's blissful rest were tenderly whispered, "Dear, dear Rebecca, I am so glad and happy that you are here!"

More than once the question has been asked, "Was there night there?" Emphatically, no! What, for want of a better word, we call *day* was full of glorious radiance, a roseate golden light which was everywhere. There is no language known to mortals that can describe this marvelous glory. It flooded the sky; it was caught up and reflected in the waters; it filled all heaven with joy and all hearts with song. After a period much longer than our longest earthly day, this glory mellowed and softened until it became a glowing light full of peace. The children ceased their playing beneath the trees, the little birds nestled among the vines, and all who had been busy in various ways sought rest and quiet. But there was no darkness, no dusky shadows even—only a restful softening of the glory.

Chapter 7

A DIVINE SPEECH

Not long after this, Frank said, "We will go to the grand auditorium. Martin Luther is speaking on 'The Reformation: Its Causes and Effects.' This will be supplemented by a talk from John Wesley. There may also be other speakers."

It was not the first time we had visited this great auditorium although I have not previously described it. It stood on a slight hill, and the mighty dome was supported by massive columns of alternate amethyst and jasper. There were no walls to the massive structure—only the great dome and supporting columns. A broad platform of precious, inlaid marbles arose from the center.

From this platform, seats ascended on three sides to form an immense amphitheater. The seats were made of highly polished cedar wood; behind the platform were heavy hangings of royal purple. An altar of solid pearl stood near the center of the platform. The great dome was deep and dark in its immensity, so that only the golden carvings around its lower border were distinctly visible. I had noticed all this on former visits.

Martin Luther Lectures

When we entered, we found the building filled with people eagerly waiting. We soon were seated. Soft strains of melody floated about us from an invisible choir. Before long, Martin Luther, in the prime of a vigorous manhood, ascended the steps and stood before us. It is not my desire to dwell on his appearance, except to say that his great intellect and spiritual strength seemed to have added to his already powerful physique. It made him a capable leader even in heavenly places.

His discourse would of itself fill a volume and could not even be outlined in this brief sketch. He held us enthralled by the power of his will and his eloquence. When he eventually retired, John Wesley took his place. The saintly beauty of his face, intensified by the heavenly light upon it, was wonderful.

His theme was "God's love." If on earth he preached on it with power, he now swept our souls with the fire of his exaltation until we were as wax in his hands. He showed us what that love had done and how an eternity of thanksgiving and praise could never repay it.

The Glory Of The Lord

Silence, except for the faint, sweet melody of the unseen choir, rested on the vast audience after he left. All seemed lost in contemplation of the theme so tenderly presented. Then, the heavy curtains behind the platform parted, and a tall form, about whom all the glory of heaven seemed to center, emerged from their folds. He advanced toward the middle of the platform. Instantly, the vast gathering of souls rose to their feet and burst forth as with one voice into that grand anthem in which we had so often joined on earth:

"All hail the power of Jesus' name,
    Let angels prostrate fall;
    Bring forth the royal diadem,
    And crown Him Lord of all."

Such a grand chorus of voices, such unity, such harmony, such volume was never heard on earth. It rose, swelled, and seemed to fill not only the great auditorium, but heaven itself. And still, above it all, we heard the voices of the angel choir, no longer breathing the soft, sweet melody, but bursting forth into hymns of triumphant praise. A flood of glory seemed to fill the place, and looking upward we beheld the great dome ablaze with golden light, and the angelic forms of the choir in its midst. Their heavenly harps, viols, and their faces were only less radiant than that of Him in whose praise they sang. And He, before whom all heaven bowed in adoration, stood with uplifted face and kingly expression—the very God of earth and heaven. He was the center of all light, and a divine radiance surrounded Him that was beyond compare.

As the hymn of praise and adoration ceased, all sank slowly to their knees, and every head was bowed and every face covered as the angel choir chanted again the familiar words, "Glory be to the Father, and to the Son, and to the Holy Ghost. As it was in the beginning, is now, and ever shall be, world without end. Amen, Amen!"

Slowly the voices died away, and a holy silence fell on us. Presently, slowly and reverently, all arose and resumed their places. No, not all. Sweet Mary Bates had accompanied us to the sanctuary, and I now noticed that she alone still knelt in our midst. With clasped hands and radiant, uplifted face, her lovely eyes were fixed on the Savior. As He stood waiting before us, her look of selfless adoration and love made her appear truly divine. She was so captivated I dared not disturb her.

But, in a moment, the Master turned and met her adoring eyes with a look of loving recognition. With a deep sigh of satisfied desire, as He turned away, she quietly resumed her seat beside me. She slipped her little hand into mine with all the confidence of a child who feels sure it is completely understood.

As I looked upon the glorious form before us, clothed in all the majesty of the Godhead, my heart asked, "Can this truly be Christ, whom Pilate condemned to die a disgraceful death upon the cross?" I could not accept it. It seemed impossible that any man, however vile, could be blind to the divinity so plainly revealed in Him.

The Savior Speaks

Then, the Savior began to speak, and the sweetness of His voice was far beyond the melody of the

58

heavenly choir. And His gracious words! If only I could, if only I dared, transcribe them as they fell from His lips. Earth has no language by which I could convey their lofty meaning. He touched lightly on the earth-life and wonderfully showed the link of light uniting the two lives—the past with the present. Then, He revealed some of the earlier mysteries of the blessed life and pointed out the joyous duties just before us.

When He ceased, we sat with bowed heads as He withdrew. Our hearts were so enfolded, our souls so uplifted, our spirits so exalted, our whole being so permeated with His divinity, that when we arose we left silently and reverently. Our hearts were filled with higher, more divine aspirations and clearer views of the blessed life upon which we were permitted to enter.

I can only lightly touch upon these heavenly joys. There is a depth, a mystery to all that pertains to the divine life, which I dare not try to describe. I could not if I wanted to; I would not if I could. A sacredness enfolds it, and curious eyes should not look upon it. Suffice it to say that no joy we know on earth, however rare, however sacred, can be more than the faintest shadow of the joy we find there. No dreams of rapture, unrealized on earth, approach the bliss of one moment in that divine world. No sorrow, no pain, no sickness, no death, no parting, no disappointments, no tears but those of joy, no broken hopes, no mislaid plans, no night, nor storm, nor shadows even. There is only light and joy and love and peace and rest forever and forever. "Amen," and again my heart says reverently, "Amen."

Chapter 8

REBECCA MEETS HER SISTER

Often, I found myself drawn to the sacred lake, sometimes alone, sometimes with one or more of my own family circle. It was always an inspiration to me. I never grew so familiar with it that I overcame the great awe with which it inspired me. On the contrary, I found that the more I bathed or floated in its clear water, the stronger I grew in spirit. I was able to more clearly comprehend the mysteries of the world about me.

My fellowship with the dear loved ones from home served to restore the greatest solace of my mortal life. I began to realize that this was indeed the true life, instead of that probationary life which we had always regarded as such.

A Special Reunion

Once, as I started to cross the lawn between my father's house and our own, I heard my name called in an affectionate manner. I turned and saw a tall, fine-looking man approaching me. His uncovered head was silvery white, and his deep blue eyes looked happily and tenderly into mine, as he drew near.

"Oliver!" I cried with outstretched hands of welcome, "dear, dear Oliver!" It was the husband of my eldest sister, whom I had always loved dearly.

"I did not know that you had come, until a few moments ago. It is delightful to have you here. It seems more like the old days to see you. We were together so much during the last years of my stay," he said as he grasped my hands warmly. "Where are you going now? Can you come with me awhile? I was thinking how much I wished you could be here before Lu came—you know her tastes so well. And now, here you are! So often our unspoken wishes are thus gratified in heaven!"

"Is my sister coming soon?" I asked a little later.

"That I cannot say for sure. But the years of her earth-life are passing, and her coming cannot be delayed much longer. Can you come with me now?"

"Gladly," I said, turning to walk with him.

"It is only a little way from here," he said. "Just where the River bends. Lu loves the water, so I chose that spot in preference to one even nearer your home."

"This is truly enchanting!" I cried, as we drew near the place. "I have not been this way before."

"I want you to see the River from the window in her room," he said. "I know you will enjoy it."

We entered the truly beautiful house, built of the purest white granite, so embedded in the foliage of the flower-laden trees that from some points only glimpses of its fine proportions could be seen.

"She loves flowers so much—will she not enjoy these trees?" He asked with almost boyish delight.

"Beyond everything," I answered.

We passed through several delightful rooms on the lower floor. Then, ascending the stairway—which in itself was a dream of beauty—we entered the room he was so anxious for me to see. I stopped upon the threshold with an exclamation of delight, while he watched the expression on my face.

"It is the most delightful room I ever saw!" I cried enthusiastically.

The framework of couches, chairs, and desk was of pure and spotless pearl, upholstered in dim gold. Soft rugs and draperies were everywhere. And, through the low window opening upon the flower-wreathed balcony, there was such an enchanting view of the broad, smooth River that again I caught my breath in delight. A thousand exquisite tints from the heavens above were reflected upon the tranquil waters, and a boat floating on the current was perfectly mirrored in the opaline-tinted ripples.

The celestial hills of the city rose far across the shining waters. Their domes, pillared temples, and sparkling fountains were visible everywhere.

We descended the stairs without a word, then I could only falter, "Only heaven could give such perfection in everything!"

Oliver held my hand sympathetically and let me depart without a word.

A Sister Comes Home

Many times I visited that lovely home and held sweet conversation with Oliver, whom I loved so well. I could not think of anything that would add to the beauty of the place, but we talked about it together and planned for and anticipated the joy of her coming.

Once, Oliver was not home, and though I waited long for his return, he did not come. I had not seen him for a while and concluded that he had been sent on a mission by the Master. As I was on my way home, I met a group of happy young girls and boys, heading the way I had come, with their arms full of beautiful flowers. As they drew near, I realized that they were the grandchildren of my dear sister—Stanley and Mary and David and Lee and little Ruth. As soon as they saw me, they all began to shout joyfully:

"Grandma is coming! Grandma is coming! We are taking flowers to scatter everywhere! We are so glad!"

"How do you know she is coming, children? I was just at the house—no one is there!"

"But she is coming," said little Lee. "We had a message from Grandpa, and he is to bring her."

"Then I will tell the others, and we will all come to welcome her," I said.

With great joy in my heart, I hurried to my father's house. I found them waiting for me, full of joyful expectation.

"Yes, we also have had word," my father said, "and were only awaiting your return that we might go together."

"Then, I will go get brother Frank, so he can also accompany us," I said.

"He is here!" said a genial voice. And, looking up, I saw him at the door.

"Colonel Springer is always present when he is needed," said my father cordially.

So we set forth to welcome this dearly loved one to her home—my father; my mother; my sister, Jodie; my brother the doctor; his two daughters; my Aunt Gray; her son, Martin; his wife and daughter; and Frank and I.

A Precious Moment

As we approached the house we heard the sound of joyous voices. Looking in, we saw my sister standing in the room with her husband's arm around her and the happy grandchildren crowded around them. But what was this? Could this radiant creature, with smooth brow and happy eyes, be the pale, wan woman I had last seen, so bowed with suffering and sorrow? I looked with eager eyes. Yes, it was my sister. But she looked as she did a full thirty years ago—the bloom of health on her face and the light of youth in her tender eyes.

I drew back into the shadows of the vines and let the others precede me, for my heart was full of a strange, triumphant joy. This truly was the "victory over death" so surely promised by our risen

Lord. I watched the happy greetings and the way she took each beloved one into her tender arms.

When, one by one, she had greeted and embraced them all, I saw her turn and look wistfully around, then whisper to my father, "Is my little sister here?" I could wait no longer and, rushing to her side, cried, "Dearest, I am here! Welcome! Welcome!"

She folded me to her heart and held me fast in her warm arms. She showered me with kisses while I returned each loving caress. I laughed and cried with gladness that she had come at last. Oh, what a family reunion that was inside the walls of heaven! And how its bliss was heightened by the sure knowledge (not the hope) that there would be no parting for us forever!

My brother-in-law, Oliver, looked on with proud and happy eyes. The hour for which he had longed and waited had come to him at last. His eternal life would now be complete forever. I told him how I had waited for him that day. He said, "We saw you as you left the house, but we were too far away to call you. I had taken her into the River, and she had looked at and admired the house even before she knew it was ours."

"What did she do when she saw her lovely room?"

"She cried like a child. Clinging to me, she said, 'This more than repays for the lost home of earth!' If the children had not come, I think she would have been at that window still!" he said laughing happily.

"I am glad you had her all to yourself at first," I whispered. "You deserved that happiness, dear, if any man ever did."

He smiled gratefully and looked over at his wife, where she stood at the center of a happy group.

A Heavenly Youthfulness

"Doesn't she look very young to you, Oliver?" I asked.

"The years rolled from her like a mask as we sat beneath the water in the River. Ah, truly in those life-giving waters we do all 'renew our youth.' But she at once became uncommonly fair and young."

"Her coming has also brought youth to you," I said, noting his fresh complexion and his sparkling eyes. "But I hope it will not change your silver hair for that is your crown of glory."

He looked at me a moment critically, then said, "I wonder if you realize the change that has likewise come to you in this wonderful place?"

"I?" I said, a little startled at the thought. "I confess I have not once thought of my personal appearance. I realize, through the Father's mercy, what this life has done for me spiritually; but as for the other, I have never given it an instant's thought."

"The change is fully as great in your case as in Lu's, though with you the change has been more gradual," he said.

I felt a strange thrill of joy in knowing that when my dear husband would come to me, he would find me with the freshness and beauty of our earlier years. It was a sweet thought. My heart was full of gratitude to the Father for this further evidence of His loving care. So we talked together as the hours sped. Then my father said, "Come, children, we must not forget that this dear daughter of mine needs rest this first day in her new home. Let us leave her and her happy husband to their new-found bliss."

So with light hearts we went our way and left them to spend their first hours in heaven together.

Chapter 9

A VISIT WITH A SPECIAL FRIEND

After we left my parents and friends, Frank hurried away on some mission, and I walked on alone toward the sacred lake. I felt the need for a rest in its soothing waters after all the excitment.

Only a few people lingered on the shore. The boats that sped across its calm surface seemed to be filled with messengers intent upon some duty rather than pleasure-seekers. I walked slowly down into the water and soon found myself floating in mid-current.

The wonderful prismatic rays blended into a golden glory, with different shades of rose and purple flashing their splendor. To me it seemed even more beautiful than the rainbow, just like the joys of our adult life caused the more frivolous pleasures of youth to fade.

I heard the chimes from the silver bell of the great city ringing an anthem as I lay there. Its notes seemed to chant, "Holy! Holy! Holy! Lord God Almighty!" The waters took up the song, and a thousand waves about me responded, "Holy!

Holy! Holy!"

Language fails me—I cannot hope to convey this experience to others. It was grand, wonderful, overpowering. I lay and listened until my whole being was filled with the divine melody, and I seemed to be a part of the great chorus. Then I, too, lifted up my voice and joined with full heart in the thrilling song of praise.

A Journey To The Far Shore

To my surprise, I found that I floated rapidly away from the shore where I had entered the water. After a time I was conscious that I was approaching a portion of the lake shore I had never yet visited. Refreshed and invigorated, I ascended the sloping banks to find myself in the midst of a lovely village, similar to the one where our own home was situated. There was some difference in the architecture or construction of the houses, though they were no less beautiful than others I had seen. Many were constructed of polished woods and somewhat resembled the finest chalets in Switzerland. Yet, they far surpassed them in artistic beauty.

As I wandered on, feasting my eyes upon the lovely views about me, I was particularly pleased by the appearance of an unusually attractive house. Its broad verandas almost overhung the waters of the lake, and the wide low steps along one side of the house met the water's edge. Several graceful swans leisurely drifted about with the current, and a delightful bird was singing and swinging in the low branches overhead. There were many larger and more imposing homes nearby, but none were as charming as this one.

I saw a woman sitting beneath one of the large flowering trees close by this cottage home. She was weaving, apparently without shuttle or needle, a snow-white, gossamer-like fabric that fell in a soft, fleecy heap at her side. She was so very small in stature that at first I thought she was a child. But a closer look showed her to be a mature woman, though the glow of youth was still on her smooth cheeks.

Something familiar in her gestures, rather than her appearance, caused me to feel that it was not the first time we had met. Growing accustomed to the delightful surprises in this world of rare delight, I drew near to her. Before I could speak, she looked up and the doubt was gone.

"Maggie!" "Mrs. Springer, dear!" we cried simultaneously. Dropping her work from her hands, she stood up to greet me.

Our greeting was warm and fervent, and her sweet face glowed with a welcome that reminded me of the happy days when we had met by the shore of a beautiful lake on earth.

"Now I know why I came this way today—to find you, dear," I said. We sat side by side, talking as we never had talked on earth. The sweet shyness of her mortal life had melted away in the refreshing air of heaven.

"What is this lovely fabric you are weaving?" I asked, lifting the silken, fleecy web in my fingers as I spoke.

Learning A Divine Art

"Some draperies for Nellie's room," she said. "You know we two have lived alone together so much, I thought it would seem more like home to her, to us both, if we did the same here. So this cottage is our special home, just a few minutes from Marie's," pointing to an imposing house a few yards distant, "and I am fixing it up as daintily as I can, especially her room."

"Oh, let me help you, Maggie dear!" I said. "It would be such a pleasure to me."

She hesitated a moment, then said, "That is so like you, dear Mrs. Springer. But I have my heart set on doing Nellie's room entirely myself—there is no hurry about it, you know. If you really would enjoy it, I would love to have you help me in the other rooms."

"And will you teach me how to weave these delicate hangings?"

"Yes, indeed."

Lifting the dainty thread, she showed me how to toss and wind it through my fingers until it fell in shining folds. It was very light and fascinating work, and I was soon weaving it almost as rapidly as she did.

"Now, I can help Frank!" was my happy thought, as I saw the shimmering fabric grow beneath my hands. "Tomorrow I will go and show him how beautifully we can drape the doors and windows."

In heaven our first thought is to give pleasure to others.

"You are a quick learner," said Maggie, laughing happily. "And what a charming visit you have given me!"

"What a charming visit you have given me, my dear!" I answered.

When we parted it was with the understanding that I would visit again.

Chapter 10

A VISIT TO THE HEAVENLY CITY

On one of my walks, I happened upon a scene that reminded me of what Mae had said about the Savior's love for little children. I found Him sitting beneath one of the flowering trees upon the lake shore with about a dozen children of all ages clustered around Him.

One dainty little tot, not more than a year old, was nestled in His arms. Her sunny head rested confidingly upon His bosom, and her tiny hands were filled with the lovely water-lilies that floated everywhere on the waters. She was too young to realize how great her privilege was, but she seemed to be enjoying His care to the utmost.

The others sat at His feet or leaned upon His knees. One dear little fellow with earnest eyes stood by Him, leaning upon His shoulder, while the Master's right arm encircled him. Every eye was fixed eagerly upon Jesus, and each child listened to every word He said. He seemed to be telling them some very absorbing story, adapted to their childish tastes and capacities.

I sat down on the lawn among a group of people, a little removed from the children, and tried to hear what He was saying. But we were too far away to catch more than a sentence now and then, and in heaven one never intrudes upon another's privilege or pleasure. So we simply enjoyed the smiles and eager questions and exclamations of the children.

Of Such Is The Kingdom

"A little child lost in the dark woods of the lower world. . ." we heard the Master say, in response to the inquiring looks of the interested children.

"Lions and bears. . ." came later on.

"Where was his papa?" asked an anxious voice. We could not hear the reply, but soon a little fellow leaning upon the Savior's knee said confidently, "I am not afraid up here!"

"No," He replied, "nothing to harm or frighten My little children here!"

Then as the story deepened and grew in interest, the children pressed more closely about the Master. He turned with a sweet smile to the little fellow with the earnest eyes who leaned on His shoulder and said, "What, Leslie, would you have done, then?"

With a bright light in his eyes and a flush on his fair cheek, the child answered quickly and emphatically, "I would have prayed to You and asked You to 'shut the lion's mouth' as You did for Daniel, and You would have done it!" (See Daniel

6:2.)

"Ah," I thought, "if only his parents could see the look the beloved Master cast upon their boy as he made his brave reply. They would be comforted in the absence of their precious child."

Lost in these thoughts, I heard no more that passed until an ecstatic shout from the children proclaimed how satisfactorily the story had ended. Looking up, I saw the Savior passing onward with the baby still in His arms and the children trooping about Him.

"Of such is the kingdom of heaven" (Matthew 19:14). How well He understood! How much He loved them!

A Special Privilege

I, too, arose and started homeward. I had not gone far before I met my brother-in-law, Frank, who greeted me with, "I am on my way to the city by the lake. Will you join me?"

"I have been hoping to visit the city. I only waited until you thought it wise for me to go," I answered.

"You are growing so fast in the knowledge of heavenly ways," he said, "that I think I could take you almost anywhere with me now. You acquire the knowledge because you love it, not because you feel bound to know what we want you to learn. Your eagerness to understand all truth, and at the same time wait in patient submission, has won you much praise and love from our dear Master. He eagerly watches the progress of us all in the divine life. I think it only right that you should know this. We need encouragement here as well as in the earth-life, though in a different way. I tell you this by divine permission. I think it will not be long before He trusts you with a mission. But I say this of myself, not by His command."

It would be impossible for me to convey, in the language of earth, the impression these words of commendation left on me. They were so unexpected, so unforeseen. I had gone on, as Frank said, eagerly gathering the knowledge imparted to me with a genuine love for the study of all things pertaining to the blessed life. I had not thought that I in any way deserved commendation for so doing. And now I had won the approval of the Master Himself! The happiness seemed almost more than I had strength to bear.

"My dear Frank!" was all I could say, in my deep joy, stopping suddenly and looking up into his face with grateful tears.

"I am so glad for you, little sister!" he said, warmly clasping my hand. "There are, you see, rewards in heaven. It does my soul good that you have unconsciously won one of these so soon."

I wish I could record in detail the precious words of wisdom that fell from his lips. I wish I could recount minutely the events of that wonderful life as it was unfolded to me. But I can only say, "I may not."

When I decided to record that never-to-be-forgotten time, I did not realize how many serious difficulties I would have to encounter. I did not consider how often I would have to pause and think if I might really reveal this truth or paint that scene as it appeared to me. The very heart has often been left out of some wonderful scene, because I dared not reveal its sacred secret.

I realize painfully that the narrative, as I am forced to give it, falls infinitely short of what I hoped to make it when I began. But bear with me. It is no fancy sketch I am drawing, but the veritable life beyond as it appeared to me when the exalted spirit rose triumphant over the impoverished flesh made subservient through suffering.

Entering The City

Frank and I walked slowly back to the margin of the lake where we stepped into a boat lying near the shore. At once we were transported to the farther shore of the lake and landed upon a marble terrace—the entrance to the city by the lake. I never knew what propelled these boats. There were no oarsman, no engine, and no sails, but it moved steadily until we landed safely at our destination.

Luxuriously cushioned seats were all around it, and upon one of them lay a musical instrument. It was something like a violin, although it had no bow, but seemed to be played by the fingers alone. Upon another seat lay a book. I picked it up and opened it. It seemed to be a continuation of the book that stirred and thrilled millions of hearts in the mortal life—"The Greatest Thing In The World." As I glanced through it while we journeyed, I learned that this great mind had already grappled with the mighty things of eternity and had given food to immortals, even as he had done for those in mortal life in the years gone by.

All Worship In Harmony

I was aroused from my thoughts by the boat touching the marble terrace and Frank waiting to assist me to the shore. Passing up a slight hill, we found ourselves in a broad street that led into the heart of the city. The streets were all very broad and smooth and paved with marble and precious stones of every kind. Though they were thronged with people intent on various duties, not a speck of debris or even dust was visible anywhere.

There seemed to be vast business offices of many kinds, though I saw nothing resembling our large, commercial establishments. There were many colleges, schools, book and music stores, and publishing houses. There were several large factories where the fine silken threads used in the weaving of the draperies I have already mentioned were spun. There were art rooms, picture galleries, libraries, many lecture halls, and vast auditoriums.

But I saw no churches of any kind. At first this somewhat confused me, until I remembered that there are no creeds or denominations in heaven. All worship together in harmony and love—the children of one and the same loving Father.

"Ah," I thought, "what a pity that this fact, if no other in the great economy of heaven, could not be proclaimed to the inhabitants of earth! How it would do away with the petty contentions, jealousies, and rivalries of the church militant! No creeds in heaven! No controverted points of doctrine! No charges of heresy brought by one professed Christian against another! No building up of one denomination upon the ruins or downfall of a different sect! But one great, universal brotherhood whose head is Christ and whose cornerstone is love."

More Heavenly Joy

I thought of the day we had listened in the great auditorium at home to the divine message of our beloved Master. I remembered the bowed heads and uplifted voices of that vast multitude as every voice joined in the glorious anthem, "Crown Him Lord of All!" I could have wept to think of the faces that must some day be bowed in shame when they remember how often they have said to a fellow-Christian, "Stand by thyself, come not near to me; I am holier than thou!" (Isaiah 65:5).

There were no homes anywhere in the midst of the city. They stood in the suburbs with great magnificence and splendor. But one pleasing fact was that every home had a large garden full of trees and flowers and pleasant walks. Indeed, these gardens were everywhere, outside of the business center of the town, like one vast park dotted with lovely houses. There was much that charmed and surprised me in this great city. I may not describe all of it, but I will never forget its beauty.

We found a very large park, with walks, drives,

fountains, miniature lakes, and shaded seats. There were no dwellings or buildings of any kind, except for an immense, circular, open temple capable of seating many hundred. Frank told me that a seraph choir assembled here and rendered the oratorios written by the great musical composers of earth and heaven. It had just departed, and the crowd who had enjoyed its divine music still lingered as though unwilling to leave a spot so hallowed.

"We will come again," Frank said, "when we can hear them."

Chapter 11

THE TEMPLE

"And the temple was filled with smoke from the glory of God, and from his power"—Revelation 15:8.

Still passing through the park, we came out upon the open country and walked some distance through flowery meadows and plains. After awhile, we entered a vast forest whose great trees towered above us like swaying giants.

Frank walked next to me, absorbed in silent thought, but with a touch beyond even his usual gentleness. I did not ask where we were going, so far from home, for fear and doubt and questionings no longer vexed the quiet of my soul. Although the forest was dense, the golden glow of the heavenly light rested beneath the trees and sifted down through the quivering branches overhead.

The Throne Of Glory

Eventually, we emerged from the forest onto a vast plain which stretched out into limitless space before us. Far away we heard the faint thunder of the breaking waves of that immortal sea of which I had heard so much but had not yet seen. Except for their faint and distant reverberation, the silence about us was intense.

We stood a moment upon the verge of the forest. As we advanced a few steps into the plain I became aware that immediately to our right the ground rose into quite an elevation.

As I turned, a sight broke upon my bewildered eyes that the eternal years of earth and heaven can never erase. Upon the summit of this gentle slope stood a Temple whose vast dome, massive pillars, and solid walls were of flawless pearl. Through the great windows of the Temple shone a white radiance that swallowed up the golden glow of the heavenly light and made it its own. I did not cry aloud nor hide my face, as at former revelations.

Instead, I sank slowly to my knees and, with my hands crossed upon my breast, an uplifted face, a stilled heart, and silent lips, laid my whole being in worship at His feet "who sitteth upon the throne" (Revelation 5:13). I don't know how long I knelt like this. Even immortal life seemed lost before that greatest of celestial mysteries.

Entering The Temple

Then Frank, who had been silently kneeling beside me, arose and, lifting me to my feet, whispered gently, "Come." I felt, rather than saw, that his face was colorless with the depth of his emotion, and I yielded to his guidance in silence.

A long flight of low, broad steps, in gradations, rose from where we stood to the door of the Temple. They, too, were of solid pearl, bordered on either side by channels paved with golden stones through which flowed crystal waters that met and mingled in one stream far out upon the plain. Ascending these steps, we entered the Temple and stood for a moment in silence.

I do not know why, but suddenly every detail of that wonderful interior was etched upon my memory as a scene is photographed and kept forever. Before this, it had taken repeated visits to a room to enable me to describe it correctly in detail. But this, in a lightning's flash, was stamped upon the tablet of my memory indelibly for all time—for eternity.

The immense dome, at that moment filled with a luminous cloud, was upheld by three rows of massive pillars of gold. The walls and floors were made of pearl, as was the great platform that took up at least one-third of the Temple on the eastern side. There were no seats of any kind. The great golden pillars stood like rows of sentinels on the shining floor.

A railing of gold ran entirely around the platform on three sides, so that it was inaccessible from the body of the Temple. Beneath this railing, on the Temple-floor, a pearl kneeling-step encircled the platform, also made of pearl. In the center of the platform an immense altar of gold arose. It was supported by seraphs of gold with outspread wings, one at each corner.

Underneath it, in a great pearl basin, a fountain of sparkling water played, and I knew intuitively it was the source of the magical River that flowed through the gardens of heaven and cleansed us of the last stains of death and sin.

The Brightness Of His Coming

Two persons knelt with bowed head beside the altar-rail on the farther side of the Temple. By the altar stood four angels, one on either side, dressed in flowing garments of white. They had long, slim trumpets of gold lifted in their hands, as though waiting for the signal to sound their trumpet call. Long draperies of silvery gossamer hung in heavy folds behind the altar platform.

Suddenly, we saw the draperies tremble and glow until a radiance far beyond the splendor of the sun at midday shone through them. The whole Temple was "filled with the glory of the Lord" (Exodus 40:34). We saw, in the midst of the luminous cloud that filled the dome, the forms of angelic harpers. As we dropped with bowed heads beside the altar-rail and hid our faces from the "brightness of His coming" (2 Thessalonians 2:8), we heard the trumpet-call of the four angels around the altar. The voices of the celestial harpers sang:

"Holy, Holy, Holy, Lord God Almighty!
All Thy works shall praise Thy name,
In earth, and sky, and sea,
Holy, Holy, Holy, merciful and mighty,
God in three persons—blessed Trinity. Amen!"

The voices softly died away, the last notes of the golden trumpets had sounded, "and there was silence in heaven" (Revelation 8:1). We knew that the visible glory of the Lord was, for the present, withdrawn from the Temple—His throne. Still we knelt with bowed heads in silent worship before Him. When we finally arose, I did not lift my eyes while I was within the Temple. I wanted it to remain in my memory as it appeared with His glory.

We walked in silence. I leaned upon Frank's arm, for I still trembled with emotion. I was surprised that we did not return into the forest, but went farther out onto the plain. But when I saw that we approached the confluence of the two streams which issued from the fountain beneath the altar, I understood that we would return by way of the River, instead of by forest and lake.

The Journey Home

We reached the stream, and, stepping into a boat that lay by the shore, we were soon floating toward home. We passed through much beautiful scenery that I had not seen before. I decided to visit these places in the future when leisure from my duties would permit. Lovely villas, surrounded by beautiful grounds stretching directly up from the water's edge, lay on both sides of the River. They formed a panorama which the eye never tired of beholding. Toward the end of the journey, we passed my sister's lovely home. We could plainly see her and her husband drinking in the scene with enraptured eyes from the window of her room.

Frank and I were both silent during most of our journey homeward. However, we each noted the signs of happy, domestic life by which we were surrounded on every side. The verandas and steps of the homes we passed were full of their happy inhabitants. Glad voices could be heard constantly, and merry shouts of laughter came from the groups of little children playing on the flowery lawns.

Once I broke our silence by saying to Frank, "I have often been delightfully surprised to hear the familiar songs of earth reproduced in heaven, but never more so than I was today. That hymn has always been a favorite of mine."

"These happy surprises do not come by chance," he answered. "One of the delights of this rare life is that no occasion is ever overlooked for reproducing the pure enjoyments of our mortal life here in heaven. It is the Father's pleasure to make us realize that this existence is a continuation of the former life, only without its imperfections and its cares."

"Frank, I believe you are the only one of our friends here who has never questioned me about the dear ones left behind. Why is that?"

He smiled a peculiarly happy smile as he answered, "Perhaps it is because I already know more than you could tell me."

"I wondered if that was why," I said. I remembered well how my dear father had said, in speaking of my brother-in-law on my arrival, "He stands very near to the Master," and I knew how often he was sent on missions to the world below.

When we returned, I lay down on my couch with a heart overflowing with joy and gratitude and love.

Chapter 12

MEETING SPECIAL FRIENDS

So much occurred, and so rapidly, since my entrance within the beautiful gates, that it is impossible for me to transcribe it all. I have only been able to record selected incidents. In so doing, many things I would gladly have related, but have unconsciously omitted.

Of the many dear friends I met, only a very few have been mentioned. The reason being that such meetings are so similar in many respects that the constant repetition, in detail, would become wearisome.

I have principally aimed to give such incidents which show the beautiful domestic life in that happy world. I have tried to illustrate the reverence and love all hearts feel toward the blessed Trinity for every good and perfect gift. I have tried to show the marvelous power of the Christ-love even in the life beyond the grave.

Renewing Old Ties

In heaven, many ties that were once severed in

the mortal life were renewed. I remember walking once near Mrs. Wickham's home, shortly after my first memorable visit there. I was attracted by an unpretentious but very beautiful house. It was almost hidden by luxurious, climbing rose vines, whose creamy white flowers were beyond compare with any roses I had yet seen in earth or heaven. Meeting Mrs. Wickham, I pointed to the house and asked, "Who lives there?"

"Suppose you go over and see," she said.

"Is it anyone I know?" I asked.

"I think so. See, someone is standing at the door expecting you."

I crossed over the snowy walk and flowery turf, and, before I could ascend the steps, I found myself in the embrace of two loving arms.

"Rebecca Springer! I was sure it was you when I saw you go to Mrs. Wickham. Did she not tell you I was here?"

"She had no opportunity until now," I said. "But dear Aunt Ann, I would have found you eventually, I am sure you know that."

"Yes, I am sure you would."

Then I told her about my visit to Mrs. Wickham's. She listened with her dear face full of sympathy, then said, "There, dear, you need not tell me. When the Master comes to gladden my eyes, I also have no thought or care for anything! Oh, the joy and peace of knowing I am safe in this blessed haven! How far beyond all our earthly dreams is this divine life!"

She sat for a moment lost in thought, then said

wistfully, "Now, tell me of my children—are they coming?"

I gladdened her heart with all the cheering news I could bring of her loved ones. We recalled many sweet memories of the earth-life, of friends and home and family ties. We expressed how we were looking forward to the future arrival of those whom even the joys of heaven could not banish from our hearts.

Another Reunion

Then, as many of our dear family circle were gathered with us in the great "flower-room," we heard a step upon the veranda. As Frank went to open the door, a gentle voice said, "Is Mrs. Springer really here?"

"She is really here. Come and see for yourself." And sweet Mary Green entered the room.

"I am so glad to welcome you home!" she said. She was coming to me with extended hands and looking at me with her tender, earnest eyes.

"My precious girl!" I cried, taking her to my heart in a warm embrace. "I have been asking about you and longing to see you."

"I could scarcely wait to reach here when I heard that you had come. Now, tell me everything—everything!" she said as I drew her to a seat close beside me.

After a long, close conversation, I took her to the library where the rest had gone to examine a new book received that day. I introduced her to them all as the daughter of dear friends still on earth, confident of the welcome she would receive. My youngest sister and she at once became interested in each other, finding similarities in many of their pursuits. I was glad to think they would see much of each other in many different ways.

There was no measurement of time as we measure it here, although many still spoke in the mortal language of *months* and *days* and *years*. I have no way of describing it as it seemed to me then. There were times for happy duties, times for joyful pleasures, and times for holy praise. I only know it was all harmony, all joy, all peace, at all times and in all conditions.

Chapter 13

A REUNION OF MOTHER AND SON

The current of my life flowed on in the heavenly ways, and my studies ascended higher in the scale of celestial mysteries. I never wearied of study, though much was taught and gained through the medium of observation in the journeys that I was permitted to take with Frank into different parts of the heavenly Kingdom.

I never lacked time for social pleasures and enjoyments, for there is no clashing of duties with inclination, no unfulfilled desires, no vain strivings for the unattainable in that life, as in the life of earth.

Many precious moments of fellowship were spent in my dear father's home. Sometimes, on rare occasions, I was permitted to accompany him to his field of labor and assist him in instructing those who recently entered the new life. They had little or no preparation for its duties and responsibilities.

On one occasion he said to me, "I am faced with the most difficult problem I have yet had to deal with in this work. It is how to enlighten and help a man who suddenly plunged from an apparently honorable life into the very depths of crime. I have never been able to get him to accompany me to the River, where these earthly cobwebs would be swept from his poor brain. His excuse is always that God's mercy is so great in allowing him inside heaven's gates at all, that he is content to remain always in its lowest scale of enjoyment and life. No argument or teaching thus far has helped him alter his decision.

"He was led astray by infatuation for a strange woman and killed his aged mother in order to secure her jewels for this wretched creature. He was executed for the crime, of which in the end he sincerely repented, but he left life with all the horror of the deed clinging to his soul."

"Has he seen his mother since coming here? Does she know of his arrival?"

"No, she is entirely alone in this world. It was not thought wise to tell her of his coming until his soul was in a better condition to receive her. He was an only child and does not lack the elements of refinement, but he was completely under the control of this vile, though fascinating, woman. It is said she drugged his wine and caused him to do the dreadful deed while under its influence, because of her hatred for his mother. When he recovered from the influence of the wine, he was horrified at what he had done. His infatuation for the woman turned to loathing—but, alas, too late! He refused to see her during his entire incarceration."

"How long was he in prison?"

"Almost a year."

"Has he seen the Master?"

"No, he begs not to see Him. He is very repentant and grateful to be saved from the wrath he feels was his just punishment. Though he is conscious that his sin is forgiven, he does not feel that he can ever stand in the presence of the Holy One. And here, as on earth, each must be willing to receive Him. His presence is never given undesired. I have not yet appealed for higher help. My ambition is to lead these weak souls upward through the strength entrusted to me. Can you suggest anything that would probably reach him?"

"His mother. May I bring her?"

He thought a moment reflectively then said, "A woman's intuition. Yes, bring her."

Mother-Love

I soon was on my way. I found the poor woman, laid the facts gently before her, and waited for her decision. There was no hesitancy on her part. In an instant she said, "My poor boy! Certainly I will go with you at once."

We found my father waiting for us and went immediately to the great house where these students stayed. It was a beautiful building in the midst of a park with shaded walks and fountains and flowers everywhere. To one just freed from earth it seemed a paradise indeed. But to those of us who had tasted heaven's rarer joys, something was lacking. We missed the lovely individual homes, the little children playing on the lawns, the music of the angel choir. It was tame, indeed, beside the pleasures we had tasted.

We found the young man seated beneath one of the flower-laden trees, intently studying a book my father had left with him. There was a peaceful look on his pale face, but it was rather the look of patient resignation than overwhelming joy. His mother approached him alone. My father and I remained in the background. After a while, he glanced up and saw his mother standing near him. A startled look came into his face, and he rose to his feet. She extended her arms toward him and cried out pathetically, "John, my dear boy, come home to me—I need you!" That was all.

With a low cry he knelt at her feet and clasped her knees, sobbing, "Mother! Mother!"

She stooped and put her tender arms around him. She drew his head gently to her breast and showered kisses on his bowed head. Oh, the warm mother-love, the same in earth and heaven! Only the Christ-love can exceed it. Here was this disheartened mother, sent into eternity by the hands of him who should have shielded and sustained her, bending above her repentant son with the mother-love. Her joy and love were shining on him from her gentle eyes.

I saw my father turn his head to conceal his emotion, and I knew that my own eyes were wet. My father had explained to the mother that the first thing to be accomplished was to get her son to the River. We now heard her say caressingly, "Come, John, my boy, take the first step upward, for your mother's sake, that in time I may have the joy of seeing you in our own home. Come, John, with mother."

She gently drew him, and to our great joy we saw him rise and go with her. Their steps led them to the River. They walked hand in hand, and as far as we could see them she seemed to be soothing and comforting him.

"There will be no further trouble now," said my father. "When they return, he will see with clearer vision." And so it was.

After this, by divine permission, I became a co-laborer with my father, and thus I enjoyed his company and his instructions more often than I might have done.

Chapter 14

THE BEST REUNION OF ALL

On one occasion, I sat resting on the upper veranda of our home. I had just returned from a somewhat strenuous journey to a distant city of the heavenly realm. From this part of the veranda, we caught rare glimpses of the River through the overhanging branches of the trees. Just below us, at a little distance, we could see the happy children playing on the lawn.

Here Frank found me and, throwing himself on a soft veranda lounge, lay for a time motionless and silent. He looked as wearied as one can ever look in that life, but I felt no anxiety about him. He had been absent on some earth-mission. I knew that some of the fatigue and care of earth will cling to us on such occasions, until we are restored by heaven's soothing air and life-giving waters.

He had not told me, as he sometimes did, where his mission had led him. And I had not asked him, feeling sure that he would tell me what I should know. My own recent duties had been unusually responsible, leading me to a distant part of the heavenly Kingdom. I had thrown all of my energies into the work assigned me by the Master.

Good News

After a time of rest, Frank arose to a sitting posture and, regarding me for a moment in silence, said gently, "I have news for you, little sister."

A thrill like an electric shock passed through me, and in an instant I cried out joyously, "He is coming!"

He nodded his head, with a sympathetic smile, but did not at once reply.

"He was stricken suddenly in the midst of his work, while apparently in perfect health, and has not regained consciousness—nor will he ever on earth."

"When was this?"

"Three days ago. I have been with him almost constantly by day and night ever since."

"Oh, why did you not tell me sooner?"

"It was thought wise to spare you the unnecessary pain of knowing he was suffering when you could not minister to him."

"Will he know me as soon as the struggle is past?"

"Yes, but he will be bewildered and weak. He will need stronger help and guidance than you alone can give. You will miss the rapture of the meeting as it would be a little later on."

"What should I do? You know I will yield to your wiser judgment even against the pleadings of my heart."

"I will not say, 'do not go.' You may accompany me, if you wish. I only think that after the first bewilderment of the change has passed, after he has bathed in the waters of the River of Life, he will be better prepared for your delightful reunion. You remember what the waters did for you and how bewildered and oppressed in spirit you were until you went into the River. It is the same with all of us. Only where there has been serious trouble with the brain, it is even more necessary than on ordinary occasions. And that is the case with my brother. He will not be himself until the cleansing waters have swept the clouds from his brain."

"You are always right, Frank. I will yield to your wise advice, although my heart cries out to rush to his side. When will you return to him?"

"Immediately. There will be little time to wait. My brave-hearted, wise, little sister, the delay will be neither sorrowful nor long."

He arose and, bending over me, dropped a kiss lightly on my brow. In a moment, he passed from my sight.

"How strange," I thought, "that even in this matter, so near to my heart, I am able to yield unmurmuringly! Father, I thank You! I thank You for the glad reunion so near at hand. But even more than that, I thank You for the sweet submission in all things that has grown into my life. I can yield to Your will even when You would permit it to be otherwise.''

I bowed my head upon my hand and gave myself up to mingled sad and happy thoughts. Was he, this dearly loved one, indeed unaware of his suffering? Would the Father mercifully spare him even the pain of the parting? Oh, that the time of his arrival were here! How could I wait even that brief while for the sight of his beloved face!

Suddenly, a soft touch rested upon my bowed head. A Voice I had learned to recognize and love beyond all things in earth or heaven said, "Have I not said truly, 'Though he were dead, yet shall he live'? (John 11:25). Of what importance are the years of separation, since the meeting again is at hand? Come, and let us reason a little together." The Master smiled down into my uplifted face. He took my extended hand into His own and, sitting down beside me, continued, "Let us consider what being here has done for you. Do you not feel that you are infinitely better prepared to bring happiness than when you parted from him whom you love?''

I nodded in glad affirmation.

"Do you not realize that you stand on a higher plane with more exalted ideas of life and its duties? In the strength of the Father, you two will walk upward together.''

Again, I gladly acquiesced.

"Is the life here less attractive than it was on earth?''

"No, no! A thousand times no!" I cried.

"Then there is nothing but joy in the reunion at

hand?"

"Nothing but joy," I echoed.

The Secret Of Marriage

Then the Savior led me on to talk of the one so soon to come. I opened my glad heart to Him and told Him of the noble life, the unselfish toil, the high aspirations, the unfaltering trust of him whom I loved. I spoke of his strength in misfortune, his courage in the face of sore trial and disappointment, his forgiveness of even malicious injury. I then concluded by saying, "He lived the Christianity many others only professed. He always surpassed me in that."

The face of the Master glowed in sympathy as I talked. When I ceased, He said, "I perceive that you have discovered the secret of marriage."

He led me on until my soul flew upward as a lark. He unfolded mysteries of the soul-life that filled my heart with rapture, but which I may not here reveal. At length, to my infinite surprise, I saw the rosy glow deepening across the sky. The Master arose and, pointing to the radiance, said: "By the time you are ready to receive them they will be here." With a smile, and a touch that made a benediction, He departed.

A Glad Song

As I arose and stood, I heard the triumphant notes of the angels' choral song. As though in sympathy with my thought, they sang, "He is risen! Hear it, ye heavens, and ye sons of earth! He is risen, and has become the firstfruits of them that slept!''

I lifted up my voice with joy and joined their thrilling song. As they swept onward, and the melody died away, I slowly descended the stairway, crossed the lawn whose flowers never crushed or withered beneath our feet, and sank beneath the pure waters of the River. I felt no haste, no unusual excitement or unrest, though I knew that he was coming. The Master's presence had filled me with such calm and peace that no power could disturb it. He had prepared me for the great happiness lying just before me.

Uplifted with a new, strange delight, I recrossed the lawn to gather a bouquet of cream-white roses, and I fastened them to my breast. Then I refilled the golden bowl in the library with the luscious scarlet carnations, laying one aside to fasten upon my husband's shoulder. I wanted to personally gather the flowers that would greet him on his coming. I twisted up my hair in the manner that he had most admired and fastened a creamy bud within the folds.

Soon I heard voices and steps. Listen! Yes, it is the same dear step which I had so often listened for in the old home-life. His steps had always brought gladness to my heart and sunshine in our home! His step in heaven! I flew to the open doorway and, in an instant, was held close to the loving, throbbing heart of my dear husband.

Frank, with thoughtful care, passed on to the upper rooms of the house. For a while we were alone together—we whose lives had been so happy through the long years of our mortal life. I led him into the house, and, in the vestibule, he again took me in his arms and drew me to his heart.

"This is heaven indeed!" he said.

We passed into the "flower-room," and he stood a moment on its threshold, entranced with its beauty. But when I began to tell him its history, as Frank had given it to me, he said, "Not today, my dear."

So we sat and talked together. Our brother, Frank, had come to us, and together we had gone through the lovely house. We stood upon the broad verandas and ate of the heavenly fruit. Then we all sat together where I had spent the time waiting in the presence of the blessed Master. I told them much that He had said to me and how He turned my waiting into triumphant rejoicing. The eyes of my dear husband were tear-filled, and he held my hand in tender sympathy.

"Oh, darling, it is a blessed, blessed life!" I said.

"I already realize the blessedness," he replied.

A Family Reunion

I said to my husband and Frank, "We must go to father and mother Springer's."

"Yes, we will go at once," they both replied.

So together we all started. I had often and with much joy visited the home of my husband's parents. I found a warm place in their hearts. Now we were taking them a favorite son. I realized how his coming would bring gladness to their hearts and home. It was a joyful meeting, especially to our mother.

When we turned to go, we met, upon the threshold, an aunt who in the earth-life—blind and helpless—had been special to us all.

"My dear children," she exclaimed, "how good it is to see you all again!"

"Aunt Cynthia!" my husband said fondly.

"Yes, Aunt Cynthia, but no longer groping helpless in the darkness. 'whereas I was blind, now I see' " (John 9:25), she quoted, smiling happily.

And so it was—the Master's touch had rested on her sightless eyes, and, closing to the darkness of earth, they had opened upon the glories of heaven. Marvelous transition! No wonder we left her singing:

Glory to Him who this marvel hath wrought,
Filling my spirit with joy and delight!
Lo, in my blindness I safely have walked
Out of the darkness into the light!

Chapter 15

THE CELESTIAL SEA

Our life was perfect, though we looked forward with joy to the future coming of our son and daughter to make its ties complete. We had often spoken of going together to the great celestial sea, but the time had never seemed quite ripe for so doing. We realized it was one of the great mysteries of heaven, although we did not know just what to expect. Once I said to Frank, "I have a strange desire to go to the sea, if you think it wise for us to do so."

"I am glad that is is your desire to go, as it is mine to have you. I was about to propose that you and my brother take this blessed journey together."

"Will you accompany us?"

"Not at this time. We will all go together another time. But it is best that you two go alone this time. You know the way. Go through the forest that leads to the Temple, until you are almost there. Then bear to the right and follow the golden path that takes you directly to the shore."

So we started. We were filled with a holy joy that we could take this special journey together. We walked through the great forest where the beautiful light fell through the quivering branches overhead. Gorgeous birds were darting everywhere. We heard the regular crashing of waves against the shore. And there were bursts of triumphant song and the harmony of many instruments of music. Eventually we emerged from the forest and stood mute and motionless before the overwhelming glory of the scene before us.

The Glory Of It All!

Can I describe it as it appeared to me that day? Not until my lips can speak and your heart can understand the language of the royal courts above. From our very feet a golden beach sloped downward toward the shore. It was many hundred feet wide and extended on either side far beyond the limits of our vision. This beach caught and radiated the light until it glittered and glimmered like the dust of diamonds and other precious stones.

The waves, as they came and went in ceaseless motion, caught up this sparkling sand and carried it on their crests. And the sea! It spread out before us in a radiance that exceeds description in any language I have ever known. It was like the white glory that shone through the windows of the Temple. Beneath this shining glory we saw the blue tint of the waters of that sea which has no limit to its depths or bounds.

Upon its shining bosom we saw, in every direction, boats representing all nations. But their beauty far surpassed anything earth has ever known. They were like great, open pleasure-barges, and they were filled with people looking eagerly toward the shore. Many, in their eagerness, were standing erect and gazing with wistful, expectant eyes into the faces of those on the shore.

Ah, the people upon the shore! "Numberless as the sands of the sea," they stood, far as the eyes could reach, far as stretched the shore of that limitless sea, a great mass of beautiful souls clad in the spotless garments of the redeemed. Many of them had golden harps and various instruments of music. When a boat touched the shore, its passengers were welcomed by the glad voices and tender embraces of their loved ones. Then the harps would be held aloft, all of the golden instruments would sound, and the vast multitude would break forth into the triumphant song of victory over death and the grave.

"Do these people always stand here, I wonder?" I said softly.

"Not the same people," said a radiant being near us who had heard my question. "But there is always a crowd of people here—those who are expecting friends from the other life, and those who assemble to share in their joy. Some of the heavenly choristers are always here, but not always the same ones. You will notice that most of those who arrive are led quietly away by their friends, and many others are constantly joining the multitude.''

He passed onward toward the shore and left us enveloped in awe and wonder.

Wonderful Reunions

We soon became deeply interested in watching the reunions and found ourselves joining with rapture in the glad songs of rejoicing. Now and then a familiar face would be among the eager faces in the boats, but there were none that had been especially dear to us. Still it made us notice more closely and sympathize more heartily with those who welcomed beloved friends. Perhaps we would see a wife caught in the close embrace of a waiting husband, or a little child with a glad cry would spring into the outstretched arms of a happy mother. Friend would clasp friend in glad reunion, and an aged mother would be folded to the heart of a beloved child.

As one boat of extraordinary strength and beauty came riding gracefully over the waves, we observed the tall figure of a man standing near the front with his arms around a graceful woman who stood by his side. Each shaded their dazzled eyes from the rare splendor and scanned, wistful and searchingly, the faces of the crowd as the boat neared the shore. Suddenly, with a great thrill of joy surging through my being, I cried out, "It is our precious son and his dear wife! They have come together!"

In an instant we were swiftly moving through the crowd which parted in ready sympathy to let us pass. And, as the boat touched the shore, they were both beside us—the dear daughter already embracing her happy parents, who were waiting near the water's edge, and our beloved son enfolding us. Soon we were all in each other's embrace. Oh, what a rapturous moment that was! Our life in heaven was complete—no partings forever! As we stood with encircling arms, scarcely realizing the unexpected bliss, the heavenly choir broke into song. With uplifted faces radiant with joy, eyes filled with happy tears, and voices trembling with emotion, we all joined in a glad anthem of praise.

Glory be unto the Father, and unto the Son!
Glory be unto the ever-blessed Three in one!
No more sorrow, no more parting, no more
grief or pain;
Christ has broken death's strong fetters,
And we are free again!
Alleluia! Amen!

The song rose and swelled triumphantly as the vast multitude caught it up. The surge of the waves made a deep undertone to the melody that increased its solemnity. With bowed heads and full hearts we passed onward hand in hand. The light that fell about was purer, holier, and more divine than it had ever been before.

Chapter 16

THE VISION ENDS

Then there came the time when I stood in my lovely room that had become a shrine to me. I walked to my couch, to lie down for a moment. But strange thoughts and ideas crept into my brain. I felt confused and bewildered. I got up, restlessly, from my pillow, only to fall back again in doubt—almost dread. What could it mean? Could the old unrest of earth enter this divine retreat?

Then I heard unfamiliar voices. Someone said, "I think her color is better than it has been for several days." "Yes, there is no doubt that she is better today. There is hope for her now, I am sure. But she came very near passing through the Gates."

"Very near passing through the Gates!" As though I had not passed through! In returning, I left heaven's gates so ajar that gleams of the heavenly radiance from beyond will fall about my life forever!

I have been in my Father's house.
"We shall know each other there!"

Chapter 17

REFLECTIONS

Let me reassert what I have already stated: I have never claimed that this strange experience is either a revelation or an inspiration. It came to me during a period of great physical suffering, and I have always considered it compensation for that suffering. Be this as it may, it has been a great comfort and help to me. Through the letters received from others, I am led to believe it has been the same to many who have read it. I am extremely gratified by this.

I wish that I could have related the entire experience just as it came to me, but our present language is wholly inadequate. There were so many mysteries, so many teachings far beyond anything we have known in this life, that I find myself bewildered and lost when I attempt to convey the marvelous things I experienced during that time.

Questions About The Vision

The question has repeatedly been asked me, "Was this a real experience or merely a fanciful sketch?'' What I have written above will answer that question. The preface and early pages are as nearly accurate as I can make them. Anything that I might add on that point would simply be superfluous.

Questions concerning the comparative distances in heaven, our powers of passing from one point to another, and if in the other life we develop wings to aid us in passage have been asked. These matter-of-fact questions are sometimes quite difficult to answer. I believe that if I were really in the other life, as during this experience I seemed to be, my thoughts would be so far above such temporal matters that I would be unable to answer such inquiries satisfactorily on my return to this life.

Looking back upon it now, and trying to gather facts from the impressions that I then received, I would say that none who have ever passed through mortal life would in any way be changed from their present personal appearance, except to be etherealized and glorified.

When I seemed to stand in that wonderful Temple filled with the glory of God the Father, four angels with uplifted trumpets stood beside the golden altar on the great platform of pearl. From their shoulders shadowy pinions enfolded them and touched the floor upon which they stood. And, in a moment of bewildering emotions, I lifted my eyes to the cloud-filled dome. There I saw shadowy pinions which half-concealed the harps and golden instruments of the heavenly choir.

Also, when I had first met the Savior, we heard the angel voices as we stood together in the great "flower-room." Looking upward, I saw the cherub faces in the golden light above us, and they, too, had delicate, shadowy wings, half-concealing their divine forms. Except for this, I have no recollection of having seen any of those glorious wings of which we so often read.

To me it seems these are given to the angels of God who have always lived in heaven. We appear to our friends when we meet them over there just as they saw us here, only purified and perfect. Still, we had powers of locomotion given us that carried us from point to point swiftly and securely, as though borne by a boat upon the waters.

A Strange Journey

I do not know how I can better illustrate this point than by giving a little incident not mentioned before. I remember sitting once on the upper terrace in the house of my sister. She said to me, "I often look across the River to those lovely hills in the distance and wonder if it is all as beautiful there as here. I intend to go soon and see."

"Why not go now?" was my reply.

"Could you go with me now?" she asked as she turned her radiant face again toward the River and the lovely fields beyond.

"With pleasure," I replied. "I have often wished to go myself. There is something very inviting in the beautiful landscape beyond the

River. Where is Frank?'' I asked. ''Will he accompany us?''

''No,'' she said, looking smilingly toward me, ''he has gone on an important mission for the Master. But you and I, dear, can go and be home again before his return.''

''Then let us do so,'' I replied, rising and giving her my hand.

She at once arose, and, instead of turning toward the stairway in the center of the building, we turned and walked deliberately toward the low, sloping wall that surrounded the upper veranda. Without a moment's hesitation, we stepped over this into the sweet air that lay about us. There was no more fear of falling than if our feet had been on solid ground. We had the power of passing through the air and water at will, just as we had the power of walking upon the crystal paths and lawn about us.

We ascended slightly until we were just above the treetops, and then—what shall I say?—we did not fly, we made no effort either with our hands or our feet. I can only think of the word ''drifting'' to describe this wonderful experience. We went as a leaf or a feather floats through the air on a beautiful day, and the sensation was most delightful. Beneath us we saw, through the green branches of the trees, the little children playing and the people walking—some for pleasure, some for duty. As we neared the River, we looked down on the pleasure-boats and the people sitting or lying or walking on the pebbly bottom. We saw them with the same distinctness as we would if we were simply looking at them through the atmosphere.

Conversing as we drifted onward, we were soon over the tops of the hills which were our destiny. For some time, we exchanged no words. Our hearts were filled with sensations that only the scenes of heaven can give. Then my sister said very softly, quoting from one of the old earth-hymns, "Sweet fields beyond the swelling flood. Stand dressed in living green."

And, in the same spirit, I answered, "It is, indeed, a rapturous scene—that rises to our sight. Sweet fields arrayed in living green, and rivers of delight."

Missionaries In Heaven

As we continued, we began to see many suburban villages similar to our own. Many of the buildings seemed quite different in architecture from our own. I suggested to my sister that we drop down a little. On doing so, we soon realized what caused this apparent difference in the architecture and surroundings. Where our homes were situated, we were surrounded by people we had known and loved on earth. And they were also of our own nationality.

Many of these villages over which we were now passing were formed from what, to us, would be termed foreign nations. Each village retained some of the peculiarities of its heritage on earth and were naturally unfamiliar. We recognized again the wisdom and goodness of the Father in thus allowing friends of the same nationality to be located near each other in heaven, as on earth.

As we drifted onward and passed over an exquisitely beautiful valley, we saw a group of people seated on the ground in a semicircle. There seemed to be hundreds, and in their midst was a man who, apparently, was talking to them. Something familiar, and yet unfamiliar, attracted us, and I said, "Let's go nearer and hear what he is saying. Let's see who these people are."

Upon doing this, we found the people to slightly resemble our own Indian tribes. Their dress, in a manner, corresponded to that worn on earth, though so etherealized as to be surpassingly beautiful. But the dusky faces and the long black hair still remained. The faces, with intense interest, were turned toward the man who was talking to them. Looking at him, we saw that he belonged to the Anglo-Saxon race. In a whisper of surprise, I said to my sister, "Why, he is a missionary!"

As so often seemed to happen when a surprise or a difficulty presented itself, there was always someone near to answer and enlighten us. And so we found on this occasion that our instructor was beside us ready to answer any surprise or question that might be asked. He said at once, "Yes, you are right. This is a missionary who gave his life to what on earth were called the heathen. He spent many years working for them and enlightening those who sat in darkness, resulting, as you see before you, in hundreds being brought into the Kingdom of the Master. But, as you will naturally suppose, they have much to learn. He still gathers them about him and leads them higher and higher into the blessed life."

"Are there many doing this type of work in this beautiful realm?" I asked.

"Many hundreds," he said. "To these poor minds, unenlightened as they were when they first came, heaven is as beautiful and happy a place as it is to any who have ascended higher, simply because we can enjoy only in the capacity to which our souls can reach. All of us have much yet to learn of this wonderful country."

In several instances as we drifted above the villages, we heard songs of praise arising from the temples and from people collected in different ways. In many cases, to our surprise, the hymns and the words were familiar, and, although sung in a strange tongue, we understood them all. That was another one of the wonderful surprises of heaven. There was no language there that we could not understand.

We passed on and on and on through wonderful scenes of beauty, finally returning to our own homes by a different way than we had come. It seemed that we almost made a circle in our pleasant journeyings. When I left my sister in her own home, she whispered to me as she said good-bye, "It has been a time of such wonderful rest and pleasure. We must do it again soon."

"Yes, dear, we will."

The Meaning Of The Vision

In answer to the question of whether I consider this experience a revelation, I can only say that I gave it as it came to me. Each person must draw his own conclusions concerning it. I can be the guide for no one.

Looking back, it seems to me to be more a series of instructions such as we give little children here in kindergarten. *It does not strive to be a revelation of what has been or what will be, in the strict sense of the word.* But, as I have already suggested, it is more like a lesson we would teach children in school.

I myself noticed, in transcribing this strange experience, the fact that the first lesson to be taught almost invariably came as an illustration. And, after my wonder and pleasure had taken in all that the picture itself would teach, then followed the revelation or a general application of its meaning.

For instance, that I may make my meaning more clear, when I myself first entered within the gates, I was shown the wonders of the celestial gardens and the beautiful River. Then came the reunions with the dear ones from whom I had been so long parted. And so I came to know the rapture of the spirit on its first entrance within heaven's gates.

Afterwards there were the instructions or first lessons concerning this life into which I seemed to have entered, until they formed one perfect lesson. And when I met and welcomed my dear sister, my husband, and my son, I knew the other side of the question—the joy that came even to the angels in heaven when they welcomed the beloved ones who came to them from the world below.

And so, all through the book, the instruction was invariably preceded by the illustration. Thus I can only think, if any meaning can be attached to this wonderful vision, that it is simply a general lesson of what we may expect and hope for when we reach the other shore.

Overflowing With Pure Water

Again, I am asked, "Does this experience retain its vividness as time passes, or does it grow unreal and dreamlike to you?" I can partially forget some of the happiest experiences of my earth-life, but time seems only to intensify the wonders of those days when my feet stood on the border of the two worlds. It seemed to me that, at every step we took in the divine life, our souls reached up toward something better. We had no inclination to look behind to that which had passed or to try to solve what in our mortal life had been intricate or perplexing questions or mysteries. Like the cup that is filled to overflowing at the fountain with pure and sparkling water, so our souls were filled—more than filled—with water from the fountain of all good. There was no longer room for anything else.

"How then," you asked, "could you reach out for more, when you had all that you could receive?" Because our souls grew and expanded and opened to receive fresh inflows of divine instruction which constantly lifted us nearer to the source of all perfection.

Some of the letters that have come to me have been so pathetic in their inquiries, that they have called forth sympathetic tears. Thus, I have an intense longing to speak with authority on the question raised. However, God has not given me that privilege. I can only tell how it seemed to me in that blissful time when earth seemed remote and heaven very near and real.

To all who have lost loved ones, I would say, "Look up, dear friends, and see the loved ones, as I saw those so dear to me, happy and blessed beyond all human conception in the house of many mansions prepared for us by our loving Father." Oh, those wonderful mansions on which my longing heart looks back! Believe in them, look forward to them, beloved friends, for we have the Savior's promise that they are there, "In My Father's house are many mansions" (John 14:2). His promises never fail. And I am sure of one thing—they will not be any less beautiful than those I saw in my vision.

In conclusion, I can only reiterate that I am no prophet; I am no seer. But, in my innermost soul, I honestly believe that if the joys of heaven are greater, if the glories "within heaven's gates" are more radiant than I beheld them in my vision, I cannot understand how even the immortal spirit could bear to look upon them.

ANOTHER POWERFUL Book
from Whitaker House

Visions of Heaven
H. A. Baker

Beggars, outcasts, homeless—such were the orphan
boys who came to the Adullam Home, a rescue mission
in China. These children asked God to reveal Himself to
them. The revelations and visions given to them are told
here and are proof of the fulfillment of God's promise
that in the last days, "young men shall see visions."

ISBN: 0-88368-401-2 • Pocket • 144 pages

Available at Your Local Christian Bookstore
Visit our web site at: www.whitakerhouse.com

ANOTHER POWERFUL BOOK

from Whitaker House

A Christian's Secret of a Happy Life
Hannah Whitall Smith

Here are practical truths that will enable you to
live above religious drudgery and enjoy the happy life
that God intended for you. The potential for a happy,
abundant Christian life is available to all who make
Jesus the Lord of their lives. This classic has
changed the lives of millions.

ISBN: 0-88368-132-3 • Pocket • 240 pages

Available at Your Local Christian Bookstore
Visit our web site at: www.whitakerhouse.com

ANOTHER POWERFUL  OOK

from Whitaker House

The God of All Comfort

Hannah Whitall Smith

God has not called anyone to lead a spiritually
uncomfortable life, but rather a life of promise and
victory! He can be with you and comfort you every step
of the way. Let Hannah Whitall Smith show you how to
become better acquainted with God and experience
all that He has for you.

ISBN: 0-88368-496-9 • Pocket • 288 pages

Available at Your Local Christian Bookstore
Visit our web site at: www.whitakerhouse.com

ANOTHER POWERFUL OOK

from Whitaker House

Experiencing God through Prayer
Jeanne Guyon

This treasure chest of wisdom contains rich nuggets of
truth that could only have been revealed by the Spirit of
God. Madame Guyon shares the secrets to experiencing
God, not just praying to Him. You will discover and
remember her easy methods of finding God
through prayer.

ISBN: 0-88368-153-6 • Pocket • 96 pages

Available at Your Local Christian Bookstore
Visit our web site at: www.whitakerhouse.com

ANOTHER POWERFUL Book

from Whitaker House

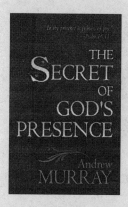

The Secret of God's Presence
Andrew Murray

In these pages, Murray discusses the idea that union
with Christ allows you to become perfect in God's
sight. As you abide in God's presence, you will blossom
into perfection. Begin now to serve God with
a willing heart, and He will do in you all that
He has done in Christ Jesus.

ISBN: 0-88368-563-9 • Trade• 144 pages

Available at Your Local Christian Bookstore
Visit our web site at: www.whitakerhouse.com

ANOTHER POWERFUL Book
from Whitaker House

Covenants and Blessings
Andrew Murray

One of the most precious of God's unbreakable
promises is to give us abundant life—not only in
eternity, but also right now. Instead of struggling to
live for God through your own efforts, you can
know the joy of the Spirit of Christ
living in and through you.

ISBN: 0-88368-748-8 • Trade • 176 pages

Available at Your Local Christian Bookstore
Visit our web site at: www.whitakerhouse.com

2 50
F
6/16

Wyatt's eyes twinkled. "We're a proud lot."

"I've heard as much."

With his finger, he pushed a barrel curl resting on her cheek behind her ear. From the second his finger glided across her skin, ridiculous yearning reared up again, putting a halt to their pleasant banter. He gazed at her with dire want, his eyes dipping down to her mouth.

"Brooke," he rasped. There was a distinct hitch in his voice that touched something powerful inside her quivering belly.

"It's okay, Wyatt," she said. Whatever he wanted, she was ready for.

A groan rose from his throat and he began shaking his head as if he couldn't believe ⬚⬚⬚ was happening. One of his hands wrapped ⬚⬚⬚⬚⬚ her waist, his fingers inching her clo⬚⬚⬚⬚⬚⬚⬚ hand was lifting her chin. His ⬚⬚⬚⬚⬚⬚⬚⬚⬚ instantly safe with Wyatt ⬚⬚⬚⬚⬚⬚⬚⬚⬚ saving her from em⬚⬚⬚⬚⬚⬚⬚⬚⬚ men. It was somethin⬚⬚⬚⬚⬚⬚⬚⬚ ever experienced before. ⬚⬚⬚

Twins for t⬚⬚⬚ is part of Harlequin Desire's #1 bestselling series, Billionaires and Babies: Powerful men...wrapped around their babies' little fingers.

Dear Reader,

I married a twin! And when we decided to have children, I always thought I'd love to have twins, *the first time around*. But after my son was born and we were contemplating having another child, I worried that, *oh no, we might have twins!*

We didn't. We had a boy, and shortly after a girl, and then ran out of bedroom space. Ha!

Without giving too much of the story away, the idea of twins plus one inspired me to write *Twins for the Texan*. I enjoyed using my knowledge of baby care and parenting to make the heroine, Brooke McKay (you met her in *One Secret Night, One Secret Baby*), somewhat of a babysitter extraordinaire. The working title of this story was *The Texan's Accidental Nanny*, so that gives you an idea where this story is heading, but if you know me and my books, you know the road to happiness for Brooke and Wyatt is paved with lots of twists, turns and detours.

With my father-in-law being a proud Texan and my husband a fraternal twin, I'm surprised it's taken me this long to write a Texas twins story. But I will say, I poured my heart and soul into this book. I hope you'll enjoy reading about these precious and precocious eighteen-month-old babies. Brett is the quieter of the two, and Brianna, "Breezy-Peezy," is quite a handful for my hunky hero, Wyatt Brandt.

As for the romance...it's sizzling hot. Brooke thinks of Wyatt as her "miracle" cowboy. Read on to find out why!

Happy reading,

Charlene Sands

CHARLENE
SANDS

———

TWINS FOR THE TEXAN

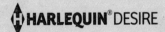

HARLEQUIN® DESIRE

If you purchased this book without a cover you should be aware
that this book is stolen property. It was reported as "unsold and
destroyed" to the publisher, and neither the author nor the
publisher has received any payment for this "stripped book."

Recycling programs
for this product may
not exist in your area

ISBN-13: 978-0-373-73456-6

Twins for the Texan

Copyright © 2016 by Charlene Swink

All rights reserved. Except for use in any review, the reproduction or
utilization of this work in whole or in part in any form by any electronic,
mechanical or other means, now known or hereinafter invented, including
xerography, photocopying and recording, or in any information storage
or retrieval system, is forbidden without the written permission of the
publisher, Harlequin Enterprises Limited, 225 Duncan Mill Road,
Don Mills, Ontario M3B 3K9, Canada.

This is a work of fiction. Names, characters, places and incidents are
either the product of the author's imagination or are used fictitiously,
and any resemblance to actual persons, living or dead, business
establishments, events or locales is entirely coincidental.

This edition published by arrangement with Harlequin Books S.A.

For questions and comments about the quality of this book,
please contact us at CustomerService@Harlequin.com.

® and TM are trademarks of Harlequin Enterprises Limited or its
corporate affiliates. Trademarks indicated with ® are registered in the
United States Patent and Trademark Office, the Canadian Intellectual
Property Office and in other countries.

Printed in U.S.A.

H HARLEQUIN®
™ www.Harlequin.com

Charlene Sands is a *USA TODAY* bestselling author of more than forty romance novels, writing sensual contemporary romances and stories of the Old West. When not writing, Charlene enjoys sunny Pacific beaches, great coffee, reading books from her favorite authors and spending time with her family. You can find her on Facebook and Twitter, write her at PO Box 4883, West Hills, CA 91308, or sign up for her newsletter for fun blogs and ongoing contests at charlenesands.com.

Books by Charlene Sands

HARLEQUIN DESIRE

Moonlight Beach Bachelors

Her Forbidden Cowboy
The Billionaire's Daddy Test
One Secret Night, One Secret Baby
Twins for the Texan

The Slades of Sunset Ranch

Sunset Surrender
Sunset Seduction
The Secret Heir of Sunset Ranch
Redeeming the CEO Cowboy

The Worths of Red Ridge

Carrying the Rancher's Heir
The Cowboy's Pride
Worth the Risk

Visit her Author Profile page at Harlequin.com, or charlenesands.com, for more titles.

To my sweet mother-in-law, Nancy, with love.

Thanks for having twins, inspiring this story
and giving me a great husband!

One

Brooke McKay had no clue where this deserted Texas road was taking her. Gazing past a dozen squished bugs on the rental car's windshield, she saw flatland stretching before her for miles and miles. After living in California near mountains and beaches, this kind of vast flatness was foreign to her.

Red warning lights blinked from the car's dashboard. She looked down at the indicator. Her gas tank was nearing empty. "Don't do it, don't do it."

Decked out in her best black lace dress with all the necessary trimmings and red heels so high they'd put the balls of her feet to the test in the walking-to-the-next-gas-station department, Brooke pushed the car to its limit.

She spotted something lying in the middle of the road. "Oh!"

Roadkill.

Apparently someone had driven on this road recently. It was good news for her, but not for the poor possum.

As she drove on, she removed her sunglasses and squinted into the afternoon sun searching for a miracle. A gas station would be nice, with an attendant who knew where in heck she was.

The car sputtered, the engine wringing out its last breaths.

She sucked in oxygen, praying that her worst nightmare wasn't coming to life.

And then the car crawled to a stop.

She pumped the gas pedal, but there was no more wringing to be had.

Oh, boy. Not only wouldn't she make it to Heather's wedding on time, she might have to camp out here in the wilderness for heaven knew how long.

She stared at her cell phone lying beside her on the seat. She already knew *that* miracle wasn't happening. She had no cell service. She hadn't for the last ten miles. She knocked her head against the leather steering wheel a few times and decided it made a good pillow, a place to rest her head and close her eyes while she thought of a way out of this predicament. She didn't have many choices. She'd have to get out and start walking.

"Excuse me, miss," came a deep voice from out of nowhere. "Are you okay?"

Her head popped up, and she looked into the bone-melting blue eyes of the man standing beside her driver-side door. Her heartbeat immediately picked up speed. There in the flesh was a dauntingly handsome, iron-jawed cowboy.

Her miracle.

"I, uh, I didn't hear anyone drive up." She glanced in her rearview mirror and sure enough, a shiny black Cadillac SUV was parked behind her car. "Yes, yes. I'm okay."

She took a closer look at him. Goodness, they grew them tall in Texas. Her miracle wore a black Western suit, a sterling silver belt buckle and one of those sexy string ties. "I th-think I took a wrong turn somewhere. Now I'm out of gas."

He nodded and scrubbed at the dark blond facial hair on his jaw. "Not a good thing to do on this road. There isn't a gas station for at least ten miles or so. I'm Wyatt Brandt, by the way." He stuck out his hand and she took it. It was a little awkward shaking hands through the car window, but his firm grip, beautiful eyes and rich Texas drawl put her at ease.

He could be a serial killer.

That thought flittered through her mind, but she dismissed it. The butterflies winging around in her stomach as he enveloped her hand, ever so briefly, told a different story. "I'm Brooke. I was heading to a friend's wedding, and now I'm afraid I'll never make it."

"Nice meeting you, Brooke," he said. "You wouldn't by any chance be heading to Blake and Heather's shindig, would you?"

Her eyebrows drew up. How did he know? *Serial killer* flashed in her mind again. Had he been stalking her? Her brother Dylan had almost lost his life to a stalker out to get revenge. Luckily, he'd survived the murder attempts and decided to get his wife away from the Hollywood scene for a while. Emma, Dylan and Brooke were all in Texas now, while Dylan was shooting a movie. She still had stalker on the brain but immediately dismissed the notion where Wyatt was concerned. How many stalkers drove Cadillacs and dressed like *GQ* models? No, Wyatt Brandt either was psychic or had been invited to the wedding, too. "Yes, that's the one. The GPS told me to take this road. I was running late, and this is supposed to be a shortcut to their wedding venue. Do you know them?"

"Sure do. I'm on my way to the nuptials, too. Blake's a friend of mine."

She smiled. This miracle was getting better and better.

"Heather and I went to college on the West Coast together. I've never met Blake."

"He's a great guy. Just so you know I'm not anyone you have to worry over. I own the Blue Horizon Ranch, about fifteen miles back that way." He pointed behind them. "And yes, this is a shortcut, if you know the roads. I'd be happy to give you a lift. I was running a bit late, too, and if we hurry, we'll make it before the ceremony begins."

"Gosh, that sounds great."

He opened the door for her and she got out. Their size difference was immediately evident. Even wearing three-inch heels, the top of her head reached his chin. His very rugged, strong chin.

"What about your car?" he asked.

"It's a rental." He closed the car door for her and she went on to explain, "I've been a little distracted lately, and forgot to fill the tank when I took off earlier. I'll lock it up and leave it here for now. I don't have much choice if I want to make the wedding."

He nodded. "Sounds good."

"Just let me get my bag." She clicked a button and the trunk popped open. He followed behind and before she could reach for her bag, he stretched a long arm around her, grazing her waist, and grabbed her suitcase. Warm shivers cascaded down her body from the contact. It was ridiculous how instantly attracted she was to him. She knew nothing about him other than his left hand was bare of a wedding ring and he had incredible eyes and pretty great manners.

"Anything else?" Her pink Gucci bag looked tiny in his grasp.

She'd heard about Southern charm, but experiencing it firsthand was refreshing. The men in other parts of the country could take a lesson from Wyatt Brandt. "No, that's it. Thank you."

"So you're staying overnight?" he asked as he guided her to his SUV.

"Yes. I figured the reception might go late, and I didn't think I'd be any good driving these roads at night. I'm not too great on them during the day either, apparently."

Rich laughter rose from his chest. "Probably a smart move." He opened the passenger-side door and she climbed into the seat.

Once she had settled in, she caught him gazing at her legs. A wave of heat passed through her as his eyes lingered just long enough not to be creepy.

After he put her suitcase in the back end, he took his seat behind the steering wheel and gave her a smile. "Do you have a last name?" he asked matter-of-factly as he started the engine. "Or are you just Brooke?"

Goodness, she didn't want to be Brooke McKay, not today, not with Wyatt. As soon as a guy got wind of who she really was, the sister of ultra-famous movie star Dylan McKay, he began treating her differently. She loved Dylan to pieces, but she'd had enough of that role, and it had caused her too much heartache with men who'd played her fast and loose just to get close to her famous brother.

Maybe it would be different in Texas than it had been in Los Angeles, where everyone it seemed, was trying to break into the movie business. But Brooke was too scarred now to test out that theory. "I'm Brooke *Johnson*."

The fib fell easily from her lips. For just one day. Was that asking too much?

"Okay, Brooke Johnson. Are you ready?"

"I think I was born ready," she said.

He laughed and they took off, leaving her little white Ford Escort in the dust.

Wyatt hadn't had a one-on-one conversation with a woman since his wife, Madelyn, had died some nine months ago. He wasn't including Henrietta in that, since his housekeeper was nearing retirement age, and besides, he was never really alone with her. Either Brett or Brianna or both of his eighteen-month-old twins were usually with them when they spoke, or rather when they tried to have a conversation. Raising twins was chaos in motion most of the time.

Yet Wyatt wasn't one for parties anymore. He preferred staying on the ranch, working long hours while trying to be a good father. But even he recognized his grief needed a swift kick in the ass, and his best friend Johnny Wilde had been the one to deliver it. "Go to that weddin', man. What you need is to get out and start livin' again."

Now he was wearing a monkey suit and heading for Blake's wedding, making conversation with a dark-haired woman with a sultry voice, great legs, and dark chocolate eyes with lids heavily shadowed and rims outlined in black.

"You're not from Texas, are you?" he asked.

"What was your first clue?"

He'd gotten a load of clues: the raven hair curling wildly down her back, the red painted lips, the dark made-up eyes and the manner of her dress. Sexy as it was, no woman in Texas would wear a skintight black lace dress to a wedding. At least none of the weddings he'd ever attended. "Oh, I don't know. Just a hunch."

"I'm from Los Angeles."

Her lips puckered as if she expected him to make some comment about her appearance. He wouldn't disrespect her that way. She was different from Madelyn, who'd been the epitome of Texas style and grace with sweet features, rosy cheeks and soft blond hair. Brooke certainly had her own style, but he wouldn't say she was unattractive. Quite the opposite, and he wished to hell he wasn't constantly noticing.

"So, you've come all this way for the wedding?" he asked.

"Yes, and for a little vacation. It just sort of worked out that I'd be able to attend Heather's wedding. I haven't seen her in years, but we've kept in touch. I'll be here for the rest of the summer."

"Where are you staying?"

"With a friend just outside of Beckon."

He nodded. "Nice."

"Yeah, it would be, but I co-own a business and I've put it in the hands of a new manager while I'm gone. It's a little nerve-racking."

"What kind of business?"

"It's called Parties-to-Go. We do all sorts of party and event planning. My partner is pregnant and well, it's a little complicated, but we both decided we needed a break. So we're here, enjoying the muggy end of the summer."

And he was enjoying her.

"What do you do, Wyatt? If you don't mind me asking? You said you owned Blue Horizon Ranch? Does that mean cattle?"

"Sure does. I've been raising cattle nearly all of my life. When my granddaddy started the ranch back in the forties, it was a small operation. My daddy built it up some, and then I took over when my folks moved to the East Coast. Blue Horizon's success had always been a dream of mine."

That and living to a ripe old age with his high school sweetheart, Madelyn.

"And now you're seeing it through."

"I am. The ranch does well, but I tinker in other things, too."

"Ah, you're an entrepreneur?"

"I suppose some might call me that."

He took pride in the investments he'd made in other companies that had paid off well. He'd made his first million before his twenty-seventh birthday, and he'd worked hard ever since to ensure a comfortable future for his family. Now he had all the money he'd ever need. Without Madelyn to share in his success, all of his hard work would've seemed pointless, but for his twins.

That was what getting off the ranch this weekend was about, him trying to move on with his life.

Start livin' again.

He glanced at Brooke, her red-lipped mouth in a pout as she tried to catch some cell service by waving her phone up in the air, putting it out the window for a few seconds. He couldn't seem to keep his eyes off her. She was a breath of fresh air and that alone stirred his juices. She was different and, he supposed, a lot of fun if he'd ever let himself find out.

"Nothing?" he asked once she gave up with her phone.

"Nope, not a blasted thing."

"We'll be at the hotel soon," he said.

The Inn at Sweetwater was known for lush gardens and scenic bridges along a natural lake. It was the destination spot for lovers and known as the ultimate venue for a romantic wedding. It was like the cherry topping on a hot fudge sundae for a bride and groom to speak their vows there. And it was why he'd resisted coming to this wedding.

Not on this day, of all days. It was Madelyn's birthday.

Hell, it was the exact reason Johnny insisted on his getting off the ranch. Wyatt needed the distraction, the time away. Wyatt had been restless and pensive and even Henrietta, bless her soul, had insisted he needed time to clear his head and gain some perspective. He'd be leaving his kids in her care overnight. Something he'd never done before, so with Johnny on his back and Henrietta pushing him, he'd accepted the invitation.

"What's wrong?" Brooke asked.

He turned to look into her pretty brown eyes. "Why do you think something's wrong?"

"Because I know you so well," she replied, grinning.

He laughed. "Sorry, just deep in thought."

"No apologies necessary. Aha! Finally, I'm getting bars on my cell. We must be nearing civilization. Excuse me while I call a tow service for my car."

"No problem." Wyatt listened to the deep, sensual lilt of her voice and tried to keep his eyes focused on the highway—not on Brooke Johnson, the engaging woman he'd picked up along the road.

As they drove through the intricate wrought iron gates of the venue, they entered a vibrant world of golf-course-green grass and tall swaying willows shading the lane leading up to the hotel. The Inn at Sweetwater was a plantation-style structure with palatial columns and snow-white shutters on every window. The gardens were ablaze with purple azaleas, pink peonies and stargazer lilies, and bluebonnets were interwoven among the stepping-stones. The paths all led to picturesque bridges arching over placid ponds. Off to the right fifty yards away, Sweetwater Lake sparkled in the late-afternoon sun.

"It looks like something out of a painting," Brooke said, hearing awe in her voice. She had an eye for creativity, and whoever landscaped these grounds knew how to set the mood. "Have you ever been here before?"

"No," Wyatt said. "But I've heard about it enough. It's my mother's favorite place. She'd have luncheons here with her friends."

"I can see why she'd like coming here."

Close to the lake's bank, there was a flowered canopy with descending wisteria vines waiting for the bride and groom. Hundreds of chairs tied with delicate satin bows were lined up in rows. Most of the guests were already seated.

Wyatt pulled the car up to a valet. And once they climbed out, he asked, "Want to make a run for it?"

"I think we have to. The wedding is supposed to start any minute."

"Okay, after you," he said, gesturing for her to take the lead.

She trotted along on her high heels, not an easy task even though the lush grass was as thick as a carpet. But after a few strides her heel dug into the rich earth and got stuck. Her leg twisted and she tipped sideways, stumbling. "Oh!"

Wyatt reached out and snagged her waist, catching her fall just in time.

"I've got you," he said, confidently. "You okay?"

They were locked together now, and her sensitive skin prickled under his touch. She liked being in his arms, and he seemed reluctant to let her go. A few seconds ticked by before he did.

"How many times are you going to save me today?" she asked breathlessly.

"As many as it takes," he offered, his blue eyes sparkling. She didn't know what to make of her miracle cowboy who'd caused her body to heat up with just one playful look. Was he teasing or flirting?

"I've got a solution to this problem," she said, snapping out of her insanity.

She slipped a finger into her shoes to pull at the straps and then wiggled out of them. Straightening, she came up holding her scarlet-red sandals between her fingers and nodded. "Okay, now I'm ready."

He blinked, grinned at her bare feet and then offered her his hand. They took off at a very brisk walk, making it to the last row of seats just seconds before the brides-maids began their trek down the aisle.

Brooke sighed in relief and sat back. A few minutes later, everyone in attendance rose to their feet as Heather glided down the aisle in an ivory satin wedding gown, her father walking beside her wearing a proud tearful smile. She held a gorgeous bouquet of new roses and fresh natural greenery that looked as though it had been handpicked just moments ago.

She met her handsome groom under the canopy, love shining in her eyes. Brooke looked on, happy for her friend who'd found love here in Texas. She'd probably start a family soon. Brooke's future wasn't quite so rosy. She didn't begrudge her friends, who'd already found happiness, but she'd always wondered what it was about her that seemed to repel any form of long-lasting relationship with a man. Being Dylan McKay's younger sister was like a noose around her neck. *Just hang me now,* she'd say to herself, whenever a man she'd dated starting hinting at meeting her celebrity brother. Of course, then came the teeny favors they'd ask of her.

Would your brother mind reading my script? I know it's gonna be a blockbuster.

I'm writing an autobiography and your brother would be perfect to star in the movie.

I'm starting a new business venture. I'm sure Dylan would love to get in on the ground floor once you tell him about it.

Riiiight.

Brooke was fed up with men who used her for their own personal gain. Leaving LA when she did had been a necessity. After the debacle with Royce Brisbane, who'd kept his cards close to the vest, and only showed his hand once she'd fallen in love with him, she'd written off relationships for the extended future. She'd been convinced her Wall Street–type boyfriend didn't give a lick about Dylan, until he handed her three scripts for her to show him. *Three*, for heaven's sake!

No man would ever use her that way again.

And then there was Wyatt Brandt, the polite, mannerly cowboy whose presence beside her made her heart pound in her chest. She didn't want to be Brooke McKay today, not while Wyatt Brandt was stealing glances at her when he didn't think she was looking. But she'd noticed, and it boosted her deflated ego to have a gorgeous hunk of a man checking her out without an ulterior motive. And if the tingles she was experiencing now weren't one-sided, this wedding could prove intriguing.

The *I do*'s were said with a flourish, and Brooke teared up as she witnessed these two people in love speak vows of undying commitment to each other. She felt Wyatt's eyes on her as a sole tear dripped down her cheek. Did he think her foolish for crying at a wedding? How cliché. Brooke wasn't a traditional kind of girl, yet weddings always seemed to get to her.

Wyatt gently placed a handkerchief in her hand. As she dabbed at her eyes, she sent him a silent nod of thanks. He gave her a brief smile.

After the vows were spoken, the loving couple garnered a round of applause as they marched down the aisle hand in hand, newly married. Row upon row of guests made their way from their seats to head toward the tented area where the cocktail hour was about to begin.

Brooke and Wyatt, seated in the back row, stood up and waited patiently for their turn. "It was a beautiful ceremony," she said, handing him his handkerchief.

"It was. But it made you cry."

She shrugged and slight embarrassment heated her skin. "I'm silly that way. Most people don't think of me as the sentimental type, but I guess I am when it comes to weddings."

"Maybe that's why you enjoy your business so much. You like seeing other people happy."

She stared into his eyes. Was he for real? How did he know that about her, after only meeting her two hours ago? Was he psychic after all? "You amaze me," she blurted.

"I do?" He rubbed at the scruffy dark blond hairs on his chin. "Well, now, it's been a while since I've amazed a woman."

"Don't stop on my account. It's been *too* long since I've been amazed by a man."

The look in his eyes suddenly grew dark and intense. "You flirting with me, Brooke Johnson?"

Yes. It was hard not to.

She glanced away for a second, making note of the two-hundred-plus guests milling about the large white wedding tent, and suddenly all she wanted was to be alone with Wyatt Brandt again.

"Just stating a fact, Wyatt."

"C'mon," he said, tamping down a smile and taking her arm gently. "Let's see if Blake and Heather had the good sense to seat us together."

She liked the sound of that.

A lot.

Two

Brooke wasn't seated with Wyatt. She sat between two of Heather's female cousins she'd met once or twice back in college. Two other male cousins and their wives rounded out the table. Everyone was pleasant. The ladies, dressed in florals and pastels appropriate for a late-afternoon wedding, were doing their best to make small talk. Brooke engaged in conversation with them and sipped white wine while giving the entire lakeside reception a cursory scan, keeping her eyes peeled for signs of Wyatt.

During the cocktail hour, she'd spent time with him, munching on appetizers and enjoying Sweetwater Lake until dinner had been called and they'd had to go their separate ways. She sensed that Wyatt had been just as disappointed as she was to discover that not only weren't they seated together, but their tables were separated by twenty others.

She spotted Wyatt standing just outside the perimeter of the decorated tent, sipping whiskey from a tumbler as he spoke to the groom. The sight of Wyatt shouldn't have made her heart race, and yet it was sprinting as if in an Olympic event. The two men shook hands and then Blake took off, most likely in search of his bride. Two women took Blake's place, sidling up next to Wyatt with giddy smiles on their faces.

She felt something possessive deep in her belly. He wasn't her date, but he seemed to want to spend more time with her, and now it didn't look as if that was going to happen.

Brooke's attention snapped back to her table when Connie, the younger of Heather's cousins, asked her a question. "Yes, I'm enjoying my stay in Texas so far," Brooke replied. "And I'm happy I was able to attend Heather's wedding. It was a beautiful ceremony."

"Heather's very happy with Blake. He's one of the good guys."

"There are so few of those," Brooke said, recognizing her tone was too cynical for a wedding.

Luckily, Connie chuckled. "I know what you mean. My mama says if you find a good one, land him and never let him go."

"She's a smart woman."

"She should know, she's been married three times. She kicked two losers to the curb before marrying my daddy. They've been married twenty-eight years now."

"I like your mother more and more."

"What about your folks?" Connie asked.

"Oh, my biological parents have issues. I don't see them much, but I was raised by foster parents and they were awesome. Without them, my life wouldn't be what it is today."

"So there's hope out there. I shouldn't be so skeptical—especially at my cousin's wedding—but my boyfriend and I have just broken up and it still stings."

She caught sight of Wyatt finally taking his seat for dinner. "I get the stinging part, Connie. I've been there." More than once. "It gets better, believe me. Just concentrate on what you enjoy doing most. That's what I do."

"Heather said you could've put this wedding together without blinking an eye."

"Heather is too kind, but if I lived here, yes, I would've loved to work on this event. There's so much natural beauty that only the fine points need accenting, and the event planner did a terrific job of not going overboard. I would've done the same."

"I guess that's the reason the inn is perfect for a wedding. It doesn't need too many added frills."

Dinner was served, toasts were given and the reception continued on smoothly. Brooke dug into her meal, enjoying the perfectly seasoned and cooked salmon, quinoa salad and freshly grilled veggies. The meal was light and tasty, and after she was finished and her plate was being cleared, a band began to make noises as they set up on a platform stage.

"Excuse me," she said to the guests at the table. She rose and walked over to the sweetheart table. This was the first chance she'd gotten to congratulate Heather and her new groom. After the ceremony, they'd been inundated by a swarm of well-meaning guests and Brooke hadn't entered the fray, deciding to bide her time until she could have a quiet conversation with the newlyweds.

"Heather, congratulations!" Brooke's friend rose and they immediately embraced.

"Brooke, my goodness, I'm so glad you were able to make it to our wedding. Blake," she said, turning to him, "I'd like you to meet my friend from Los Angeles. We went to UCLA together, back in the day."

Blake stood up and took her hand. "Nice meeting you, Brooke, and thanks for being here."

"It's a special day and I'm glad I could make it. Heather has been trying to get me to make a trip to Texas for years."

"Oh, yeah? I hope you're getting a big Texas welcome."

"I am. Everyone's been gracious and nice. I'm on vacation, staying with friends in Beckon, so I'll be here for several more weeks."

"That's wonderful," Heather said. "Maybe we can get together when Blake and I get back from our honeymoon."

"I'm taking her on a cruise of the Mediterranean. We'll be gone ten days."

"Sounds perfect. And I'd love to see you when you return. Heather, you look stunning and it's not just the gown…you're glowing. Blake must be doing something right," Brooke said, giving him a wink.

"You know it." Blake took Heather's hand. "I like your friend already."

"I told you you would," Heather said.

The master of ceremonies called for the newlyweds' first dance. "Well, I guess you're on, you two. Congratulations again. I'll speak to you later."

A crowd formed around the parquet dance floor set up under the glorious white tent. Brooke took a position in the outer circle as the two lovebirds danced to a George Strait ballad. The lights were dimmed, and a sole spotlight shone on them like a halo. Heather really was glowing now.

Once the dance was over, there was a round of applause, and the bandleader urged the guests to join the bride and groom on the dance floor. Brooke headed to her table. Before she reached her seat, a man approached. He was in his midforties, she guessed, his tie crooked, his entire body seemingly angled to the left, as if he'd fall over any second. "W-would…you like to d-dance?"

His breath reeked of alcohol. "Uh, no thank you."

"Just one dance, missy, is all I'm asking."

"No, thank you," Brooke said as politely as she could

manage. She turned away from him and started for her table again. But he snagged her arm from behind, thick fingers digging deep into her skin. She whirled on him and yanked her arm free. "What part of no don't you get?" she said quietly. The last thing she wanted was to make a scene at Heather's wedding.

"You're a f-feisty little th-thing." He reached for her again and it was easy to step out of his grasp.

"And you've obviously had too much to drink."

"Is there a problem here?" Wyatt got between her and the pesky man, towering a good six inches above the guy. Wyatt's glare made it clear he wasn't one to mess with.

The man leaned way over, nearly toppling, and Wyatt quickly caught him.

"No p-problem. Nope. N-not a one," he said, chuckling.

"I think you need some air." Wyatt held the man upright and turned to Brooke, his mouth twisting in a smirk. He winked at her. "I'll be back as soon as I can."

He escorted—or rather supported—the guy out of the tent and Brooke returned to her seat. The man was probably harmless, but Brooke didn't like being manhandled that way. She'd been ready to raise her voice and call security, which would've dampened the festive mood. Once again, Wyatt was there, stepping in to save the day.

A quiet hum strummed through her body and she smiled.

"That's weird Uncle Hal," Connie said into her ear as Brooke lowered down into the chair beside her. "I caught some of what happened out there and my whole family apologizes to you." Connie made a face. "Hal likes to drink…when the liquor is free. Heather almost didn't invite him to the wedding. She was afraid he'd cause a scene. But he seems to have been neutralized."

"Neutralized?"

"Yeah, once he's been set straight, he doesn't cause any more trouble. He'll probably come over to say he's sorry."

"I hope not." Brooke shivered.

"Who was that hunk who took him outside?"

"Oh, um, he's a friend of the groom's. I met him earlier today."

"Does he have a younger brother, if you know what I mean?"

Brooke sighed. "Yeah, I do know what you mean. And honestly, I don't know."

"You're three for three, Wyatt," Brooke said.

Wyatt held her at arm's length as they danced to a light and breezy love song. His touch, though highly appropriate, thrilled her from head to toe. There was something steady and sturdy about him. He made her feel female, which seemed silly, but those deep blue eyes studied her with keen intent, as if she were a secret art treasure or a delicious hot fudge sundae. Either way, she was happy to be the object of his attention.

"How's that?" he asked.

"You saved me thrice, my lord," she said with a mock curtsy. "The last time with big Uncle Hal."

He laughed. "You were handling the situation just fine."

"You think so?"

"I do. But I also saw the indecision on your face. Where I come from, a man doesn't lay a hand on a woman 'less he's invited. When he didn't back down I figured you didn't want to make a scene."

"You're right about that. I don't like to draw attention to myself."

He drew her closer and spoke into her ear softly, "Then you shouldn't have worn that dress."

His gaze dipped past the lace on her scooped neckline

and touched upon her breasts. From under the material, her nipples tightened. Wyatt could do that to her with one look.

"You don't like it?" she asked, a little uncertain. "Or was that a compliment?"

Emma, her bestie, business partner and sister-in-law, was always telling her to put some color in her wardrobe, but black was her thing. She wasn't a floral kind of girl.

"Every guy in this place has his sights set on you. And I'm the one dancing with you." Appreciation shone in his eyes and she almost forgot all about Royce what's-his-name. "I like it, all right."

"Thank you."

"Welcome." His hands snaked around her waist, and the space between them lessened to inches. Brooke wasn't complaining. He smelled like whiskey and something woodsy and natural. She took deep breaths of him, drinking in his scent and enjoying the way his dark blond hair curled at his collar.

"I have a confession," he said in a quiet rasp. "I'm glad your car ran out of gas today."

Something broke apart inside her then, and her cynicism crumbled away. At least for the present, she wasn't going to question her actions. Or his. This perfect guy seemed to come straight out of her dreams, and she wasn't going to play it safe tonight. Not with Wyatt. She brought her fingers to the curls at the back of his neck and smiled, titling her chin up. Her eyes had to be gleaming now. "I'm glad, too," she said.

Wyatt's gaze heated. Thrills ran up and down her spine as she waited for him to do something bold, something daring.

He brought his head closer, never losing eye contact with her. "Are you inviting me?" he said, but he didn't wait for her answer. The connection they had was real and happening fast. He had to feel it, too.

His lips brushed hers softly, once, twice. Shock waves traveled the length of her body. She hadn't realized how much she'd needed this, how much she'd missed the simple reality of connecting with a man on an elemental level. The pure masculine taste of him washed completely through her, and a soft purr escaped her lips. She kissed him back and things got hot and heavy really fast. He cupped the back of her head, weaving fingers through her long, wild hair. "Oh, man," he murmured, pressing his lips more forcefully to hers, making exquisite demands on her. Demands she was eager to answer.

Was it lust? She'd been attracted to Wyatt from the second she'd laid her eyes on him. And now he was kissing her as if he'd been starving, and let's face it, she hadn't even nibbled in a very long time. Now she was ravenous.

Wyatt broke off the kiss before things got completely out of control on the dance floor and sighed loud enough for her to hear his frustration. Her ego was lifted to new heights as he tugged her tightly into his embrace, pressing their bodies closer. The slow ballad continued, but she barely heard the music. All she knew, all she felt, was her connection to Wyatt. They were so close, so incredibly in tune with each other.

Tension sizzled between them in a crazy way that upset her newly regained balance. She wasn't ready for this, for him. But when the dance ended and he stared into her eyes, she was lost.

"Let's get some air, darlin'."

She gave him a tiny nod, and he grabbed her hand and tugged her toward the edge of the draped tent that led to the lake.

Soft blades of grass tickled her ankles as Wyatt wove a path to the bank of Sweetwater Lake. Moonlight reflected off the rippling waters now, the sun having long ago bid farewell to the day. The air was still damp with humidity, but since sunset the temperature had cooled considerably. They stood facing the lake.

"Better," he said, taking gulps of air into his lungs. "It got a little heavy in there."

He dropped her hand, seeming to compose himself.

"It did."

"You surprised me, is all," he said, looking away from the lake to connect with her again. "I mean, I didn't expect…"

"I know. I'm different." He didn't have to say it. He didn't expect to be attracted to her. "I'm no Texas girl. I dress weird most of the time. Believe it or not, I toned it down for the wedding." No leather wrist bracelets, giant hoop earrings or multiple long chains around her neck for this shindig. As a matter of fact, she'd left most of that stuff back home in LA. Maybe she was entering a new phase in her life.

"I like your style, Brooke. There's nothing weird about you."

"Thanks for that."

"I mean it. When I saw you with Uncle Hal on the dance floor, I had an irrational urge to knock his block off."

"Is that equivalent to punching his lights out?"

"It is," he stated plainly.

"Why, Wyatt, that's the nicest thing anyone's ever said to me." She stood toe-to-toe with him, grinning. It felt good to break the tension and get back to easy conversation with him.

He laughed loud and deep and she joined in, too.

"I like you, Brooke," he said easily.

"Feeling's mutual," Brooke said. "Isn't that how they say it out here?"

"Stop poking fun at Texans." Wyatt's eyes twinkled. "We're a proud lot."

"I've heard as much."

A wicked Texas breeze blew strands of hair into her face.

With his finger, Wyatt innocently pushed a barrel curl resting on her cheek behind her ear. From the second his finger glided across her skin, the ridiculous yearning reared up again, putting a halt to their pleasant banter. Her laughter died in her throat, and as she focused on the man touching her tenderly, his smile changed into something less animated and playful. He gazed at her with dire want, his eyes dipping down to her pursed and needy mouth.

"Brooke," he rasped. There was a distinct hitch in his voice.

"It's okay, Wyatt," she said. Whatever he wanted, she was ready for.

A groan rose from his throat and he began shaking his head as if he couldn't believe what was happening. Brooke was in the same boat. They were sailing along at breakneck speed. She wasn't about to throw down the anchor; she wanted the wind at her back taking her wherever this was leading.

Wyatt wrapped one of his hands firmly around her waist, his fingers inching her closer, while he lifted her chin to meet his beautiful giving mouth with the other. The kiss was sweeter, more leisurely than before. She instantly felt safe with Wyatt; it wasn't about his saving her from empty gas tanks or pesky older men. It was something more, something she'd never experienced before. Utter trust.

The little voice in her head said, *It's because he doesn't know who you really are.*

But that wasn't it. A Texas rancher couldn't care less about her being a celebrity's sister. Wyatt had no agenda in that regard, and this uncanny faith she had in him came from a deeper, more soulful place within her.

Only seconds later, Wyatt whispered a curse over her lips and deepened the kiss, making it hard for Brooke to think straight. Helpless to curtail the sizzling connection between them, she flung her arms around his neck and his kisses immediately became inferno hot. Her lips were on fire, set ablaze by this amazingly strong, gorgeous man. He walked her backward until she met with the solid breadth of a cottonwood tree. She leaned against it, out of view of the wedding tent and the two hundred other guests.

He urged her mouth open and their tongues tangled. Explosive sensations rocked her back and a potent stream of desire coursed through her body, making her feel more alive than she'd felt in a long, long time. Wyatt had her trapped, his arms on either side of the thick tree. There wasn't any place else she'd rather be.

He brought his arms down to cup her face and tilted her head at an angle that was to his liking. His kiss was more deliberate this time, packed with intensity and precision. Oh, he was a yummy kisser.

He began an exploration of her body with both hands grazing her shoulders and traveling down her sides, along the inward curve of her torso and caressing the slight flare of her hips. She could tell he wanted to touch her in more intimate places but his keen sense of propriety wouldn't allow it. She wanted more, but couldn't deny how incredibly sweet and sensitive he was to her.

They came up for air a minute later, both shaking, both completely turned on. The music inside the tent stopped and the bandleader's gleeful voice carried over the microphone, announcing it was time for the bride and groom to cut the cake.

"Brooke." He whispered her name on a sigh and touched his forehead to hers, his warm breath caressing her cheek. "We should really go back inside."

"Mmm." He was right, of course, but how on earth would she stop her legs from trembling, her body from quivering? "I think so, too."

"You go first," he said, encouraging her wit.
"I'll need a minute. Oh, and be sure to save the last
for me."

She straightened her disheveled dress, took a swallow,
steadied her out-of-whack nerves and then headed up the
embankment toward the tent. Halfway there, she swiveled her head around to find Wyatt's discerning eyes still
on her.

She turned to continue her trek, purring with quiet delight like a kitten lapping up a bowl of rich cream.

"Here you go," Wyatt said so quietly she barely heard
him. He set her luggage down outside her hotel room door
as she slid the key card into the lock.

"Thank you," she said, turning to him. "I, um, had a
great time tonight. The wedding was pretty cool."

"I had a good time, too. Thanks to you."

She stared at him, quaking inside. She didn't want to
make another mistake. But looking into Wyatt's eyes,
she didn't believe him to be one. "You give me too much
credit."

"I don't think so. I was dreading coming here today.
And then I met you."

She blinked. He had a way of saying the right things.
He wasn't a clever charmer, but he was charming. And he
was a gentleman, in every way that counted. "Why were
you dreading it?"

Pain entered his eyes. "Let's just say I'm new to bachelorhood and leave it at that."

"Oh." She got that. She didn't want to rehash her past
relationships, either. One of the best parts of meeting Wyatt
tonight was not having to think about the Royce Brisbanes
of the world. She was fine with forgetting all about her
own lousy relationships. "Okay."

Wyatt tilted his head. "You're not like most women."

"That doesn't sound like a compliment, Wyatt."

"Believe me, it is. Most women want to nose around and fix what's broken, but I'm not into that right now."

He was broken? Now that was a revelation, because from where she stood all of his parts seemed to be in excellent working order. "Wyatt," she said softly. She didn't want him to leave. Gosh, how she didn't want to say goodnight to him.

"I'd better get to my room."

She didn't miss the reluctance in his voice. "Okay. Thanks for being my miracle cowboy today."

He blinked, seemingly surprised at her comment.

She smiled and lifted up on tiptoes to brush a soft kiss to his cheek.

He kissed her back, a gentle peck on the mouth. "Welcome."

She loved the taste of him, the way he smelled, the sturdy breadth of him.

He gazed at her mouth, his eyes holding a lingering dark gleam as if he wanted more. As if he wanted to devour her. The bone-melting effect reached all the way down to the tips of her toes. If he touched her again, she would be lost.

And then he did just that. He splayed his hands on her waist and drew her closer. "I need one more kiss, Brooke."

His rich baritone voice did crazy things to her, especially when he was asking to kiss her again. *Oh, man.* "Anything you need." Her voice was a breathless whisper.

And then their mouths came together in an amazing onslaught of potency and possession. Heat immediately rose up and flared like a lit match. It was as if everything fell into place again. His hands wound tighter around her waist. Her arms wrapped around his neck. Their lips smacked, and moans and sweet sighs of pleasure surrounded them.

"Take it inside, you two," a passerby said, chuckling as

he headed down the hallway, obviously having had one too many.

"Good idea," Wyatt stated softly over her lips.

"Yes, Wyatt. Yes."

With one hand, he pushed the heavy door open and then lifted her luggage and plunked it down just inside the room. Then the door closed behind him and they were alone in the dark hotel room.

"Just tell me you want this," he said, bracing her against the wall.

"I want this."

"God, Brooke. You're the one who's the miracle."

It was the sweetest, most beautiful thing anyone had ever said to her. She squeezed her eyes closed briefly and drank it all in. She drank *him* all in, too. His kisses set her body on fire, and now that they were out of the public eye, they were free to unleash their passion full force.

"I need to touch you," he whispered.

"Touch me."

His palms traveled over the slopes and curves of her body. His hands were large and rough, but he was gentle in his approach, making her want him all the more. He lifted her leg up under the knee, and she gasped as he slid his hand under the tight confines of her dress, stroking her thigh back and forth, over and over. "You're soft," he murmured between kisses. His body pressed to hers was a wall of granite, so big and hard, and she was overwhelmed with sensation after sensation. Between her thighs, pulsing heat gathered and her breaths came in short, rapid bursts.

He lowered her leg to the floor and flipped her around to face the wall, her back to his front. He probed her backside, skimming his hands over black lace. Through the material of her dress, the heat of his palms scorched her skin and she sighed, surrendering her body to him.

Finally, he inched the zipper of her dress down. She felt

the cooling fresh air on her skin as he pushed her dress away. Planting kisses on her shoulders, he undid her bra and then reached around to cup her breasts. He filled his hands, massaging and caressing her until she could barely stand the pleasure, tiny moans escaping her lips.

He skimmed his hands down her torso and back up again, navigating her body as if he were exploring points on a map. "You're soft everywhere."

She loved the quiet words he spoke over her shoulder and the way he held her so preciously. She breathed in the aroused scent of him as he reclaimed her aching breasts, his body pressed to hers, fully aroused, his scent intoxicating.

"We need to move this onto the bed," he said. "Unless you like—"

"No, the bed is fine," she managed.

He helped her remove the remainder of her clothes and then lifted her into his strong arms. He carried her to the turned-down bed and laid her there carefully.

Without saying a word, he kicked off his shoes and undressed for her, undoing his string tie, removing his jacket, shirt, belt and pants.

From what she could see from the sliver of moonlight streaming into the window, Wyatt met and exceeded her expectations. God, he was glorious above the waist, with brick shoulders and hard abs. And below, well, she took a huge gulp. He was definitely all man.

"Don't ask me why," he said, quite earnestly, "but I have protection."

"That's a relief," she said softly. "I don't."

She hadn't exactly planned on hitting the jackpot tonight, but she thought it odd that he would be apologizing for carrying protection. He'd said he was new to bachelorhood. She assumed he was divorced, yet she needed to ask. "Wyatt, just tell me one thing. You're not married, are you?"

He stared into her eyes for a beat of a second and then shook his head. "No, I can promise you that."

Relief took on a new meaning with that promise. "Then, as much as I like looking at you, I'd like to touch, too."

He sighed, perhaps equally relieved. "Absolutely, darlin'."

The first time Wyatt made love to her, it was an exploration of newness. They were careful with each other as she learned what he liked, while he provided what she wanted. There was heat and pleasure and a development of trust. She did trust Wyatt. She knew he wouldn't abuse her in any way; he was far too much of a gentleman for that. But now, after a short respite, Wyatt was pulling her atop him, kissing her senseless again, and this time both of their guards were down.

"I want you again." The urgent plea tore from his throat.

"I'm here," she whispered, climbing up his body and giving him access to her breasts.

"I'm glad you are," he said, tickling her nipple with the tip of his tongue. Both peaks pebbled up immediately, and wild stirrings began at the apex of her thighs.

Wyatt was the best lover she'd ever had. He could take her from zero to ninety with just a heated look or a bold caress. And he was doing just that with exquisite strokes of his tongue on her breast, the full circle of his mouth drawing her out, making every nerve ending ping and jump.

When he was through making her squirm in delight, he moved down her body, his hand gliding past her waist and his fingers tucking into her sensitive folds. He knew exactly how to caress her. He knew where she needed to be stroked and oh, he was merciless. She cried out, the pleasure so exquisite it was almost painful. Electric sensations rocked her back and forth until she could barely take it another second.

"Kiss me," he ordered, and she obeyed.

And just as their tongues met, her body splintered apart, the amazing orgasm rocketing through her body with enough force to jerk her off the bed. She came down panting, the effects of her release almost mystifying her until she opened her eyes and saw Wyatt staring at her, his darkened gaze hot as fired metal.

He rolled her over onto her back and lifted her hips, positioning her. And then he was inside her again, this time without hesitation. He began thrusting, his erection hard and thick, pulsing with new life. He moved deeper and harder and brought her to the brink of insanity once more. "Come with me this time," he rasped, his throat thick.

And they moved together, arching, aching, a beautiful joining of bodies in complete sync with each other. And when she was primed and eager and staring into his eyes, he tipped his head in acknowledgment. He knew she was ready. Then they rose up and bucked and cried out, her sighs meeting his groans. Her body shattered, just as his came apart.

It was glorious.

She was in heaven.

And she stayed up there awhile before slowly easing down.

Her limbs were weightless now. She felt like a sated rag doll, too limp to move. Wyatt scooped her up in his strong arms and surrounded her with his hot, perfect body. He kissed her cheeks, wove his fingers through her hair.

"Brooke," he whispered over her lips.

"Mmm." She'd never been happier. Or more tired.

"Sleep, darlin'."

"Sorry, can't help it."

"It's okay," he said.

Wrapped up in his arms, she closed her eyes.

Wyatt opened his eyes to a dawn that had long ago broken through the shuttered windows of Brooke's hotel room, streaming bright light inside. The digital clock read eight o'clock and he cursed silently as he untangled himself carefully from Brooke. His heart thumped in his chest as he glanced down at her, looking so peaceful, her eyes closed, that mane of raven hair falling down her back. His body strummed to life again, but he had no time to indulge or to say goodbye to Brooke. No time to look into those pretty brown eyes or hear the sultry tone of her voice.

He should've been on the road an hour ago. He was late, and he'd made Henrietta a promise. He couldn't take advantage of her good nature. Weekends were precious to her.

"Dammit," he muttered as he scrambled to step into his clothes. He hated leaving this way. There was a reason widowers shouldn't have one-night stands. He was out of his element here. He had seconds to make a decision and God only knew if it was the right one, but time was wasting. He scribbled a note to Brooke and left it on the nightstand.

He had nothing to offer Brooke. He was still in love with Madelyn and he had no room for another woman in his life. Not that Brooke seemed to want anything but this one night together. She hadn't asked him a bunch of questions the way women tended to do, and she hadn't hinted at anything more. She was vacationing in Texas and had a life and a business on the West Coast.

The thoughts crowded his mind as he gave her one last glance.

He'd be forever grateful to her for this night. Brooke

had helped him get through a tough day and they'd had a good time.

Actually, they'd had *multiple* good times during the evening.

End of story.

He walked to the door, not surprised by the regret burning a hole in his stomach. He didn't usually walk out on women. But he couldn't stay, either. It was better this way. For her. For both of them.

He turned the doorknob and strode out of the room, leaving Brooke and the Inn at Sweetwater behind.

More than an hour later he'd reached the gates of Blue Horizon Ranch. He was home, back where he belonged. But he'd thought about Brooke most of the way and he'd cursed his best friend, Johnny Wilde, for practically daring him to go to the wedding. Now he had guilt. And memories he couldn't wash from his mind.

Was he a fool to think he was betraying his late wife by enjoying himself with another woman? Johnny would certainly think so. But then, what did he know? He'd been with too many women to count and he'd never found the right one, while Wyatt had met the love of his life and had married her. For that short time—only five years—they'd had together, he'd been happier than he thought possible.

And now he had his precious twins to think about.

He parked the car in front of the house and gave it a quick glance, just as a wave of pain jabbed his gut. He'd never quite gotten over the fact that Madelyn wouldn't be here, greeting him after a trip. That her birthday had come and gone yesterday and there would be no more sweet kisses between them, no emerald sparks of joy in her eyes when he surprised her with a gift. "Sorry, Maddy."

That day nine months ago had ripped his gut in two. Seeing the sheriff at his front door, hat in hand, his face solemn. *Madelyn's had an accident. I'm sorry, Mr. Brandt.*

Wyatt shook off the memory. He had to get his ass inside the house. Henrietta's youngest niece was coming to help him with the twins, so Henrietta could spend the weekend camping in their fifth wheel camper up at the river. Ralph, her husband, wasn't a patient man. He'd been pressing her to retire, and she'd promised him she would as soon as Wyatt found a suitable nanny for the twins. Henrietta was as loyal as they came, and she was good with his kids, but she was exhausted lately. He'd catch her rubbing at her back and taking short naps in those rare times when the twins were both asleep. She'd been here since his folks lived at the ranch, and she was more like family than the help. Clearly, she didn't want to leave Wyatt in the lurch without someone he trusted to care for his children, but the search wasn't going well.

He entered his house and stood in the foyer, listening for baby sounds. "I'm home," he said quietly, just in case Brett and Brianna were napping. And then he heard their voices coming from the great room, which substituted now as a giant playroom, and strode in that direction. His heart warmed immediately when he spotted his kids. The twins were toddling around on the floor, paying Carly no mind as she read them their favorite book, *Goodnight Moon*.

"Hi, Carly," he said to the teenager.

"Oh, hi," she said, glancing at him through her black-rimmed glasses.

At the sound of his voice, Brett, who was scooting a Lego truck along the hardwood floor, and Brianna, who was clutching her doll, abandoned their toys, flapped their arms excitedly and toddled over to him, their smiles lighting him up inside. He scooped both twins up in his arms. "Hello, my babies."

He gave each a kiss on the cheek.

Brianna was more vocal than little Brett. "Daddy! Home. Daddy kisses."

Brett stared at his sister first and then hugged Wyatt around the neck. Nothing was sweeter. Nothing helped his healing more than their unconditional love. He was constantly enveloped in sadness thinking that Madelyn would never know her children. And that his twins had been cheated out of a wonderful mother.

Henrietta walked into the room. Her sturdy build and cinnamon red hair piled in a tight bun atop her head gave her the appearance of a stern woman, but nothing was further from the truth. She was an old softy at heart. "Sorry I'm late," he said, feeling like a heel.

"Not a problem, Wyatt. I hope you had a nice time at the wedding."

An image of Brooke Johnson, naked and asleep in the bed he'd just left, popped into his head. "I did. It was good to see Blake again."

"That's nice. My Ralph is on his way. Carly's been here, playing with the kids. She'll help with feeding them later, and getting them down for their naps. I've got the weekend's meals ready for you in the fridge."

"Thanks, Etta."

Carly stood, picking up a few toys from the floor as she rose. "I can stay overnight if you need me to, Mr. Brandt."

"Thanks, Carly. Let's see how the day goes. I might just need you to come back tomorrow, if you can."

"I can do that, too," she said.

"Okay, great." Wyatt set the kids down and squatted onto the floor next to them. It was a tough balancing act, being in charge of a huge ranch corporation and being Daddy to his children. But he couldn't let them down. They needed the stability of having him here most of the time, knowing that they came first, no matter what.

After Madelyn's death, he'd relied heavily on Henrietta

for support with the kids. But if he didn't find a suitable nanny soon, old Ralph would march in here one day and threaten to knock his block off…with a shotgun.

He had three interviews with potential nannies later this week.

He could only hope.

Three

Brooke
You'll never know how much last night meant to me.
If you ever need me for anything, you can find me at
the Blue Horizon Ranch. Thank you.
Wyatt

Brooke sat on her bed in the guest room of Zane Williams's brand-new gorgeous ranch estate and reread the note for the tenth time this month. She hadn't been able to toss it away. The paper was crumpled and creased, but the words rang out loud and clear. Wyatt had blown her off.

The morning after the wedding, when she'd woken up alone at the inn, she'd read his words and been baffled. She'd been certain Wyatt wasn't the love-'em-and-leave-'em type. She'd been certain they'd wake up together and exchange phone numbers, at the very least. Maybe have breakfast together. Their connection had been powerful, so strong, in fact, it sort of scared her. She'd been sure it wasn't one-sided. Had her BS meter gone on the fritz?

After what Royce Brisbane did to her, she'd turned on her protective radar with all shields up. She'd come to Texas partly to forget about men and romance. And then Wyatt appeared, seemingly out of the blue, and gave her one miraculous day…and night.

Maybe that's all there'd ever be for her, snippets of passion, spread out here and there, but nothing real, nothing permanent. Oddly enough, it was the "thank you" at the end of the note that pissed her off more than anything. As if she'd done him a service.

If you ever need me for anything, you can find me at the Blue Horizon Ranch.

Hell, yeah, she needed him. But right now, her pride interfered with good judgment. Tears entered her eyes. Tears she didn't want. Tears that embarrassed her. She wasn't a teary-eyed romantic fool, but her hormones were out of whack and had been pretty much since she'd missed her last period.

She knew what it meant. She'd taken the test yesterday. She was going to have Wyatt's baby—a result of too much passion and not enough good sense.

She'd slept on the news last night, hoping when she woke up today it would've all gone away, like a bad dream you eventually forget. She hadn't told a soul, but Emma was raising her eyebrows at her lately, asking her why she was tired and looking pale. She blamed it on the Texas heat and humidity. She wasn't used to the sweltering temperatures, but Emma was five months pregnant and having just gone through these early months, she knew the signs all too well.

Dylan popped his head into her room. "Are you gonna come out to the set today, sis?"

"Oh, I don't think so. But thanks."

"What are you gonna do? Stay alone here all day?"

Zane and his new wife, Jessica, had graciously offered for the three of them to stay as his houseguests in the glorious new home Adam Chase had designed as a wedding present, while Dylan shot a Western movie here. Zane had been a neighbor for a time back in Moonlight Beach, California, and Dylan, Zane and Adam were all good friends now. But newlyweds Zane and Jessica were inseparable, and a few days back, they'd left on Zane's spectacular tour bus, heading toward New Orleans to do a round of country music concerts.

Now Dylan, Emma and Brooke had the house all to themselves for the next few weeks.

Emma barged into the room, her growing belly covered by a breezy floral handkerchief dress. "No, she's not spending the day alone. She's going to help me pick out baby girl clothes!"

Brooke forgot about her own problems and jumped up. "You're having a girl?"

Emma nodded, her laughter infectious. She lifted the pointed hem of her dress with both hands, and danced around the room singing, "Yes, yes, we're having a baby girl."

Brooke caught her midstride and hugged her tight. "Oh, this is wonderful. Boy or girl, it doesn't matter, but now we know!"

She peered over Emma's shoulder at her brother. His eyes were gleaming with love for his wife and new child. One would never know the child Emma carried wasn't his. But he loved both mother and child with all of his heart. And that's all that mattered.

Brooke stepped away from Emma and with arms reaching up, walked over to Dylan to give him a giant warm hug. Her big brother was happier than she'd ever seen him. "Congratulations."

Dylan kissed her forehead. "Thanks. We're excited."

"You're going to be outnumbered, you know, with all these women around."

"He's used to it," Emma said, her eyes sparkling with mischief.

"That's right, the big mega movie star has women falling at his feet," Brooke said.

"Not anymore. They know I'm taken." Dylan went to Emma and took her hand. She smiled and then both of them looked Brooke's way. "So, you'll drop by the set with Emma later?" he asked.

"Sure, we'll come by and see you."

She couldn't burst his bubble. She'd been a downer lately, and hadn't been able to concentrate on having a good time. They sensed something was up with her, but hadn't pried. Not yet, anyway. She didn't want to raise any more suspicion. She was having enough trouble accepting the fact that Emma wouldn't be the only new mother around here. And she had no clue of how or when to tell Wyatt Brandt he was going to be a father.

Wyatt sat upon a black gelding with white socks named Oreo and faced the rushing waters of the Willow Springs River. Twenty miles north of Beckon and even farther from his ranch, he was doing Johnny a favor today by coming here. Aside from Johnny Wilde, no one else in the area had as much commonsense knowledge about horseflesh and cattle as Wyatt did. Not that he'd wanted this job. Hell, he was no consultant, but his friend had called him in a panic. Johnny had come down with the flu, hopefully just the twenty-four-hour kind, and he'd needed a replacement, pronto. "You're the only one I trust to do the job," he'd said.

It wasn't the plea, but the weakness in Johnny's voice that had Wyatt agreeing to haul his butt away from Blue Horizon Ranch and his kids today.

He glanced at the men milling around, decked out in fringed leather chaps, Stetsons and snakeskin boots. Actors.

Dressing room trailers—honey wagons, Johnny had called them—were set up in the outlying area and a crew of about fifty were pulling wires, setting up cameras and shouting orders. He'd already spoken with the director today about the scene they were to shoot along the river's edge. The horses and cattle would be crossing in shallow waters, but it was a key concern that no animals or actors be hurt in the highly technical shot.

From a distance, he spotted the star of the movie, Dylan McKay, stepping out of his trailer decked out in a chambray shirt, jeans and a red paisley kerchief around his neck. And then Wyatt froze. He blinked and refocused.

Yep, he wasn't imagining it. Dylan was with a woman.

It was *her*.

Brooke Johnson.

What was she doing here? She looked awfully chummy with Dylan, laughing at something he'd said and walking along with him as though she was accustomed to being close to the mega superstar.

Seeing her again sent blazing fireworks off in Wyatt's head. "Uh, Tony?" He took his eyes off Brooke for a second to get the assistant wrangler's attention. "Do you know who that woman is walking with Dylan McKay?" He pointed. "Is her name Brooke Johnson?"

The wrangler scrubbed his jaw, his eyes narrowing a bit to gain a good look. "It's Brooke all right. All the single guys on the crew have been eyeing her. But her name's not Johnson. That's Mr. McKay's sister, Brooke McKay."

"She's Dylan McKay's sister?"

"Yep, that's what they tell me. She's a looker, but she's not the friendly type, if you know what I mean."

No, he didn't know what Tony meant. A knot formed

in the pit of his stomach. The woman he'd met on the road had been friendly and fun and sassy. He'd never describe Brooke as unfriendly. But then, he hadn't known the real Brooke, had he? She'd given him a fake name. Now that wasn't cool.

And just like that, Brooke turned her head and met his gaze. She halted abruptly, her face going as white as newly plowed snow. Dylan kept walking, but Brooke stood there, some twenty feet away, staring at him as if she couldn't believe it. As if she wanted to hide under a rock.

God, when had his effect on women taken a turn for the worse?

She said something to her brother, and then did a one-eighty and hightailed it back to the trailer. Before stepping inside she glanced in Wyatt's direction. To see if he was watching? Their eyes met again and for all he was worth, he couldn't, wouldn't stop looking at her. Then she was gone, the trailer door slamming shut behind her.

"Crap," he muttered, climbing down from his horse. He planted his feet on solid ground and held the reins in his hand, trying to decide what to do. He'd worked hard to put Brooke out of his mind, and now here she was infiltrating, invading and trying her best to take up space again.

He was so busy being in his own head, he didn't notice Dylan McKay until he was standing right in front of him. "Hello, I'm Dylan. I understand you're taking over for Johnny Wilde today?"

"Yes," Wyatt said, distracted. He got it together enough to refocus and pay the star some attention. "Wyatt Brandt."

Dylan put out his hand. "Nice meeting you."

"Same here."

They shook hands. "I understand you think the river's too fast to do the crossing scene today?"

"That's right. I told the director we should wait. I know the area, and that current is only going to get stronger as the day progresses. It's not safe for the animals. Clouds are starting to gather and those breezes are gonna turn ugly in a few hours. The winds will only complicate things. Sorry, I know it's not the news you hoped to hear."

"No need to apologize. We can shoot around it. Keeping the animals and crew safe is a priority. I just wanted to hear it from you."

"Sure thing."

"So, you're from around here?"

"I've lived in Texas all my life. I own Blue Horizon Ranch some twenty-five miles from here."

"Horses?"

"Cattle, but we have a string of Arabians and cutting horses on the ranch, too."

They spoke about horses and Texas for a while, and Wyatt came away thinking that Dylan McKay wasn't a stereotypical prima donna celebrity. It was on the tip of his tongue during the conversation to ask him about Brooke. But that didn't happen. Dylan had been called away. Just as well. Wyatt had come to the conclusion that he needed to speak to Brooke himself.

Sure, she'd lied to him about who she was.

But he'd left her alone in a hotel room after a wild night of sex, without much of an explanation.

He marched over to the honey wagon with a clear vision of what needed saying, but as he came close to knocking on the trailer door, his mind began to blur. Visions of Brooke slapping his face a good one flashed in his head. She might call security to toss him off the property.

He'd like to see them try.

But his hand clenched into a fist and he rapped on the door regardless. Things needed saying. It was as simple as that.

The door opened, and he was shell-shocked when a

pretty, pregnant redhead stood facing him. "Hi, can I help you?"

"Uh, sure. I wanted to speak with Brooke. I'm Wyatt Brandt."

"Okay, Wyatt. Let me see if Brooke is available. What can I tell her this is about?"

Hell, the wagon wasn't that big. Brooke was probably hearing this whole conversation. "Just mention my name. Tell her I hope she'll see me."

"I'll see him, Emma." Brooke said, her voice stony. And then she appeared in the doorway. She wasn't happy about seeing him, yet her beautiful brown eyes widened a bit when she looked at him, turning his brain to mush. The words he wanted to say fled him faster than a jackrabbit running from a hound.

"Hello, Brooke."

"Wyatt."

Emma gave them both a curious glance. "You know, I just remembered I have an errand to run."

Out here? There wasn't a town for miles.

"You don't have to leave, Emma. This won't take long," Brooke told her.

"No, no. I've really got to, to, uh…talk to Dylan. He's waiting on me to meet him down by the river."

Emma ducked her head and scooted down the steps quickly, giving them privacy.

Brooke's curvy body blocked the doorway. "I'm not inviting you in."

"There's no need for that. I just wanted to say…" Brooke's arms were folded and any minute now, she'd be tapping her foot, schoolteacher style. "Listen, I have some explaining to do. But so do you. You lied to me."

"About what?"

"About your name. You faked your identity."

"I have my reasons for that. But you skipped out…and oh, never mind."

"Can we talk?"

"I thought that's what we're doing."

"No, I mean really talk. I feel badly about how I had to leave you that morning. I do, and I want to make it up to you."

If body language had anything to do with it, she'd surely refuse him, but something stopped her. Instead, she seemed to be considering it. "What did you have in mind?"

"Come out to the ranch and have dinner with me. We can talk there, uninterrupted." Well, that depended on two little rascals and their sleep schedule, but he couldn't offer her anything more right now. His sense of honor was at stake. He didn't usually treat women the way he'd treated Brooke, and he wanted to make amends. "I can pick you up later and take you to the ranch."

"No. I don't think so," she said, and he felt the disappointment all the way to his toes. "I'll drive out. Just give me directions…*easy directions*, or I may not find it," she said.

She was agreeing? Why was he so damn happy about that?

"Great. It's about half an hour's drive from here and it's practically a straight run. I'll write down the directions. But I'd be happy to pick you up."

"No, I'll drive to you," she said, in a tone that meant business.

He got it. She wanted to be able to leave at a moment's notice. He didn't care. At least the nagging thoughts plaguing his mind would be put to rest after he explained the whole one-night-stand business.

The trick was trying to sort it all out in his own head first.

With her windows rolled down and a light drizzle dotting her windshield, Brooke was actually enjoying the ride.

The muggy Texas day had given way to an evening of fresh scents and cooler temperatures. Her windshield wipers clicked on and off and her driving arm was hit with an occasional raindrop as she steered over remote terrain toward Wyatt Brandt's ranch.

If it weren't for the baby she was carrying, she wouldn't be making this drive, but the opportunity to tell Wyatt the truth presented itself today when he shown up on the set of *The Price of Glory*. Seeing pigs fly would've shocked her less than having Wyatt Brandt appear at the river.

But as luck or bad karma would have it—she wasn't sure which—Wyatt had come out of nowhere again, her not-so-miraculous cowboy. Talking to him had become inevitable. She certainly couldn't speak with him on Dylan's set; there were too many opportunities to trigger gossip and speculation. And at Zane's home, there'd be too many eyes and ears around to have a private conversation, namely her brother's and Emma's.

Country music filled the silence of the road. Brooke sang along with Reba to keep her mind off what she was about to do. The words of "Cowgirls Don't Cry" poured out of her as she traveled over a lovely wooden bridge, the creek below surging with water. Alongside the water's edge, a carpet of healthy bluebonnets stretched out as far as the eye could see.

The picturesque image stayed with her and gave her a sense of peace. Soon white fences lined with Mexican oaks standing tall and probably designed for privacy came into view. Long branches with leathery leaves waved at her as she drove by. Within a minute, she came upon brick columns and iron gates and a pretty metal sign embossed with the sun rising over the land, welcoming her to Blue Horizon Ranch.

She sighed. Grateful to have made it without getting lost or running out of gas, she now had to contend with the fact that she was *here*. And one way or another, her life was going to change forever when she revealed her pregnancy to Wyatt Brandt.

As she drove through the open gates, the sudden strong scent of cattle filled her nostrils. Texans told her she'd get used to the smells around these parts, but it wasn't exactly vanilla sugar she was breathing in and she sincerely doubted that smell would be a treat to her nose anytime soon.

But oh man, the ranch was beautiful. The branches of whispering oaks formed a canopy over the road leading to a beautiful slate-gray stone ranch house. Wide windows gave the place an open feel. Across the way, the barns and outer buildings were faced with white wood and gray-toned shutters. It was homey and contemporary at the same time. Brooke immediately loved Wyatt's home. From the outside.

What lay in store for her on the inside was another matter.

She drove the circular drive and parked the car. She was on time for a change.

She'd dressed for dinner in old Brooke style, wearing basic black hip-hugging slacks, a silver-and-black shimmery top, and a wide belt. Her shoes were skyscrapers in red suede. She wasn't entirely sure she'd dressed this way out of defiance or as a shield of armor. She knew one thing: she felt comfortable in her own skin, and right now she needed that burst of confidence to confront Wyatt and tell him the truth.

She knocked at the door, and when nothing happened, she hit the doorbell. Inside, she heard the chimes ring out. A moment later, the door opened and she stood face-to-face with Wyatt.

Holding a squirming baby boy dressed in tiny denim overalls.

It was the last thing she expected. The child's melt-your-heart blue eyes were a perfect match to Wyatt's. The baby took one look at her and turned his head into Wyatt's shoulder and clung on for dear life.

"Wyatt?" She was rendered speechless after that, staring at the man who'd made her insides quiver just one month ago. Now he looked the picture of domesticity, his pale blue shirtsleeves rolled up, a stain that looked like sweet potato on his collar, his short blond hair disheveled.

"Come in, Brooke. I'm glad you made it okay."

She stared at him, still not believing what she was seeing. He'd never mentioned having a child. Although there'd seemed to be a silent agreement between them not to delve too deeply into their private lives. But being a father? Having a child was news he should've shared with her.

When she stood rooted to the spot, Wyatt moved aside and nodded, encouraging her to enter the house.

She stepped inside, instantly aware of her surroundings: the planks of light gray flooring under her feet, the brightness of the rooms even as dusk was settling. But what struck her the most was seeing the parlor crowded with toys: a fire truck and princess car suitable for a toddler and musical instruments and blocks everywhere. Everything was tidy and yet, it was *there*.

Wyatt closed the door behind her. "This is Brett, my son. He was supposed to be sleeping by the time you arrived. Obviously that didn't happen. Babies tend to make liars of their parents."

"You never mentioned you had a child, Wyatt." She tried hard not to put accusation in her tone.

"Would that have made a difference?"

"I don't know." It was the truth. She'd been so incredibly drawn to Wyatt that if he'd been open with her and told her he was a father, would she have fallen so easily into bed with him? She wasn't sure.

The baby inclined his head toward her, his rosy face so sweet, so curious. "Hello, Brett."

Brett clung tighter to Wyatt's neck.

"He's not much of a talker yet."

"How old is he?"

"Going on nineteen months."

"He's beautiful, Wyatt."

"Thanks, he's the best part of me. Well, him and his twin sister, Brianna."

"There's two of them?" Her ears twitched at the sound of her own voice. Twins? Wyatt had two children. This was all a bit much for her to take in. Her crazy hormones brought the threat of tears. She forced them down and tried not to think about what his reaction would be when she told him her news.

"Yes, and they're a handful, believe me. Listen, I want to explain all this to you. Why don't you have a seat in the dining room?" He started walking and she followed. "There's wine and cheese and other snacks ready. My housekeeper, Henrietta, is gone for the day, but she put out a nice spread for us. It'll just take me a few minutes to put Brett down to sleep and change my clothes."

He gave her another cursory glance. "You look pretty, by the way," he said, his miracle cowboy charm taking hold again. He was such a freaking gentleman, she had trouble remembering how he'd dumped her after a spectacular night of sex.

A night that they'd conceived a child.

"Please," he was saying, "have a seat."

Robotically she obeyed. And once he excused himself, she sat there stunned and feeling foolish. Her perfect miracle cowboy had engaged in lies of omission. Was he at that wedding just to hook up with a woman? Was her man radar off that much that she couldn't recognize a player?

But deep inside, she kept telling herself it wasn't true.

She couldn't have been that much off the mark with Wyatt. He'd been wonderful that night, and today, he'd invited her to his ranch to explain. Yet it nagged at her that if they hadn't accidentally met today, it would've been solely up to her to seek him out. It put her in an awkward spot.

A waterfall of rain poured over the gutter above the dining room bay window, drawing her attention. Lit by surrounding lights, it was a pretty distraction even if the skies were dark and filled with dreary clouds. It sort of mirrored her mood right now. Her nerves were jumping, and she bounded up to walk around the room, stopping to look at the pretty things in the china hutch, expensive yet tasteful pieces of crystal, delicate dishes and gold-rimmed teacups.

"That teacup set dates back to post-Civil War," Wyatt said quietly.

She hadn't heard him enter the room, but he stood behind her now and when she turned around, he was a breath away, staring into her eyes. The faint hint of his cologne brought reminders of being naked with him, of his hands on her and...

"It was my grandmother's favorite..." His voice trailed off as his gaze dipped down to her mouth.

Brooke felt the jolt down to her toes and looked away, pretending interest in the rain.

She wasn't going there with him, not again. There was too much unsaid between them.

He sighed and stepped away, pulling out a chair for her. The table was set perfectly, with some of the same fine china from the cabinet. She sat back down. Before he took a seat, he offered her a glass of wine.

"No thanks," she said. No alcohol for her.

He nodded, probably thinking she was being careful because she'd have to drive home. Well, there was that, too.

"You haven't touched anything," he noted.

"I'm not hungry right now, Wyatt." She was queasy about being here and queasy in general due to being pregnant.

"Okay, we can wait on dinner."

He braced his elbows on the table, matched the fingers of both hands in a steeple under his chin and sighed. "Brooke, I'm very glad you're here. The way I left you that morning was…unforgivable. I was out of my element and unsure what to do."

"You didn't appear unsure of anything the night we were together."

"Maybe it was you…"

"Don't butter me up, Wyatt. I can't get past the fact that if we hadn't accidentally met today, I would've never heard from you."

"You gave me a fake name."

"And you ran out on me after we…" She shook off the thought. She'd been over this in her mind a hundred times.

"I guess we both have explaining to do."

"You go first," she said. "And then I'll let you know if I want to share my reasons with you."

He nodded. Of the two sins, his was by far the worst, and he seemed to know it by the miserable look on his face. "My explanation is simple, but hard to admit. I lost my wife about ten months ago. She got in the car one day to pick up diapers for the twins and she never returned. She was pushed off the road by a semitruck. Her car plummeted off the shoulder and crashed into a tree."

Brooke gasped quietly, surprised to learn of Wyatt's loss. It explained a lot about why he hadn't spoken much about his past. He was probably still in a great deal of pain. When she'd met him he'd told her he was newly single. She'd thought that meant he had broken up with a girlfriend, or he was divorced. It never occurred to her that he might be a widower.

"That's awful, Wyatt. I'm so incredibly sorry."

She couldn't imagine losing someone she loved that way. One minute they were alive and vital and then in the blink of an eye, they're gone. How terribly sad it was for the mother who would never know her children. And those poor little babies, too. It was tragic all the way around.

She'd never forget how she felt when Dylan's life was in danger. She'd been absolutely terrified for him and she couldn't imagine losing him. But Wyatt had had to face that reality. He'd become a widower at a very young age.

"Thanks. I've been wallowing in self-pity and grief and as you can see, I have my hands full with the twins. They're about all I can handle. Two is like having four. Henrietta keeps reminding me how hard it is on her. I'm trying my best to find a suitable nanny, but it isn't easy. The last two who worked for me were mediocre at best. The babies didn't seem to respond to them, and they flaked on us a few times. I can't have that. I need someone reliable. Henrietta is sticking with me for the short term. She's getting on in age and she just can't do both jobs. I offered to hire more help so she could take the kids on full-time, but her hubby is chomping at the bit for her to retire. I can't say as I blame him."

Wyatt's shoulders lifted in a shrug that spoke volumes about his frustration. "My friend Johnny Wilde pressed me to go to that wedding. He said I had to get out and start living my life again. So, between him and Henrietta urging me on, I decided to go. The wedding was a way to distract me from the real issue that day. It was Madelyn's birthday. She would've been thirty."

Brooke was beginning to get the picture. "Was *I* your distraction, Wyatt?"

He gazed into her eyes, and his head made a slight movement. Was that a yes or a no? She couldn't tell what she was thinking or what he was about to say by the solemn expression on his face. "You were…but in an unexpected way."

"What does that mean?" She found herself speaking quietly, and not because of the sleeping children. This was delicate subject matter and Wyatt was looking so miserable.

"I thought I'd attend the nuptials, wish Blake well and bide my time during the reception. There'd be some drowning of my sorrows in whiskey, too, and then I'd planned on turning in early. I didn't go there with anything else in mind. I couldn't stop thinking about Madelyn and how we would've spent the day celebrating her birthday together. But then I found you broken down on the road, and I couldn't drive on by. I stopped and well, that's the unexpected part. For the first time since Madelyn died, I started enjoying myself again. Just being in your company changed my outlook and made me glad I'd made the trip to the inn. You made me forget some pretty awful days and I…well damn, this isn't easy to admit."

He pushed his fingers through his hair and sighed from deep in his chest. "I was attracted to you, Brooke. Madelyn was my whole life and I can't even remember a time that I wasn't infatuated with her. But then I had this one day with you."

"So I was a hall pass from your grief and guilt?"

He nodded. "Sounds awful, but maybe that's exactly how it was."

"So you woke up the next day and ran…because the guilt came back? You couldn't face me? Why didn't you wake me or at least wait until we could say goodbye?"

Wyatt reached across the wide table and touched her fingers, as if he needed the connection with her. Sparks ran up her arm, but she wouldn't make anything out of it. Wyatt was clearly still in love with his wife.

"No, Brooke. It wasn't that. It was Henrietta. She'd

stayed overnight with the babies, and I'd promised her I'd be back early in the morning. She had a trip planned and I didn't want to ruin her day or abuse her good nature. I woke up later than expected that morning. Believe me, there was so much I wanted to say to you. But that note was all I had time for, and that's the honest truth. On my babies' lives, I swear to you."

Brooke was quiet for a time. He was giving her time to absorb it all. She took a swallow of her drink and began nodding her head. "Okay, I get that. But you know what part of the note insulted me more than anything? The thank-you at the end."

Wyatt stared at her and shook his head. "You're mad because I thanked you?"

"It was as if…as if I'd done a service for you or something. I can't explain it, but that's how I felt when I woke up alone and found your thank-you note."

"Oh, man." He rubbed his forehead and closed his eyes. "I had no idea it would come off that way. I wasn't proud of how I left that day. It's bothered me all this time. Believe me, Brooke, I never intended to hurt you."

Thunder boomed off in the distance and she jumped. Was it a heavenly omen, a sign to take Wyatt at his word?

"I'm out of practice with women, Brooke. And I never expected to have…"

"Sex?"

He nodded. It wasn't in his wheelhouse to be crude; she'd already figured that out about him. But she had no problem telling it like it is.

"It was an amazing night, Brooke. But I didn't think past that night or what the next day would bring."

"I didn't either, if I'm being honest."

"But you didn't expect me to run out on you."

She nodded. "It made what could've been a good memory for me feel cheap."

"No!" Wyatt scraped his chair back and stood. "No, Brooke. That night…it was real and honest. I needed to feel alive again…and it was you, and only you, who helped me with that. And if I'm not mistaken, you needed the same from me, too. Am I right?"

She opened her mouth, but her denial didn't come. Slowly, she closed her trap and nodded. She would give Wyatt that. She'd needed someone who'd cared—if only in the moment—for her. She was still healing from Royce's duplicity. She would've almost rather had her ex throw her over for another woman than to use her the way he had.

Wyatt was a different breed of man. That much she knew. "You didn't tell me you had children."

"I didn't. I just wanted to be me, not a father, not a widower, that night. My pain-in-the-ass pal Johnny is forever saying I need to find myself again. That's what I was trying to do."

She inhaled a sharp breath, everything becoming clear in her mind now. He was lost without his wife.

A flash of lightning lit up the night sky behind Wyatt and reflected off the window. The bright beam illuminated a backyard filled with patio tables and chairs, toys and a gated pool. This was a home for a family to live and love and thrive in, but sadly there was a missing piece now. The family wasn't whole anymore.

Her anger faded as fast as the lightning. Oddly, she understood how Wyatt wanted to be private about his past when they'd met, wanting one night to just be himself and not a responsible father, not a grieving widower. Wasn't that the same reason she hadn't been totally honest with him? She just wanted to be Brooke, not Dylan McKay's younger sister, not the girl who'd had men use her to get close to her famous brother.

If she were brave, she'd reveal her pregnancy to Wyatt and try to cope with the decisions they would make together. But her courage failed her. She couldn't lay this on Wyatt right now.

As she grappled with her decision to cut and run, a baby's wail broke into her thoughts, loud and panicky.

Wyatt's squeezed his eyes shut momentarily. "That's Brianna. Sorry. I think she's having a bad dream. I've got to check on her. "

"Of course. Go."

As soon as Wyatt took a step out of the dining room, another howl erupted, the second one huskier and deeper than the first. Both babies had woken up. And their cries blasted through the house without interval. Double trouble. Brooke rose and followed Wyatt up the stairs.

At least this was one crisis she could help manage.

Four

Brett and Brianna both howled, one in each crib, their little bodies facing up toward glow-in-the-dark neon stars illuminating the ceiling. Madelyn had chosen nursery decor that would bring a sense of peace and calm, but there were times that nothing much soothed cranky twins. Thunder boomed outside, rattling the windows, and their cries grew louder. Wyatt picked up Brett first, bouncing him in his arms, and then turned to Brianna. But Brooke was already picking up his little girl.

Brianna was groggy at best, her eyes half closed. But she looked so sweet, her blond curls falling onto her face as she clung to Brooke's neck. She had no clue she was in the arms of a stranger. Heaven help them all when she discovered that fact. Bri was his wild child. She didn't take to newcomers, which was something her previous nannies had learned the hard way.

Brooke bounced Brianna in her arms, taking her cue from him. Not that he knew exactly what he was doing.

His kids were a constant bafflement to him. One minute they were happy as clams, the next, they'd be wailing about something he couldn't begin to fathom.

Bouncing them was clearly not working. Tears continued to fall, and then Brooke began to sing as she rocked the baby in her arms. Not just *sing*: her lilting voice filled the room with sweetness, a serene siren's song that mesmerized with its beauty. And damn if Brianna didn't stop crying right then and there. Her big blue eyes opened wide and she sniffled a few times, stunned into silence by her own curiosity and…awe.

Brett followed suit, and Wyatt walked him closer to Brooke, so he, too, could be enchanted. Brooke clearly had a talent, which seemed to pour out of her effortlessly. Within minutes, his crab apple little ones were quieted. Brooke rocked Bri and he rocked Brett and once they'd fallen asleep in their arms, Wyatt nodded to Brooke. Carefully, she laid the baby down in her crib. Then Wyatt kissed Brett on the forehead and also set him in his crib.

Brooke tiptoed out of the room, allowing Wyatt a minute to simply stare at his babies. God, he loved them. They were all he had left of Madelyn, and they truly were the best part of him. He would do just about anything to ensure their happiness. But with one strike against them already—losing their beautiful mother—the weight of his responsibility sometimes scared the stuffing out of him.

He left the nursery door open and went in search of Brooke. He found her at the top of the stairs, waiting for him. "They're both sweet," she whispered. "You're very lucky."

"Thanks. You have a beautiful voice, Brooke. Hidden talent? Or did you lie to me about your profession?"

Her body went rigid. Fueled by anger, her brown eyes lit up. "I didn't lie to you about anything but my name."

"Yeah, and why was that? You feel like telling me

now?" he asked softly, trying to tread carefully. He'd pissed her off unintentionally, but he really wanted to know.

Her shoulders relaxed some, and she studied him a moment, then nodded. "All right. I'll explain."

"Great. Let's talk downstairs." He took her arm and led her to the parlor sofa. "Have a seat."

She sat on the couch and he took a seat on the opposite end.

"It's not a big deal," she began, "that I lied about my last name. My brother is famous and it gets old real fast, having people act nice to me only because of him."

"That's it? That's why you lied? You get tired of answering questions about him?"

"No, Wyatt. I get tired of men using me, getting my hopes up and pretending to care about me only to get close to *him*. I get tired of men giving me scripts or screenplays to show him or using me to ask him to invest in their pet projects."

Wyatt shook his head, finally getting the picture. It wasn't pretty. It would take a strong, secure woman not to be affected, but then, Brooke was all those things, which made the creeps using her horrible slugs. "You've been burned."

"To a crisp."

"Man, that's rough. I'm sorry. Was it someone in particular, someone special?"

"I thought he was special at the time. It was a man who worked in finance, a real pencil pusher, a numbers man, a guy I thought wouldn't care who my brother was. As it turned out Royce was a closet wannabe screenwriter. And when he lowered the boom I didn't see it coming. It floored me and hurt me, and coming to Texas was a way to mend and heal. And gain some perspective. So, what I did that day by lying to you wasn't too different than what you'd done. I just wanted a day without questions. One day to be me. Just plain Brooke."

"You could never be plain," he said, and realized how much he meant it. From the get-go, he'd found something unique in Brooke.

"Thanks." She shrugged and looked away as if she didn't believe him, as if what he was saying to her was merely a platitude to make her feel better. Yes, he wanted her to feel better, but he wasn't lying.

"It's the truth. And I do understand. I'm sorry you got hurt, Brooke. Honestly, it makes me feel awful about running out on you the way I did."

She snapped off a quick smile. "Story of my life."

"You're terrific, Brooke. I mean that. And any creep who would use you isn't fit to call himself a man."

"Present company excluded?"

"I didn't use you. Tell me you don't think that."

Her eyes squeezed closed and she shook her head. "No. I don't think that. Not anymore."

Which meant she'd gone the entire month thinking he had. Crap.

Wyatt closed the gap between them on the sofa. He had to get closer to her now, and make sure she was okay. Hell, she was more than okay. She was amazing. It wasn't easy being this close without touching her, holding her in his arms and making her feel better. But sanity prevailed just in time and took over his brain. Touching her again would be a colossal mistake. A change of subject was needed.

"You're very good with children. Do you have a big family?"

"Not really. I'm Dylan's foster sister—his folks are my folks. It was just me and him growing up. He's always been my rock, my best friend, and sometimes, my bitter enemy. You know, your usual brother/sister dynamic."

"Sounds like fun."

"Yeah, it was. Still is. I love him to death. What about you? Brothers or sisters?"

"Nope, just me and those two powerhouses you helped put to sleep. They're a handful and a half. I don't know how people with big families do it. One boy, one girl, and I'm done. Especially now."

"You mean because you're doing it without their mother?" Brooke's voice lowered and nearly cracked. She wouldn't look him in the face.

"Two's enough, when both parents are in the picture. But yeah, I suppose it's because I'm trying to move on and it's tough going sometimes. That's why when I met you…well, it was nice. *You* were nice, and I suppose I—"

"Don't, Wyatt. I get the picture."

She went rigid all over and lowered her lids to her red suede shoes. They looked great on her feet, but weren't exactly perfect footwear for a rainy night. "Maybe you don't."

"Oh, believe me, I do." Her voice was stronger now, but pained, as if he'd hurt her all over again.

Just then, lightning flashed, and a second later thunder cracked, the loud boom shaking the house. Wyatt bounded up quickly and moved to the window. Rain was coming down in buckets. This raging storm wasn't moving on anytime soon. "Dammit. I should've been paying closer attention."

"To what?" Brooke asked.

He turned to her while releasing a you're-a-fool sigh aimed at himself. "The rain. The storm. This isn't good, Brooke."

"Won't it pass?" She rose and marched over to the window.

"Not before doing a lot of damage. The bridge is washed out by now. Happens every time we have a major storm."

"What bridge? Not that pretty little bridge I drove over a couple of hours ago?"

"That's the one. It's the only way in and out of the ranch. Can't get to the highway without it. You're going to have to spend the night here."

Her face twisted up, and those chocolate eyes went dark as coal. "That's ridiculous, Wyatt. I. Am. Not. Spending the night here."

"Hey, I know you don't want to, but this storm is dangerous. And you won't get over that bridge. Trust me."

She shook her head. "I'm betting it's not too late. If I leave now, I'll make it. The rain only just started coming down hard."

"Nope, not happening. I can't let you do it."

"You can't order me to stay here." Her voice rose. "I'm going to try, Wyatt."

She found her purse, grabbed her car keys and made a dash for the front door.

He followed her. "Brooke, be reasonable." But the determined look on her face said reason wasn't a factor.

"Thanks for dinner."

"You didn't eat a thing."

"Thanks anyway. I'll...we'll talk. I have to go."

He blocked the door with his arm. "Don't. It's not safe."

It wasn't safe for her to stay overnight either, but he wasn't going there.

She gazed into his eyes. There was something more going on with her. Something that he didn't understand. Was she worried about a repeat of the night they'd shared? He'd hurt her, and she wasn't forgetting that anytime soon, but for some reason he didn't believe that was it. He thought they'd cleared the air. They'd talked openly and honestly, but something had jarred her and he wasn't sure what it was.

"You don't have to worry about, about..."

"Don't be an idiot, Wyatt. You think you're that irresistible?"

She blinked her eyes; her sarcasm was hiding something else. Something she wasn't saying. Having her spend the night here wouldn't be easy on him. He wasn't immune to her, the way she claimed to be to him. She was the only other woman beside Madelyn to touch something deep inside him and bring out his protective instincts. Was it a bad case of lust? He'd gone months without sex, and Brooke had been the perfect partner, guileless and beautiful and giving. Having her here would test his willpower, but the very thought of her going out in that storm gave him hives. She didn't know the roads like he did. She didn't know the treachery that lay in her path. She came from California, where a few sprinkles meant storm watch. But here in Texas, they had real storms, ones that could wipe out entire towns.

"Brooke, listen to me. You're being stubborn."

"And you're wasting my time. You can't keep me here against my will," she hissed out.

Holy hell, she was right. "I am trying to keep you safe."

"I don't need you to rescue me anymore. You're through being my miracle cowboy, Wyatt. Now, unblock the door."

Slowly and against his God-given good judgment, he stepped away from the door.

She exited quickly, and he watched her get into her car, start the engine and pull away.

The windshield wipers weren't doing a very good job. Or was it her tears causing her vision to blur? She slowed the car down to a snail's crawl and inched her way along the dark road leading her away from Wyatt, his kids, his grief and his declaration that he wanted no more children. Period. *Two's enough.* Two, as in his adorable twins who were motherless now, and being raised by a dad who was lost in his own way.

And where did that leave her?

More tears spilled onto her cheeks, mingling with the raindrops that had slashed across her face just minutes ago as she got into her car. Damn her hormones. She was usually stronger than this. But usually, she wasn't pregnant by a virtual stranger whose only sin, other than running out on her in the morning after a one-night stand, was that he had no clue how her heart had shattered and was still shattering when she realized that he wasn't going to jump for joy at having another child.

And dammit, her child deserved more than that. Her child didn't deserve being cast aside. She should know. The McKays had taken her in and loved her like their own. She was grateful every day of her life, but it still didn't heal her secret pain of knowing that she'd been unwanted. Unloved. It was classic foster-child syndrome. But now, her baby, the sweet life growing inside her, wouldn't have what Brooke had vowed any child she bore would have: two loving parents.

"Not fair," she mumbled while trying to slosh along the flooded, muddy road.

A flash of lightning lit up the skies and thunder followed, the loudest she'd ever heard. Her hands trembled on the steering wheel, and she sobered. Maybe Wyatt wasn't trying to be Prince Charming again. Maybe this storm was really as bad as he'd said.

An animal skittered across the road and she braked hard. "Oh!" She barely missed the critter, and the car skidded, careering to the right. She gripped the steering wheel tighter, her knuckles white, as the car spun out of control. The back end dipped into a muddy ditch and hit a brick fence post. The force pitched her forward and her thick skull slammed into the steering wheel.

The jolt startled her, and her forehead immediately throbbed. She sat there, dazed, as big drops of rain pelted the windshield. Her head pounded, her eyes burned and she felt as if she'd been hit by a giant dump truck rather than mixing it up with a fence post. She closed her eyes, a sense of déjà vu hitting her. She'd been in this car once before and laid her head on the steering wheel, clueless as to how to proceed. God, she was an idiot.

Tears sprang anew from her eyes, and she welcomed them this time. She needed a good cry. What secretly pregnant girl didn't?

She took a tissue out of her purse and blew her nose. That's when she realized it wasn't just tears streaking her face. Blood colored the white tissue. Not a lot, but enough for her to take another tissue out and adjust the mirror in the dark to catch a glimpse of the damage. She had a knot the size of a plum erupting and a scrape two inches long. No doubt tomorrow, it would turn from hot red to dark purple. Wonderful. Now she'd have to explain all this to Dylan and Emma and endure their worry and concern.

If she ever got home tonight.

A knock came on the driver's side window, startling her out of her self-pity. Oh, no. It couldn't be. The man wearing a rain slicker and big Western hat gestured for her to roll down her window.

She did. He shone a flashlight on her face and then quickly lowered it. But it must have been enough for him to see her stricken expression and bruised forehead. Curses spilled from his mouth. Really ugly words hissed out, not exactly the words of a knight in shining armor. Lucky for her, the pound of the rain washed away the worst of them from her delicate ears.

"Wyatt."

"Dammit, Brooke. You're bleeding."

"Not that much," she said numbly.

"Are you okay?"

"I… I think so."

He yanked the door open and reached for her.

"I can walk."

"Quiet, Brooke," he said through clenched teeth. There was fierceness in his voice she'd never heard before. So she clamped her trap shut as he lifted her out of the car and carried her to a big four-wheel-drive Jeep. He dumped her in the front seat, but not before her eyes drifted to the backseat. And her stomach plummeted. Two beautiful children, strapped into their car seats wearing pajamas and shivering, were rustling around back there, restless, cold and sleepy-eyed.

Brett rubbed his eyes and Brianna was barely holding back sleep-deprived tears.

Wyatt had risked going out in the storm with his babies to save her sorry butt.

He slammed the door shut behind him and didn't look at her. "I'm…sorry about this, Wyatt."

Nothing.

She bit her lip. His seething anger was almost tangible, and she felt the slap of his silence as he pulled out onto the road and slowly navigated his way through the storm. The rain didn't let up, and the windshield wipers fought a crazy swish and slosh of water. But she felt safe again and knew he would steer them cautiously home. Lights from the ranch house appeared out of the darkness like a beacon of all things good, and Wyatt drove into the attached garage and killed the engine. He would've probably liked to kill her, too, at the moment. Brett had started crying halfway through the drive home and Brianna had joined in shortly after. The cacophony of their cries only added weight to her blunder.

She was a heel.

A thoughtless fool.

She hadn't once thought of the risk to her own baby in all this.

And Wyatt's innocent kids had been dragged through the storm in the dead of night.

Of course, she'd thought of none of this beforehand. She'd only wanted to make a clean getaway. She didn't think she could bear staying the night under Wyatt's roof, and guess what? *Hello.* Now she had no choice in the matter. And instead of Wyatt being a gracious host, she'd be privy to his wrath.

Which she deserved.

Wyatt gave her a cursory look, only to gauge her injuries. "Stay put in the Jeep. I'll be back for you," he ordered.

"You don't need to do that," she said, opening the door and practically falling out. It was a long way down, and she'd been in a hurry. "I'm helping with the kids. You take Brett, I'll get Brianna."

"Brooke," he said, his sigh weary and frustrated, but he didn't argue the point. It was too loud in the garage to hear much beyond the babies' cries.

"Let me help, Wyatt," she said softly. "It's the least I can do."

"You're not dizzy?"

She was dizzy in the brain lately, but that wasn't what Wyatt meant. "No. I'm not. It's just a little bump."

He grunted and she took that as a yes to helping with the kids.

She opened the back door of the Jeep, ignoring the throbbing pain in her head, and concentrated on unfastening Brianna from the car seat. The baby was pushing the heels of her hands into her tired eyes, whimpering. "Come with me, Bri baby. We'll get you warm and back to sleep."

Apparently at some point, Wyatt had tossed two blankets over them, but now they lay on the Jeep's floor. She grabbed one and wrapped it around the baby, while Wyatt was doing his best with Brett. Once they had their two unruly packages all bundled up, they entered the house. Im-

mediate warmth settled around them as they made their
way up the stairs.

The nursery was illuminated by a night-light. Brooke
and Wyatt stood quietly in the center of the room rocking the babies. Their cries simmered some, but they were
still restless.

"Wyatt?" she whispered.

"Hmm?"

"Do you have your cell phone handy?"

"Yeah, why?" he whispered, still swaying little Brett
in his arms.

"I need it for a minute."

He gave her a look, but then handed it to her.

"Thanks."

She set Brianna down in her crib and covered her with
a blanket. Brooke then fidgeted with the phone until she
found what she was looking for. "Okay," she said, "put
Brett in his crib."

Wyatt gave her a dubious look, but set the baby down
and covered him.

Then she turned up the volume on the phone and the
gentle humming of a box fan filled the room.

"They should be asleep in minutes," she whispered to
Wyatt.

"What in hell is that?" he asked, staring at her as if
she'd grown horns.

"White noise."

She tiptoed out of the room. Wyatt glanced at his quieted babies, not quite asleep yet, but soothed and calmer
now, before following behind her.

In the hallway, he grabbed her hand. "Come with me."

His grip was tight, but not in a loving way. She felt a
lecture coming on. But to her surprise, he led her into his
master bedroom. It was a beautiful room filled with white
oak furniture in tasteful shades of cream and lilac. Made-

lyn's touch was all around, from the top-notch drapes and
bed linens to the delicate crystal perfume bottles on the
dresser to the impressionist pastel artworks on the wall. It
was hardly a manly rancher's room, and Brooke had trouble picturing Wyatt in here. Yet it was a testament to his
love for his wife. He'd let her decorate, allowing her to do
whatever made her happy.

"Wyatt, what are you doing?"

They bypassed the bed and entered a foyer that led to
a massive master bathroom. She was sure she could put
her whole apartment in this room. There were two of everything, which was the way Wyatt seemed to roll, having
twins and all: two long granite counters with dual sinks,
two toilets and two walk-in closets. Just one tub though,
sunken and luxurious, surely big enough for two consent-
ing adults to share. The thought made her hot all over.

He picked her up and set her on the countertop. "Gosh,
you've got to stop doing that," she blurted.

"Doing what?" he asked, distracted. He was busy gathering supplies, peroxide, washcloths and a first aid kit.

"Carrying me places."

"You don't seem to have sense enough to keep yourself
out of harm's way."

"I keep out of harm's way."

He snorted.

"I said I was sorry. I never meant to endanger your children. I wasn't…thinking."

"There's a lot of that going around."

Did he mean the night they'd slept together? Was he
regretting it? Of course he was. She'd been nothing but
trouble from the moment they'd met.

He placed a warm washcloth on her forehead, and she
flinched.

"Sorry, Brooke. I've got to clean this wound."

"It's nothing."

"Nothing?" He placed his hands on her shoulders and swiveled her partway around. She got a good look at her wound in the light.

"Oh!" It was three times the size she'd seen in the car's mirror. Blood had caked on her forehead. It looked like a red rose atop a lumpy cupcake. Only this was not sweet. "I didn't realize."

"You could've been seriously hurt," he said through tight lips. He dabbed at the blood some more.

"But I wasn't. I never expected you to drag your babies out into the storm to rescue me."

"You left me no choice. What else was I supposed to do? Let you crash your car and get hurt or...or—"

"You put your children in danger for me."

"I could let you believe that. It would serve you right. But the truth is, I know the land and the four-wheel-drive Jeep has weathered lots of storms. I wouldn't deliberately put my kids in danger."

"But still, you dragged them out of bed to come get me."

"I won't be disagreeing with you."

"I'm so sorry, Wyatt. I promise you won't know I'm here and in the morning I'll—"

"You're not going anywhere in the morning, Brooke. This storm is pounding the land, and the weather reports aren't good. Looks like we're in for a few more days of it. There's another storm right behind this one."

"There is?" She took a swallow.

"I'm afraid so."

He finished washing her wound and dried her forehead, then took a pad of gauze and soaked it with peroxide. "This is gonna sting a bit," he said.

"You're going to love every second of it."

He leaned back to look into her eyes. His were still cold, hard and so amazingly blue, she wanted to cry. But she'd already done enough crying. She'd take her medicine like a big girl and pay the price for her stupidity.

"You should've listened to me. Then none of this would've happened. You put your life in danger, Brooke."

And then she got it. She knew why he'd come after her. She'd put him in a terrible position. Shoot. She wished she was wrong on this, but her heart told her the truth. He couldn't let her go it alone to possibly crash her car or worse. His wife had died in a car crash. Those memories must have tortured him tonight. Wyatt couldn't stand by and let another woman die on his watch. He had to come after her; his conscience wouldn't allow anything else. And whatever he'd said to the contrary, he *had* risked his kids and his own safety to rescue her.

"Ouch!"

The hardness in his eyes evaporated some. "I told you it would sting."

She almost choked on the pungent smell of peroxide. When he finished ministering to her gash, he capped the bottle and put it away. She jumped down from the counter before he picked her up again.

"It only lasts a minute or two," he said.

She nodded. "I'm really sorry I behaved so selfishly. Really, Wyatt. I wish there was a way for me to make it up to you."

His dark blond brows rose and the intense glint in his eyes put wicked thoughts in her head. Was he thinking about their night together? When they had labored long and hard to satisfy each other's hunger? When they'd spoken of nothing consequential and yet said so many things in the heat of passion?

Wyatt's landline phone rang in the master bedroom, breaking up the moment.

He walked over to it and glanced at the number, then

winced, his frown even deeper than the one he had for Brooke.

"I'll leave you so you can answer that."

"No, it's not necessary. I'll return that call in the morning. Right now, you're going to eat something."

"I'm not—" She was about to say she wasn't hungry, but then she remembered the life inside her needed nourishing. She'd been selfish enough tonight. She needed to eat, if only to maintain her strength for the baby. "Okay, yes. It's a shame to let the dinner go to waste."

"Fine," he said. "And you should put some ice on that bump."

"Right. Ice. Just what I need. Gotcha."

He turned around at her sarcasm, and that brow rose again. Did he have to be so darn appealing, even when he was scowling at her?

She made the gesture of zipping her lip with her fingers.

Wyatt's eyes gleamed and a smile threatened to emerge on his face, before he turned around and kept going.

She followed behind without another word.

Dinner was a quiet affair of stilted conversation and reheated food. Nevertheless, she downed her meal with gusto. It was either a result of Henrietta's expert cooking or the fact that Brooke was eating for two now. She filled her tummy with chicken piccata, scalloped potatoes, yeast rolls and salad until she thought she would explode. "My compliments to the cook," she said once she was all through.

"I'll tell Henrietta. It'll earn me brownie points, relaying the compliment," Wyatt said, sipping coffee. He hadn't looked at her during the dinner. The vibe she got was that she'd pissed him off and now he was stuck with her. What was his demeanor saying? Don't mess with Texas? Or Texans, for that matter.

She kept her lips buttoned and spoke only when spoken to.

"How do you know about white noise?" he asked finally, pushing away his empty coffee cup.

She shrugged. "Years of babysitting, I guess. You pick up hints and tricks along the way. And I've been doing some reading. My, uh, sister-in-law Emma is pregnant."

And so am I. If only she had the courage to make that announcement.

"I'd never heard of it," he said, staring at her mystified. "There's so much…"

"You learn as you go, Wyatt."

"I suppose. But sometimes I feel behind the eight ball on all this."

"You're a businessman with a company to run. You can't possibly keep up on the latest baby trends. And the old ways of doing things aren't so bad."

He pushed his hands through his hair. "You mean like rocking a baby to sleep instead of brainwashing them with digital noise?"

She laughed. "Yes. Both ways work."

He chuckled, too, and his whole demeanor changed. It was nice to see his smile again, if only for a few seconds. She could faint dead away from how his eyes touched upon hers. They lingered for a while, sparkling brilliant blue like the sea on a sunny day. It was killer to see him unguarded and free of any pain or anger.

"So are you hating me right now, or have I moved up the scale to mild dislike?" she finally asked.

A deep sigh broke from his throat. "Brooke."

"I'm sorry. But we are going to be stuck here together for a few days."

He shook his head at her comment. "I don't hate anyone. Dislike is reserved for my enemies."

"You have enemies?" Now that was a surprise.

"A few. You can't get to this level in business without ruffling feathers and pissing people off. I've done my share of negotiating but I've always done it fairly. Some of my competitors haven't been so scrupulous. I don't abide ruthlessness in business or anywhere else."

"So, you dislike your competitors. That's probably the case for a lot of business owners. What did they do, undermine your good name?"

"I can fend for myself. And my name is just fine. But they hit me the hardest when Madelyn died. I was struggling with her loss and my babies being motherless, and my rivals swooped in during a vulnerable time in my life to steal contracts away. At the time, I was too grief-stricken to take much notice or to care."

"That sucks, Wyatt. That's a really rotten thing to do. Okay, so I'm not in that category. Thank God."

"Brooke, there's no need to put a name on any of this. I sure as hell don't know what to call…us." He gestured with his hands to both of them.

Us? As in, the two of them? Brooke wouldn't get her hopes up that he meant anything serious by using the term. There was just no other way to describe the two of them. Still, while they were on the subject of babies and white noise and all, why couldn't she bring herself to tell him she was carrying his child?

And the devil's voice in her head was only too glad to explain, *Because you couldn't bear for your baby to be unwanted, the way you were.* And that was the crux of the matter. She was just coming to terms with being pregnant herself, and having Wyatt rebuff and reject the baby would be a knife to her heart.

Outside, the storm didn't let up. Windows rattled and winds howled with frenetic energy. It was the gloomiest of gloomy and yet there they were having a cozy meal together in the warmth of the house with two sweet babies asleep in their cribs upstairs.

"Do you have to check on the animals or anything?"

Wyatt ground his teeth and nodded as if she'd hit upon the very thing he'd been thinking. "I probably should, but I…"

But he didn't want to leave the babies alone with a stranger. She would remedy that right now. If there was one thing she could do for him, it was that. "I'll watch the twins, Wyatt. I'll sit in their room if you'd like. And I promise no more stunts. I'll be right there if they need something. Although I wasn't hinting for you to go out in this god-awful weather."

"The weather doesn't bother me, but I should check on the horses in the barn at the very least. I've gotta make sure they have feed and water. And it's not necessary for you to sit with the babies. I'll look in on them before I go out. They should sleep the rest of the night. Why don't you get ready for bed? You must be tired. You can listen for them in the guest bedroom."

She was exhausted. And the idea of cuddling up with a pillow and a warm blanket over her suddenly became appealing. Usually a night owl, her energy cells shut down after nine o'clock these days.

"Sounds good. But first, let me help put some of these things away," she said.

Wyatt didn't stop her from picking up plates and taking them to the kitchen. They worked silently, moving about the room tidying up and making very sure they didn't accidentally bump into each other. She couldn't have him touching her tonight, not while the storm raged outside and her innermost feelings were so close to the surface. She liked Wyatt a whole lot, and the iron barriers she usually put up with men seemed to falter when he was near. And that was a bad, bad thing.

"Follow me. I'll get you something to wear for the night."

He was halfway up the stairs before she started the climb, trying to keep her eyes down and not on the precise cut of his jeans and the rear end that was pretty near perfection. It was darn hard not to notice as his boots clicked and clacked upon the shiny wood steps, accentuating what was going on with every long-legged stride he took. Then she caught a glimpse of his shoulders in the tight cotton shirt. He was one of those cowboys whose muscles bunched under the shirtsleeves.

It wasn't as if she hadn't seen him naked. But somehow this was more intimate: being alone with him in his home with his children sleeping just steps away from her room.

"Here we are," he said, once he reached the room that was two doors down from the nursery and on the opposite side of the hallway from his master bedroom. "You can bed down in here. There's new toothbrushes and towels and everything you might need. If you don't find something, just let me know."

"I'm sure it's fine. Thanks."

"Oh," he said, remembering something. "Just a sec."

He walked away and then came back holding a red plaid flannel shirt. "This is the best I can do right now. It's clean."

She'd wondered if he would give her one of his wife's garments to wear, or if he still had any of her clothes around. Wearing something that was Madelyn's would be too darn weird, so the flannel shirt was a good choice.

He handed it to her and she hugged it to her chest. "Thanks."

Maybe hugging his shirt wasn't the brightest idea. His gaze dipped down to her chest and his eyes flickered like a newly lit flame.

She took a big breath.

He did the same. "Well," he said, lifting his eyes to meet hers.

"Well," she said, captivated.

He made a face, then pushed his hand through his hair. "I'd best go see to the animals."

"And the twins?"

"Are sleeping tight. But you can check on them if you'd like while I'm gone. I hope to be only ten minutes or so."

"Fine, I'll be listening for them."

"Appreciate that."

Five

It was a mother of a storm. Wyatt wasn't a small man, and yet as he exited the warmth of his home, he was thrashed about quite handily by sweeping thirty-mile-an-hour gusts that nearly stole his hat from his head. He pushed it down with the flat of his hand and trudged toward the barns. He had a string of Arabians that wouldn't take kindly to Mother Nature's outburst. A few years back, he'd installed floor heating in the barn, but those animals were feisty and high-strung and they sure as hell didn't like the boom of thunder and the sound of rain pelting the rooftops overhead. It was not quite hurricane weather, and he was grateful he had the means and the cash to provide the best structures for the animals. If the cattle had any sense, they'd take shelter in the overhangs on the property he'd set up every forty acres or so to provide a source of cover for his crew.

He reached the barn and made quick work of checking on the horses, pitchforking a layer of extra straw in their stalls, and making sure they had enough alfalfa and oats to fill their bellies. It would be at least two days before his crew would return. His weekend crew couldn't get onto the ranch anyway, and he'd texted them all earlier, telling them not to try. It was too dangerous.

With his work done, he latched the barn doors. He fought his way back, putting his head down and trudging through winds that could likely lift him off the ground and carry him to parts unknown. But he made it to the house just fine.

He stood in the foyer, shedding his cold, rain-soaked coat and gloves. The warmth inside the house seeped into his bones. It would take a hot shower to completely thaw him out.

He climbed the stairs two at a time, ready for this night to be over, and checked on the babies. But he damn well wasn't prepared for the sight before his eyes. He halted and swallowed hard.

Brooke.

She was leaning over Brianna's crib, her mile-long tanned legs giving him quite a show. As she bent further, he caught a powerful glimpse of the slip of white cotton panties she wore and the plump, perfect cheeks peeking out.

He blew breath out of his lungs and admired the view, his groin tightening up, his heart racing. What he wouldn't give to have her here under different circumstances. To have the freedom to take her to his bed and make wild love to her again and again.

He groaned, the sound penetrating the room, to his chagrin.

Brooke startled and turned around, catching him in the act of lusting after her. She gasped, a beautiful breathy sound that stirred his senses even more as they met eye to eye across the darkened room.

Brianna quieted back to sleep, thanks to Brooke, and then Wyatt remembered his place, the fact that Brooke wasn't here by choice and that he wasn't available to her. Not in the way he craved. But judging by the spark of heat in Brooke's eyes she tried to conceal, she might be craving him, too.

She tiptoed out of the room, edging her way past him in the doorway, her breasts teasing his chest as she passed by. That wisp of a touch nearly undid him.

"Brooke."

She whirled around, her eyes knowing and hungry. "She was fussing. I calmed her back to sleep."

"Thanks."

"You're cold and wet," she said. He liked having her eyes on him.

"I'm getting ready for a warm shower."

She nibbled on her very plump bottom lip and drew his attention there. "Good idea."

Crap. Did she have to have such a kissable mouth? Now all he could think about was kissing her senseless, stripping her of his shirt and having her join him in the shower.

"I'll be off to bed now," she said, without making a move.

"I, uh…okay."

The staring match continued. Wyatt could look into her pretty coffee-brown eyes all night. Her hair was falling off one shoulder, all those lush rich raven strands close enough to reach out and touch.

"Brooke," he said again, giving his head a regretful shake.

"I know, Wyatt. It's okay… Good night."

He sucked in air. She felt it, too, and there wasn't a damn thing either of them could do about it. "Night."

Finally, she turned and headed down the hallway to

her own room. Before closing the door, she wiggled her fingers at him.

Once she was out of sight, Wyatt breathed a sigh of relief. Two more days of this could mean trouble. What a freaking mess he was. Hungering for another woman in the very home he'd once shared with Madelyn.

It wasn't going to happen.

But oh, it wasn't going to be easy, either.

When morning dawned, the sky was just as dreary as the night before. There was no sign of sunshine, just gray threatening clouds. A steady light cascade thudded against the roof, but without the theatrics of thunder and lightning. Today's storm was the second-class citizen to yesterday's deluge.

Wyatt pulled himself out of bed, splashed water on his face and shoulders, toweled off, threw on a pair of jeans and a shirt, and padded barefoot to the nursery. Would Brooke be in there again wearing his shirt and nothing else? A small tortured part of him sorta hoped so, crazy glutton for punishment that he was. But as he stepped into the room, he saw that only his precious two were in there, still sleeping. Brianna was on her back, looking so much like her mother it pained him. Her hair was the same honey blond with slight curls and her eyes were shaped like almonds, wide across her little face. She had the same fair complexion and sweet smile as her mother, and it melted his heart every time he looked at her. Brett was blond, too, but his hair was a darker shade that might just change to light brown when he got older. He was a good mix of both Wyatt and Madelyn, although people who didn't know Madelyn thought his son looked exactly like him, which made him puff up with pride.

He smiled and exited the room. Any minute now, they'd wake and all hell would break loose. It was always the same, the welcome quiet before the toddler storm. And he'd learned to take advantage of these quiet times. Having a cup of coffee in peace was a luxury. He descended the staircase, smacking his lips over the prospect of a simple bowl of cereal and a steamy brew. As he neared the kitchen, the scent of coffee filled his nostrils.

Before he could gather his thoughts, a sassy female voice greeted him. "Morning, sleepyhead."

He entered the kitchen, smiling. But his fantasies were extinguished quickly. Brooke was wearing the same clothes she'd been in last night, only this time, her silvery silk blouse wasn't tucked in. "Sleepyhead? It's six in the morning."

"I thought cowboys rose at the crack of dawn."

He glanced out the window. "Today, who could tell?"

She chuckled. "You got me there. It's nasty out there. Want some coffee? Oh, I hope you don't mind, but I sort of helped myself to your kitchen. I've got bacon under the broiler and I was going to crack some eggs. Are you in?"

"I don't mind at all. I figured cereal would be my breakfast and lunch of choice without Henrietta. Hell yeah to coffee, and I'm *all* in. How's the head?"

"Surprisingly, not bad. I thought I'd wake up to a huge headache. I guess I got lucky."

"You got damn lucky." Her hair covered her bruise. He imagined it had turned fifty shades of purple by now.

"How long do you suppose we have?" she asked.

Wyatt knew exactly what she meant. "Maybe fifteen minutes, maybe half an hour. The kids usually wake up around six thirty."

"Do they eat anything special?" she asked, pouring the coffee into the one mug she'd laid out on the counter.

"Well, they've been eating just about everything these days. So eggs and a bit of bacon is fine. I think Henrietta used to make them baby oatmeal or something. "

"Okay, we'll figure it out."

He liked the way Brooke took over his kitchen. She wasn't a wilting flower who needed to have everything handed to her. She'd stepped in and helped out and didn't seem uncomfortable in her surroundings.

"How did you sleep?" he asked, being a good host, though his mind automatically flashed back to an image of her lying next to him in that hotel bed. Things were different now and he knew it for fact, but his groin was having issues that didn't surprise him. He switched gears, thinking about his children sleeping innocently in their nursery right now. They were his splash of ice-cold water. They were the buffer he needed.

"Like a baby," she said. "The bed is comfy and the sound of the rain sorta lulled me to sleep. How about you?"

"Good. I slept good."

He removed the bacon from the broiler while she cooked the eggs. He made toast, too, and within a few minutes, they were sitting in the kitchen eating breakfast. "You're not having coffee?"

She shook her head, her gaze dipping to his chest. He hadn't buttoned up, and now he caught her stealing a glimpse. When his lips curved up in a smile, she pulled her gaze off him immediately and made a production of buttering her toast. "No, I, uh… I'm not one for coffee. I'm fine with orange juice. Want some?"

Her dark hair was in wild disarray, looking natural and untamed and gorgeous falling past her shoulders. He hadn't thought to give her a hairbrush last night. He had other things on his mind, such as how in hell he was going to steer clear of her this weekend.

"No thanks. I'm good." He sipped his coffee and they both concentrated on the meal, keeping the conversation to a minimum.

Cries erupted upstairs ten minutes later. "Peace as you

know it has just ended." He rose from his seat. "I'll go get them."

"I'll go with you."

Wyatt wasn't going to argue. When it came to his kids, without Henrietta here to guide him, he was on a bucking wild horse without a saddle.

Brooke scooped Brett up just before he slung his taxi-cab-yellow dump truck at Brianna's head. She took the truck out of his hands and twirled him around and around. "Here we go," she said, giving Brett an airplane ride. "Zoom, zoom." Brett's legs shot out and his giggles made Brianna stop attacking the seventy-inch flat screen's remote controller with a spoon to look up at her brother in envy.

"Your turn next," Brooke said, almost out of breath. The little ones weighed a good twenty-five pounds if they weighed one pound. Brooke figured this was the best workout she'd get while she was here. Wyatt had offered her his private gym in the basement of the house, and maybe when the twins napped, she'd head down there to check it out, but until she got the okay from a doctor to do some mild exercise, all she would be doing was looking.

Brianna raced around the great room, which seemed to have inadvertently become the twins' playroom. As a matter of fact, every room downstairs had signs of toddler-dom. There were dolls and trucks, cars and dress-up clothes everywhere, though neatly arranged, thanks to Henrietta, Brooke presumed. Yet the entire stunning ranch home, with all the latest perks and privileges and modern digital conveniences, showed signs of children.

Not a bad thing at all. Maybe that's why Brooke felt comfortable instead of out of place here. The house was grand not but austere. So what if she didn't want to be here. She was stuck and she might as well make the best of it.

Brianna came running into her arms and she lifted her up and flew her across the room. "Zoom, zoom, zoom. You're flying, Bri." Sweet laughter poured from the child's tiny mouth and her joyous smile put a sparkle in her blue-bonnet eyes.

"Daddy, lookee me."

"I see, Bri. You're flying," Wyatt said. His eyes were filled with so much love, Brooke's heart lurched. This family was missing one vital part and she saw the hint of that sadness, even as Wyatt smiled at his daughter and held his son.

"I flied too," Brett said.

"Yes, you did," Brooke said, setting Brianna down and drawing deep breaths into her lungs.

Wyatt made note of her labored breathing and announced, "Okay, flying school is closed for today."

The children protested with whines and whimpers.

"But maybe if Daddy says it's okay, we can have ice cream?" She gave Wyatt a sheepish smile. "Is that okay?

"Yay, Daddy, pleeeeze," from Brianna.

"Pleeeeze, pleeeeze," Brett parroted.

"Oh, um…" He glanced at his watch. The children had eaten a good breakfast and lunch, and it was now approaching dinnertime. "Sure, why not?"

The twins squealed with joy. Wyatt lifted Brett in one arm, and picked up Brianna in the other, giving Brooke a break as they headed for the kitchen.

Twenty minutes later, the ceiling had nearly caved in from Brianna's screams and Brett was covered from head to toe in fudgy ice cream. There wasn't a clean spot on his shirt, despite the bib. Apparently bibs weren't fool-proof, not with little hands pulling and tugging at them constantly.

"Okay, well, maybe ice cream wasn't such a bright idea," Brooke said.

"You think?" Wyatt frowned at the mess that was his kitchen, splattered walls and all.

"I'll take care of it. You mentioned you have work to do?"

"I can't leave you with this…them." He spread his arms out wide. Which only made her want to jump into them. Getting away from him today would be imperative for her peace of mind. They'd been together all day, dealing with the children, and she'd been all too aware of him. His presence beside her. His heart-stealing blue eyes. The intoxicating scent of his cologne. When he was close she felt safe, and that scared her most of all. She couldn't give up her heart again. She was scarred by Royce's deception and didn't trust herself to make the right decisions when it came to men. Especially since she had no idea what Wyatt would say about the baby she carried. And she was too chicken to find out.

At times, she'd catch him ogling her with an intense look that even she, a novice when it came to knowing a man's mind, understood as hunger and desire. And her ego would rocket like a shooting star.

Wyatt looked ready to escape the chaos. He was struggling to balance his fatherly duties with tending to business.

"Wyatt, I can manage just fine. Piece of cake."

"Oh, yeah? What's your plan?"

"My plan? Well, a bubble bath works wonders."

His brows arched and he gave her a sardonic smile. "Sounds perfect."

"For them, Wyatt."

"Oh, right." At least he could tease about the tension that sizzled between them, despite the double kid duty. "I knew that."

Her ego soared again.

"I don't know." He scrubbed his face, pulling at the

golden stubble on his jaw. "It's a lot to ask of you. They're a handful and a half."

"Hey, it's not as if you're far away. Your office is down here, isn't it?" she asked over Brianna's meltdown.

"Yep, but it's in another wing of the house."

"You have an intercom system, right? I'll use it if I need to. And that's a promise. Now go, and let me put these little ones out of their misery."

And you out of yours.

He finally agreed. After he helped get the twins upstairs, she took over, giving them both a bath full of light airy bubbles. The kids immediately simmered down, their sugar high from the ice cream leveling off. Brooke splashed them silly, until the room filled with their giggles, until their little fingers and toes shriveled to wrinkled raisins. When the bath was over, Brooke wrapped each one in a My Little Pony towel and snuggled them to her chest, drying them off. She dressed them in their jammies and then all three squatted on the floor to play. The twins had so many toys, and they played with each and every one before they got bored of the games. Then Brooke laid them down on a pastel-colored quilt and sang them silly songs. When she couldn't remember the lyrics, she made up the words, and every song brought big grins to their faces.

"Piece of cake?"

She swiveled her head to find Wyatt blocking the doorway, his arms folded across his chest, blue eyes filled with admiration.

"Putty in my hands," she said.

"I know the feeling," he said under his breath.

Oh, God.

"Actually, I know the *secret*," she said.

"And what's that?"

He came to sit beside her and ruffled both of the children's hair. Again, those blue eyes were alight with love for his kids.

"Play with them 24/7. Entertain and delight them, give them what they want."

"And exhaust yourself…"

"Do I look exhausted?" She turned her face to him. When their eyes met, his nearness suddenly made it very hot in the room. It was a mistake to ask him that leading question, because his expression went dewy soft and he reached out to touch a strand of her hair. Focusing on the dark lock, he shook his head. "No," he rasped. "You look beautiful."

He touched her then, with his smile.

She gave him an uncertain smile back. "Thank you."

He backed off, noting her hesitation. "You've been up here two hours."

"Really? I lost track of time. Probably should think about dinner."

He nodded and cleared his throat before standing up. He reached for her hand and helped her rise. Pretending nonchalance, she pulled her hand away and made a fuss about cleaning up the room when all she wanted was for him to touch her and keep on touching her.

Dangerous thoughts.

"Come on, you two. Let's race and see who can put the toys away the fastest." She dumped the first one into the toy box and the twins followed suit, grabbing toys two at a time, competing in another fun game.

Forty-five minutes later, Brooke and Wyatt were eating spaghetti in the kitchen with the twins. "Good move, not giving them sauce," Wyatt said.

"Butter and cheese keep the bath monster away."

He chuckled. "Yeah, you sure are an arsenal of helpful hints."

"Maybe when dealing with children." The same couldn't

be said in her dealings with men. In that regard, she was clueless.

Wyatt tipped his head to stare at her, a question in his eyes.

"That didn't come out right," she said, easing diced pasta into Brett's mouth as Wyatt fed Bri. It was a subject that needed changing quickly. "Hey, looks like these guys are ready to conk out. I bet they go to sleep right after dinner. Then you can finish up your work."

"I'm finished for the day," he said.

Oh, great. It was coming up on eight o'clock. Too early to turn in. Of course, Brooke could claim fatigue and watch television in her room or read a book.

"I thought I'd get a fire going, relax some and have hot chocolate," he said, giving her a glance.

"With marshmallows? Gosh, that sounds like heaven," she cooed, thinking out loud. Peace and quiet by a crackling fire, sipping hot chocolate, and relaxing with Wyatt after a long, tiresome day would be pretty amazing. Hot chocolate was something she *could* drink and not endanger her baby. But uh-oh, she'd just stepped in it. Now there was no legitimate way out without sounding lame.

"With marshmallows," he said on a nod. "Then you'll join me?"

When would she ever learn to button her lips?

"Uh, yeah. For a little while. Unless you'd rather be alone, with your, uh, thoughts?"

He grinned. "Men never want to be alone with their thoughts."

"Okay, then."

As expected, the twins had fallen asleep right after dinner without much coaxing. Now the big ranch house was quiet. She padded on bare feet down the stairs, wearing Wyatt's ginormous flannel plaid robe, which tied around her waist twice. The robe hugged her like a big teddy bear, a teddy bear that sported Wyatt's appealing scent. She'd been wearing the same outfit for two days straight and had asked Wyatt for something to throw on over his shirt while she laundered her clothes. The rain hadn't let up; just as the weatherman had predicted, a new storm had piggybacked on this one.

She entered the living room, where a floor-to-ceiling bedrock fireplace blazed. "It's beautiful in here," she said, hugging herself around the middle. The entire room was softly lit by the glow of the fire. Wyatt looked up from his place on the floor and gave her a heart-melting smile. Two mugs of steamy hot chocolate sat on the hearth, a bag of marshmallows beside them. "Have a seat," he said, and arched a brow when she sat down on the floor, leaning her body against the part of the sofa farthest away from him. He couldn't think she'd sit directly next to him, could he? Not in this lifetime. It was hard enough seeing him all day, as he interacted with his children and sauntered about in those perfect-fitting jeans, with that sexy pirate beard going on. A girl could only take so much.

"At least move closer to the fire," he said, a knowing tone in his voice. "It'll warm you."

"I'm warm enough, thank you very much."

"Suit yourself."

He sprinkled mini marshmallows into both mugs and handed her one. Then he leaned back against the sofa and stretched out his long legs. Sipping the cocoa, he quietly watched the fire for a while. "Don't get much peace around here. This is nice."

"It is."

"You're good with the little ones," he said.

"They're precious, Wyatt."

"They're all I have left…"

She let that comment go, but she knew he was thinking of their mother, Madelyn. Oh, to be loved like that, so strongly that even in death the bond couldn't be broken.

He put his head down. "Sorry."

"No need to be, Wyatt. You went through a trauma. All of you did, and I get it."

"It's just that… I'm feeling all this guilt now." His eyes lost their gleam, and he looked absolutely miserable.

"Guilt? About what happened between us?" Her stomach clenched. At times, she forgot she was carrying his child, but the baby made his presence known. Her breasts were becoming increasingly tender. She got tired more easily now, and she often bordered on nausea, especially in the morning. As far as symptoms went, hers were mild, but they were there reminding her daily that she couldn't just pretend all was right with the world. Not until she shed her secret. She wanted to tell him to forget about what had happened between them, to put it in the past and save himself from his torment, but she couldn't. She couldn't say those words when she had more profound words to say.

"About what I'm feeling now. About how much I want you, Brooke."

Her hand shook and the mug nearly tipped on its way to her mouth. Goodness, he'd just come right out and spoken his mind. She wished it would be that easy for her. She set her mug down and stared at the marshmallow circles melting as fast as her heart. "What if I said…the feeling is mutual, but we both know better?"

"Do we?" he asked, his voice registering doubt. She glanced at him again, and his dubious expression caught her off guard. Firelight reflected in his eyes and she noted the torment in them. His expression gave her pause.

"What do I say to that, Wyatt?"

"I don't know. Maybe one of us needs to be reckless," he added.

"I thought both of us were, at the wedding."

His Adam's apple bobbed up and down as he swallowed. "Meeting you that night was the best thing that happened to me in nine months. You helped me through a rough time, and I'll be forever grateful."

She didn't want his gratitude. What exactly did she want from Wyatt? She knew the score. He was emotionally unavailable and she'd be fooling herself to think anything else. She was pregnant and a little bit frightened about telling him, because then they'd have to face reality and make appropriate arrangements for custody and all the ugly painstaking plans that went along with a child being born out of wedlock. Gosh, it was so much easier to put her head in the sand and not deal with any of this. Pretty soon, her body would betray her with a belly bump that would expand, and then she'd have no choice but to reveal her pregnancy. But tonight she wanted to sip hot chocolate with Wyatt and just *be*.

She heard one of the babies' cries from upstairs and just *being* was immediately eighty-sixed. "Is that Brianna crying?" she asked softly, her ears perking up.

"I think it's Brett," Wyatt said, putting his mug down and listening. "Yep, that's him. Bri will be right behind him. She doesn't sleep when he's in a state. Stay here by the fire. I'll see to them." Wyatt popped up.

"I'll help." She rose and nodded. "It's okay. I want to."

"Appreciate that. Double rocking them doesn't always work."

"I can't see how it ever works, Wyatt. What do you do, hold one in each arm?"

"I try." He sighed. "Usually Henrietta is here to help out."

He really did need a nanny. Or two. How could one aging housekeeper keep pace with twins? Brooke was younger by thirty years, and even she was exhausted after watching them most of the day.

As she followed him up the staircase, Brianna started wailing. Now both babies were rocking the nursery walls. Wyatt and Brooke entered the room and she took one quick, assessing look at Brett. "He's soaked through his jammies."

"Ah," Wyatt said. "That explains it."

"I'll change him and get him back to sleep," she said. "Why don't you rock Brianna?"

"Sounds good. If you're sure…"

"I'm sure."

And then on an afterthought, a storm of indecision crossed his face. "Their mother didn't want the babies separated. In a house this size, they could each have their own room, but Madelyn thought this way was best."

"There's time for them to have their own rooms later in life. I think it's a good plan for now, Wyatt. Twins have a special bond, I think."

He let out a relieved sigh. "Okay."

The poor guy. He was second-guessing his decisions regarding his kids and trying like mad to honor his late wife's wishes.

"You take the rocker, Brooke. I'll walk Brianna in my arms. She likes that."

Twenty minutes later, Brett was dressed in clean pajamas and sleeping soundly. Wyatt wasn't far behind putting his daughter back into her crib and covering her. He kissed her forehead so lightly, it might have been an air kiss, and then did the same to Brett.

With a hand to Brooke's back, he guided her out of the room and down the hall. "Thanks," he said. She found herself wrapped in his cushy robe, standing just outside her bedroom door. "You've been pretty darn great. I'd kiss you good-night, but we both know where that would lead."

Her lips formed into a pout. She couldn't hide her disappointment. She felt closer to Wyatt tonight. Maybe it was the intimacy of putting his little ones to sleep and working as a team, sharing meals and personal thoughts. Maybe it was the strong pull of his deep gaze that told her beyond words how much he wished things were different.

Maybe it was his body language and the way his eyes were on her mouth now, looking as if he'd devour her if given the chance.

"What if *I* kissed *you*, Wyatt?" She rose up on tiptoes, absorbing the heat of his skin as she laid her palm on his jaw. Not giving him a chance to answer, she brushed her lips over his.

"Good night," she whispered, and as she backed away, Wyatt's lids lowered, his breath rushed out in a groan, and before she knew what was happening, he reached out and pulled her into his arms. As he crushed her against his chest, his mouth came down on hers and his kiss stole her very breath. It wasn't hard to melt into him, to give up her denials and simply feel. And oh, how good it was.

"God, Brooke," he rasped over her lips, and then drove into her mouth in a fiery surge that she met with equal eagerness and enthusiasm.

"Wyatt," she murmured, raking her fingers through the short tufts of his hair.

The connection between them might only be physical but it was strong, real and overpowering, judging by how fast her heart was racing, how every nerve in her body was standing on end.

He cupped her face with both hands and positioned her head to give him more access.

His kisses went deep, and raw, elemental lust rose up. Suddenly, she wanted his hands all over her again; she wanted to feel his flesh against hers and have him inside her making her splinter apart.

He gripped the tie of her robe to pull her closer. "I've been wondering all night what you have on under here."

"Not too much," she offered softly, the need in her voice ringing in her ears.

A painful groan emerged from his throat. "That's what I thought."

He kissed her again, his mouth ravaging and greedy. She didn't mind being the recipient of his hot, passionate hunger. She wasn't going to stop him. She wasn't going to let any rational thoughts enter her head. Not tonight.

"I don't think I can walk away from you tonight, Brooke."

Her chin up, she captured his gaze. "I don't think I'd let you."

She turned the knob on her bedroom door and entered backward, keeping his face in her line of vision the entire time. He followed her, and the door flew shut with a kick of his foot.

He came toward her, stalking her like a wild animal, limber in his approach. His blue gaze was as dark as midnight. He tugged her forward by the sash on her robe. It opened and hung from her shoulders, the cool evening air replacing the warm furnace of material and leaving her naked but for the panties she wore.

Wyatt sucked in a breath and gave her a glowing look of admiration. Then he sifted through the material of the robe and laid his hand on her breast. She closed her eyes from the pleasure of his touch. And when he began a slow, deliberate massage with the flat of his palm, squeezing the skin together and flicking her nipple, everything below her waist began to throb. Like crazy. Sweat broke out on her forehead.

"Are you sure about this?" he asked.

Totally not fair of him to ask. "Yes. Oh, yes."

Six

Wyatt's hands roamed her body as his kisses drove her to the brink. It wasn't any different, any less urgent, than the night they'd shared at the inn. In the guest room of his beautiful ranch home, amid horses and cattle and yes, children sleeping a few rooms away, she gave in to the storm of desire enveloping her with a force that she could no longer fight. If she was being stupid and foolish, then so be it. She'd pay the price later, but for now, in this moment, she wanted Wyatt. No, she *needed* Wyatt.

A shudder passed through her entire body. Wanting was one thing, but needing him? Fear slammed into her heart and brought her up short momentarily. The blood froze in her veins.

Wyatt immediately stopped midkiss. He sensed something was up, and didn't that tell her all she needed to know about him? He was sensitive enough to know she'd balked. "What's wrong, darlin'?"

The corners of her mouth lifted as she touched his

cheek, her palm grazing the rough stubble of his beard. His eyes bore down on her, waiting. "Nothing."

He pulled her palm to his mouth and kissed the inside of her hand. "You sure?"

She nodded, plastering on a smile. "Positive."

Other than she was falling hard for the Texan, the father of twins and her unborn baby, and there was nothing she could do to stop it.

He gave her a soft, loving kiss and murmured. "Climb into bed, sweetheart. Stay warm. I'll be right back."

She was pretty sure he was going to his room to get protection. Oh, man.

After he left, she gazed out the window at threatening stark gray clouds and the pouring rain that was keeping her trapped here. Now, that was a notion: being shut in with a gorgeous guy who you're pretty sure is the best man you'd ever met in your life. Only he was still hung up on his late wife. And he'd made it clear in no uncertain terms, quite a few times, that having two children was quite enough for him.

The debate in her head raged like the storm outside. She pulled the material of her robe together tightly, and crossed her arms over her chest, ready to tell Wyatt everything and pay the consequences.

And then, there he was standing in the doorway, shirtless, bootless, in jeans riding low on his waist, holding a batch of purple-hued flowers in his hand. His hair was damp and there were raindrops sprinkled on his bare shoulders.

"These are for you, Brooke," he said. His eyes blazed bright blue as he sauntered over to her and set the flowers in her hand.

"They're beautiful," she said. "Where did you get them?"

"Out back. There's a garden, and these are pretty hardy

this time of year. Asters and violets. This one here is a tiger lily."

She stared at the flowers as he pointed them out.

"I figured you might like them."

She pressed them to her chest and felt tears coming on. "I love them, Wyatt. You went out in the rain for these?"

"You deserve them," he said. "I, uh, wanted you to know, I'm not the jerk who ran out on you at the inn."

"I think I know that now."

As her arms slid down her sides, the robe opened again. Now both of them were standing in the middle of the room, nearly naked. He began rubbing her arms up and down briskly, getting her circulation going and heating her up inside. "I thought you'd be in bed. Aren't you freezing?"

"I, uh, no. You're pretty good at keeping me warm."

"Ah, Brooke," he said, circling his arms around her entire body, warming her with his own heat. "I like the sound of that."

And then his kisses rained down on her and for all those beautiful minutes, she kissed him back, loving the taste of him, loving the poignant sound of his passion-filled groans, loving the way he held her as though she was precious and sacred.

They moved to the bed together, locked in each other's arms. Wyatt gently removed the robe from her shoulders and lowered her down until the mattress met with her bare back and the pillow cradled her head. He loomed above her, all those straining muscles holding him back from crushing her with his body, and brought his mouth down to hers. He smelled of fresh rain and outdoors, and she roped her arms around his neck and played with the dark blond strands of his hair.

He began to lightly massage her shoulders. His fingertips dug in to release tension there before he moved lower still to caress her tender breasts. Smoothing them over with gentle hands brought relief, and then he molded them with a propping motion making ready to take her into his mouth. She held her breath, waiting. And then he dipped his head and sucked on her, his tongue circling the round orb and lashing her with moisture. An almost painful pleasure coursed down to her belly, and a tiny moan escaped her lips.

Down below, his erection strained against his jeans and ground into her body, pulsing and ready. She thrashed her head against the pillow, biting her lip as electric currents outraced her heartbeats. "Wyatt," she breathed.

He tore his mouth away from her now-aching breast and slid down her body, pulling her free of her panties. Lifting her legs up, he positioned himself, and the hot, wet slide of his tongue teased her core. She stilled, absorbing the sensations washing through her like waves on the ocean, one right after another, his stroking creating tingles and light shocks.

"Oh," she whimpered, biting her lip.

Everything inside her tightened up and as his relentless tongue bathed her, her body absorbed the pleasure until it was too, too much. The pulses grew heavier, tighter, and then, then a spasm burst inside her and claimed her breath.

She hurtled back down to earth, sated, her body limp and her endorphins causing the highest high.

Wyatt released her then, his eyes glazed and hungry.

"So good," she said, instead of admitting it was the best.

He brought himself up, kissed her soundly on the lips and then rolled away to unzip his jeans. "I'm glad. It was for me, too."

He moved his pants down his legs and a sigh escaped her throat as she caught a glimpse of him in all his glory.

She rolled on her side and took him in her hand. "Thank you for the flowers," she whispered, and began long, slow, deliberate strokes. He was hot silk in her hands, so smooth, so inspiring. Scooting closer, she pressed her mouth to his and began kissing him. "Lie back and enjoy."

And if the grunts and noisy sounds he made were any indication, she was giving Wyatt just as much pleasure as he'd given her tonight.

"I'll never make it," he rasped, "if you go on doing what you're doing."

He gave her no time to respond. He flipped her over onto her back then, and she was captured by the inferno in Wyatt's eyes. With his knee, he parted her legs and rose over her. A heady rush of adrenaline pulsed through her veins. She remembered the last time they were joined; this was going to be equally good, if not better. She saw the promise in Wyatt's eyes and believed it.

He touched the tip of his manhood to her. "Oh, man, Brooke," he murmured so quietly, it was more of a sigh. Her breath caught in her throat. She couldn't manage a reply; she couldn't utter a word. Sensations rippled through her as he pushed deeper, giving her time to adjust, time to accept him.

She pulled him down to her mouth and kissed him. It was beautiful and crazy good and from then on, Wyatt locked in on her body and she was done for. Completely and utterly in his zone. She gave everything she had to him and then some.

The furious passion in his eyes, his hands exploring every part of her and his magnificent erection kept her body on the brink. She was close to combusting in the very best way. He pumped and she bucked, he grated and she rubbed, he climbed and she followed.

A vivid curse pushed from his lips and the word vibrated in her ears. Everything below her waist tightened. *Talk dirty to me, Wyatt. I can take it.*

The fact that he'd lost a bit of control pushed her over

the edge. There was nothing higher, or better, than being at this same place with him. Going the distance together.

He lifted her hips from the bed, squeezing her cheeks tight with his powerful hands as he thrust deeper still.

"Oh…oh, Wyatt."

"We're here, Brooke."

Her spasms of release joined his, a continuing series of shudders and moans that filled her ears. They were in their own place now, a few moments of exquisite flurry shared equally. Her heart was racing like mad, her body tight.

Wyatt kissed her gently, his hands softly tangling in her hair as he whispered sweet words in her ear. When he lifted up and moved beside her on the bed, his heat evaporated and cool air touched her skin. But it didn't matter; she was flushed and hot enough to warm up Wyatt's entire ranch house.

Wyatt brushed hair from her cheeks. "You're beautiful, Brooke."

If he kept saying it, she might just believe it.

"And this was…"

He didn't finish. Brooke understood his dilemma, how he must be feeling. What happened between them was better than good, better than great. It was freaking amazing. But Wyatt's admitting that would be disrespectful to Madelyn in his eyes. That had to be it.

Right now, as she came down from the most satisfying blissful sex of her life, she didn't want to think too much. She hugged a pillow to her chest and faced him. "Wyatt, you don't have to say anything. I think we both know."

He stared up at the ceiling and when she thought he'd checked out, he slipped his hand over hers and held on until her eyes closed and she drifted off.

Wyatt was sex-starved and Brooke's appearance in his life was a scratch to his itch. Or so he thought. But as he lay beside her on the bed they'd shared last night, watching her chest rise and fall in deep slumber, the rosy hue he'd put on her face making her appear even more beautiful, he realized he was full of crap.

He wasn't going to get her out of his system anytime soon.

He wanted her here. But as Sunday morning dawned, the worst of the storm was gone, leaving only a light drizzle in its place that would slow to a stop sometime this afternoon. Texas sunshine would dry the land, and the bridge would be repaired and drivable again. By tomorrow, Brooke would be heading away from Blue Horizon Ranch and he would have to let her go.

As she rolled over, the sheet covering her fell away and her breasts teased his chest. The gentle scraping of her nipples stirred everything male inside him. *Shoot.* He was hard again and ready to take her once more.

Lazy eyes opened to him and she smiled. It was a sweet, aftermath-of-good-loving smile that tugged at his heart. She blew her messy brown locks out of her eyes on a soft puff of breath.

"Mornin'," he croaked.

She chuckled, stretching her arms over her head. "Yes, it is," she said on a long, sexy sigh. "You look good enough to eat, Wyatt."

His lips curved up in a smile. Brooke always surprised him. "I was thinking the same about you."

She rose on her elbows, and his gaze drifted to her small, round, perfect breasts. "Have you checked on the babies?" she asked.

"I have. Ten minutes ago. They're asleep."

"Is it still raining?" she asked, taking a peek out the window.

"Yep, drizzling."

"Guess you're stuck with me another day."

"Guess so." He leaned in, inches from her mouth, and whispered, "It's a hardship."

She tried to swat at him, but he was too fast and caught her wrist midmotion. "Now that I've snagged you, what will I do with you?"

"Whatever you want," she said coyly.

He snapped his eyes to her. "God, Brooke. You're killing me."

"Am I?" she asked, her smile gone, her dark brown eyes soft and steady on him.

"Yeah."

She looked under the sheet draped at his waist. "You seem very much alive from where I'm sitting."

"I am alive, when I'm with you." Rising over her, her pinned her arms above her head and held her there. Her lips parted slightly, and the intake of her breath told him she wanted him again. There would be no protest, and he wasn't gonna leave this bed without making love to her again.

One minute later, his cell phone buzzed. He had a mind to ignore it. But he gazed over at the lit-up screen on the nightstand and bit back a curse. It was his mother again. Man, she had bad timing. He'd dodged her call the other night and managed to leave her a voice mail afterward telling her everything was all right.

But Mom was nothing but persistent.

Brooke looked at the phone. "It's your mother. You should answer it, Wyatt. She's probably worried about the kids and the storm."

He backed away from Brooke and sat up on the bed, gritting his teeth. "Yeah, you're right. I'm sorry I have to get this."

"It's okay," Brooke assured him.

"Don't move a muscle. Not an inch. Okay?" he asked.

Her arms were above her head, her breasts exposed and gorgeous. "I promise."

Releasing a low guttural groan from his throat, he picked up the phone, walked out of the room and ducked into another bedroom.

"Yeah, hi, Mom."

"Wyatt. I've been trying to reach you. Is everything all right? The storm is all over the news here in New York. Lord, I remember those hurricanes. I know how dangerous they can be. How are my grandbabies?"

"The babies are fine. We're staying in and the storm's ready to pass. Did you get my message?"

"Yes, but, honey, I needed to speak with you in person. You have to understand how I worry. I haven't seen Brett and Brianna in months. You know that I was planning on coming to Texas for the cancer foundation's big fund-raiser in Dallas, right?"

"Yes, I know, Mom."

"And I was going to come to the ranch for a visit after that?"

"Uh-huh." He began to feel an ache in the pit of his stomach. Something was up with her, and he wasn't going to like it.

"Well, my plans have changed. I'll be coming to Blue Horizon before the fund-raiser, rather than after. I should arrive day after tomorrow. I'll stay about a week."

His heart stopped. He'd thought he had at least a month before she arrived. "What?"

"Sorry for the short notice, but it's just worked out better this way."

"For who?" he asked.

"Now, Wyatt, you know I have a busy schedule. You're all alone there, except for my Henrietta, and well, I miss the babies so. Have you managed to find a nanny yet?"

"It's in the works, Mom. I'm getting close." It was a

lie. He had some interviews scheduled, but nothing was concrete yet.

"That's what you said the last time we spoke. And poor Henrietta is being run into the ground trying to keep pace with my precious grandkids. Honey, I know you don't think I'd do a good job, but my offer still stands. I'll come back to Texas to live. I'm willing to help out. There's nothing I'm doing here that can't be postponed or canceled if you really need me."

Wyatt always thought her offer was an idle threat, but lately, she'd been speaking more and more about moving back to Texas and leaving high society behind to care for her grandchildren. It was an offer that he'd patiently and tactfully refused on several occasions.

She'd hate it here. Genevieve Brandt wasn't meant for country living, and when Wyatt was growing up, she'd reminded him and his father daily of the sacrifice she'd made for love. She was a city girl, through and through. As soon as his father retired from Blue Horizon, she'd dragged him off the ranch and moved him to her hometown and the faster-paced city life of New York. George Taylor Brandt passed on three years ago, and Wyatt was convinced that if he'd stayed on the ranch he loved after his retirement, he would still be alive today.

"Mom, we're managing just fine." It was a blatant lie.

"We'll see, honey," she said, a dubious tone in her voice. "I can't wait to see you and the babies."

"Uh, same here, Mom."

After the call ended, Wyatt stared at the phone as dozens of thoughts filled his head. He had to do right by his kids. But having his mother move in with him wasn't the answer. Oh, yeah, he loved her. She'd been a good mother, and she did adore his children, but she was also high-maintenance and somewhat self-centered. And she would drive him absolutely nuts.

He shook his head and remembered Brooke, the stunner he had waiting for him in bed just steps away. She, too, drove him nuts, in another way entirely.

He left all that behind and returned to the bedroom.

"What's wrong?" Brooke asked the second he walked in. She read his expression and must've seen his concern.

He sat down on the bed and ran a hand through his hair, staring at the opposite wall. "You don't want to hear it."

"Sure I do." She covered up and took a place next to him on the bed.

"My mother is coming for a visit."

"That's a good thing, isn't it?"

"It is if it was only that. But I get the feeling she's coming to check up on me and the kids. And if she doesn't like what she sees, she might just stay on *to help out*."

He shuddered and Brooke bit back a laugh.

"It's not funny," he said, focusing on the Dalí print on the wall.

"I know." He appreciated that she managed not to chuckle again, though he must've looked pretty comical, sitting almost buck naked on the bed, twitching because his mother was coming for a visit.

"I've been trying to find just the right nanny to relieve Henrietta of her duties. A new housekeeper I can always find, but a nanny, someone to watch my kids all day, that person has to be special. And I haven't had any luck finding anyone that meets my requirements."

Someone who could stand in for Madelyn.

"Sorry, Wyatt. Those children are treasures and they do deserve someone special." Brooke laid her hand on his shoulder, and her warmth and comfort seeped into his skin. Her touch, or maybe just having her understand his situation, helped a great deal. With Brooke beside him, he didn't feel quite so alone and devastated.

He covered her hand and turned to give her a smile.

When she returned the smile, his body stirred and his mouth sought hers again. Kissing her helped untangle his mind, and he indulged over and over again. It seemed that he needed lots of untangling. And when kissing wasn't enough, he pushed her down onto the bed, pulled off the sheets and fell headlong into Brooke's willing arms.

Making love to Brooke McKay was the best medicine for what ailed him.

"I'll do it," Brooke announced, coming to stand over Wyatt on the bed. He looked edible, lying with his arms over his head, his eyes still dusted with sleep and his luscious muscled chest calling for her touch. Dawn was long since gone. She'd just finished checking on the twins. They rustled about and made sweet noises, on the verge of waking. Any second now, they'd be up and ready to start the day, and she and Wyatt wouldn't have a moment to gather their thoughts. That's when the idea came to her. She wasn't ready to leave Blue Horizon yet. She needed more time with Wyatt. "I'll stay on during your mother's visit and pretend to be the twins' nanny."

"What are you talking about, darlin'?"

"You need a nanny, Wyatt. I'm here. I've got nothing on my agenda until Dylan's movie wraps, and I owe you."

Wyatt sat up, hung his legs over the side of the bed and planted his hands on the edge of the mattress. "After last night, and this morning, I'm thinking I'm the one owing you."

He was teasing. They'd satisfied each other and there was no measure to that, no payment for deeds. "That was mutual and equal. Wasn't it?"

He gave her an earnest look. "Yeah. So what do think you owe me?"

"You came after me in the storm with your kids in the

car. I'll never forget that. You risked them to save me. It's the least I can do. I want to help."

He heaved a big sigh and ran his hands through his hair, tousling it even more. Bed head looked incredibly sexy on him. "How can I ask you to do that for me?"

"You're not asking. I'm offering."

He thought about it awhile as she stood there, her heart in her throat. God, he had to say yes. Once the offer was out there, she realized how very much she wanted him to agree. She wasn't ready to leave him. She wasn't ready to reveal her secret and part company, all businesslike. She was falling in love with him. More time would confirm her feelings, and she could test out her new and wishful theory that Wyatt was getting over his late wife's death. Silly her. At the very least, she could bide her time and try to find the exact right moment to tell him she was carrying his child.

He lifted his eyes to her. "My mother isn't easy."

"I can handle her."

"She's got a mouth on her."

"So do I."

His gaze dipped to her lips. "Lord, I know."

She smiled.

"She's impetuous, rude sometimes, and likes to get her way."

"Sounds like my kind of girl."

"She'll drive you crazy."

"I won't hold it against you."

"You're determined then? You want to do this?"

Brooke nodded.

"I mean, hell… I'd be lying if I said I didn't want you here longer."

That was encouraging. "Ah, but if I stay, Wyatt, we can't…"

"Yeah, yeah, I get it. I agree. It won't be easy."

No, it wouldn't be easy going to bed at night, knowing that forbidden pleasure and the satisfaction of being in Wyatt's arms were just down the hallway.

Wyatt rose from the bed, shedding the sheet, and stood before her, fully aroused. "You think we can pull this off?"

Her bones melted. She wanted him so badly. She gulped air and nodded. "Yeah, I think we can. It's only for a week, right?"

"Yeah, a week should convince her." He sighed. "Now I'd best get me a cold shower. Seems I'm gonna be taking a lot of those from now on."

Seven

The stage was set. The sun had come out. The land was dry. The roads were clear. All was back to normal.

Well, sort of.

To Genevieve Brandt, Brooke would be Brooke Johnson, the newly hired nanny. The very best Wyatt had ever found. The twins loved her. She had all the right credentials. Wyatt made her a promise to take care of any probing questions his mother might ask when she arrived.

Brooke wasn't a liar by choice. In fact, she hated people who bent the truth to suit their needs. And wasn't she sliding right into that persona now, pretending to be someone she wasn't? In essence, she was also fibbing by omission to Wyatt, too.

By the end of the week, she promised herself, one way or another, Wyatt would know the truth about her pregnancy and all would be settled. A shiver ran through her. She was in deep now and she would have to wade through the days hoping to convince Genevieve that the babies were in good hands. Hoping that Wyatt would…what? Beg her to stay?

Her cell rang and she muttered a choice word as she glanced at the screen. Putting pep in her voice, she answered the call. "Hi, Dylan. How's it going?"

"How's it going? I'm sitting here in my trailer, trying to read lines, wondering why the hell my sister is spending the week with a total stranger. A man with two kids, no less."

"Oh, I explained it all to Emma when I picked up some of my clothes yesterday. He's a good guy really. You know him. He's the consultant to the film. Wyatt Brandt. The storm struck while we were having dinner and I sorta got stuck here."

"It's not raining anymore. Aren't you coming back to Zane's place?"

"Well, as I told Emma, I'm staying here helping him with his twins this week. It's a long story, but trust me, I'm fine."

"Is this a paying job?" Dylan knew damn well it wasn't.

"Hey, I'm a big girl, Dylan. I can take care of myself."

"It's not a job. Oh, right, because you have a job waiting for you back home in California. Are you forgetting that we're leaving for home in less than two weeks? So what's really going on, Brooke?"

"Nothing. God, Dylan. Please, back off. I…kn-know what I'm doing. I'm helping someone out."

Her brother's overprotective groan traveled through the receiver. "All right, I'll back off. I'm only looking out for you, you know."

She sank into the bed Henrietta had made sometime while Brooke was feeding Brianna and Brett their lunch. "I know. I'm… I'm going to be fine." Even to her ears, she sounded uncertain.

"I'm trusting that you are. But I want to hear from you every day, Brooke."

"I'll call. I promise to check in with you and Emma."

Dylan grunted his farewell, and after she hung up, she was torn between loving Dylan to death and wishing he wouldn't treat her like a child. She was twenty-six years old, for heaven's sake. And yes, granted, she'd had a tough year and he didn't want to see her hurt again, but that might happen anyway. Regardless.

The sound of tires crunching gravel on the road put her on alert. She rose and walked to the window. Outside, Wyatt was opening the Jeep door for Genevieve. At first glance, Brooke's eyes widened. Wyatt's mother was beautiful, with sterling platinum hair and a tan complexion complemented by just the right amount of makeup. Wearing a blue silk blouse, a flowing crepe scarf, cream slacks and ankle boots, Genevieve looked every bit the part of New York high society.

Bolstering herself with a pep talk, Brooke headed toward the nursery. Brett and Brianna fidgeted in their cribs, waking from their naps. Just in time.

Brooke made fast work of cuddling them with hugs and kisses, then diapering and changing them into clean clothes. Brianna wore a pink dress with ruffles at the skirt, and Brett wore a new pair of blue jeans, à la Wyatt Brandt, and a little man shirt in red. She was just putting a bow in Brianna's hair when she heard footsteps on the polished wood floors.

"My babies." Genevieve rushed into the room—her pleasant floral scent following her—and picked up Brett immediately. She smothered the boy with kisses, and Brett, love his soul, watched her carefully, as if trying to piece together who this woman was exactly. Genevieve turned to Brooke, looking her up and down. Had she passed the test? "And how's my little Breezy Peezy doing?"

"She's on the verge of being a crank pot. I think she woke up too soon from her nap." Brooke held a fussing Brianna to her chest. "Hello, I'm Brooke," she said to Genevieve.

Genevieve's chin rose. "Wyatt tells me you're good with the children."

From behind his mother, Wyatt shook his head, his lips twitching. Brooke wasn't fazed. She'd dealt with tough cookies from her Parties-to-Go business. "We think alike."

Genevieve laughed. "Do you, now?" She ruffled Brianna's light blond locks and bent to kiss her cheek. Anyone with that much love shining in her eyes couldn't be that bad. "I'm Genevieve. Their grammy."

"Nice to meet you, Grammy Genevieve."

"You can call me Mrs. Brandt."

On the other hand...

"Mom." Wyatt pushed into the room. "Brooke doesn't have to—"

"No, it's okay, Mr. Brandt," Brooke said, giving him a big smile. His eyes bugged out and she almost laughed. They hadn't spoken about what she should call him, but now, it was clear in her mind, she needed to distance herself from him while Grammy was here. "I most certainly will call you Mrs. Brandt. It's not a problem. I was guessing it might be confusing for Brett and Brianna. There's so many names being jostled about, but I'm sure the twins know exactly who you are."

"Of course they do," Genevieve said, just as Brett kicked away from her, reaching for his daddy's arms.

Wyatt grabbed his son and Brett immediately turned his head into his daddy's chest. Genevieve's confident expression slipped a little. "Well, they may need a little reminder," she said. "It's been too long. I miss them."

"I'm sure they miss you, too," Brooke said, swaying her

hips and rocking Brianna side to side. "Bri, would you like your grandmother to hold you now?"

Brianna didn't make up her mind right away, and Mrs. Brandt began smiling and encouraging her. "Come on, Bri Bri. Grammy will rock you."

Genevieve clapped her hands, wiggled her fingers and twirled around in a circle. "And I don't mean on my hip. Wanna dance, Breezy Peezy?"

Brianna giggled, the sweet sound penetrating the tension radiating off Wyatt's body. He needed to lighten up. His mother wasn't all that bad. A bit huffy and pretentious maybe, but she did love her grandchildren.

"Maybe we can all dance," Brooke said, handing Brianna over to her grandmother and giving Wyatt a big nod as she began singing a Taylor Swift song about shaking it off. Wyatt grinned for half a second and began to move. He wasn't light on his feet—that was for sure—but he did have good moves elsewhere. And she loved that he didn't balk at the idea of acting silly with his kids.

The children cackled as they moved throughout the room.

Just then her stomach notched up, a weird kind of hollow, dull ache pulling her out of the dance mentally. Was this what morning sickness was like?

And wasn't that supposed to happen in the morning?

Then she remembered Emma telling her it can hit at any time, day or night. Something would set it off, the smell of food or too much activity or nothing at all. It would just sweep in and make you feel like you could empty your lunch at any second.

Lucky for her, Genevieve put a halt to the fun, claiming fatigue, and Wyatt showed her to her room. It was the second master suite down the hall. Henrietta had told her that after the Brandts retired to the East Coast, Wyatt had a contractor tear down walls in two rooms and construct his very own master suite. The house was certainly large enough for two master bedrooms, and Wyatt had wanted to keep his mother's room intact. Or as Brooke imagined, Genevieve wouldn't have it any other way.

Henrietta walked into the nursery carrying folded baby laundry. Brooke's savior. "Oh, um, Henrietta, can you watch the babies for a few minutes?"

"Of course." Henrietta had gentle eyes and a kind heart. Brooke had only met her yesterday, but she could tell the woman was a nurturer. And loyal to the Brandt household. She didn't know the truth—the less deceit the better—yet she had to be suspicious of how Wyatt had pulled a new nanny out of his cowboy hat over the weekend. But she hadn't said a word about it. Instead she'd readily accepted Brooke, probably greatly relieved to have additional help.

The children were playing with giant interlocking blocks on the floor. Well, munching on them was more like it, giving them a good toothy chew. Henrietta set the laundry aside and squatted on the floor. "Oof."

If Brooke didn't get out of this room immediately, the three of them would witness her double over. "I promise I'll only be a minute," she called, racing out of the room. She sprinted to her bathroom, leaned up against the wall, her hand on her tummy, and took deep solid breaths, praying she could hold it together.

Minutes later and lucky for her, the need to empty her stomach had passed. Only slight tremors rocked her belly now. She splashed water on her face, took a comb to her hair, pulling it back into a ponytail. She felt much better now. She opened her bedroom door.

To Wyatt. He blocked the doorway, his hand fisted, ready to knock. Her jaw dropped and he seemed quite pleased that he'd startled her.

"Wyatt, I'm sorry, I can't talk to you right now. I've got to get back to—"

He shoved at her chest and followed her as she stumbled into her room. He gave the door a quick kick and it quietly clicked behind him. The next thing she knew, she was pinned to the back of the door, Wyatt's hands on her wrists, his beautiful face inches from hers, wearing a wry smile. "I'll show you *Mr. Brandt*," he whispered. And then his mouth was on hers, hungry, possessive and wild.

God, payback was a bitch. She should've known he wouldn't let that go. Her bones liquefied instantly and she kissed him back with a fire that started from deep inside her belly. She was helpless to push him away. "We can't," she pleaded blandly, between kisses. "Your mother—"

"Is locked far away in her room, probably already napping."

Was the locked part wishful thinking? "But the children?"

"Henrietta is doing fine with them."

"But we agreed…"

He nibbled on her throat and then ran his tongue down to her collarbone, taking bites there, too. The secrecy of meeting him like this was a turn-on, but then so was *he*— anywhere, anytime. Just one touch from him turned her brain to jelly. "I'm breaking the agreement. Just for now."

"Wyatt," she sighed, giving in to sensations driving her crazy. They groped at each other like teenagers hiding out behind the stairwell.

If only her teen years had been this exciting.

Finally she put a stop to it. Wyatt, breathing heavy, clunked his forehead to hers. "I don't want my mother bullying you."

"Is that why you came in here?"

"Yes. No."

Something about his confusion tugged at her heart. He wanted her, and that gave her all kinds of happy butterflies, but he wasn't ready and he was clearly battling with his emotions. "I've got your mom pegged already, Wyatt. She's not all that. I can handle her. Now, I've got to get back to the twins."

She made a move, but his hands were still splayed around her waist, and he didn't let go. He gave a yank and their bodies met, thigh to thigh, hip to hip, pulse to pulse. He kissed her once more, a killer kiss that left her trembling. His gaze sharpened on her, a hot blaze of blue lashing her as he opened the bedroom door. "*Mr. Brandt* is leaving now."

Then he walked out of the room.

The land was dry enough to take the children outside. Lord knew, they all had cabin fever. Getting out of the house for some fresh air seemed like a great idea. Until Mrs. Brandt got wind of it and decided to come along.

"Too bad my son couldn't join us today," she said, pushing the double stroller toward the stables. "We could've spent some time together, just the four of us."

Brooke let the comment pass. In Genevieve's eyes, she was just the nanny and didn't rate in a family outing. Wyatt had a meeting this morning and he wouldn't be back from Beckon until later this afternoon.

It was silly how much she missed him. They'd spent the entire weekend together and it had been like a dream. But reality was staring her in the face now. "I'm sure you'll be able to have more time together before you leave. I think Mr. Brandt would like that. I used to love family outings with my folks."

"You're from Ohio, right?"

"Yes, born and raised there."

"Do you have any siblings?"

"Just one brother. Well, technically, we're not related, but we're as close as any brother and sister could be. I was in the foster care system and then was adopted by the...

the Johnson family." Eek. She didn't want to expand on the lies. "But my family is solid and tight. It was my lucky day when Mom and Dad took me in and then adopted me."

"I did some charity work for the foster care program. It appears the system worked for you."

"I was one of the lucky ones. My good friend was in the system and wasn't as lucky as I was, but she's doing well now. She married my brother and life is good."

"Is that why you became a nanny?"

"Oh… I guess. And because I adore children. I babysat my way through high school."

"Madelyn was the same way. She adored children. It breaks my heart that the twins will never know their mother. Wyatt was crushed when she died."

"It had to be rough."

"She was a sweet girl, the perfect match for my son." Sadness seemed to steal Genevieve's breath. "I still can't believe she's gone. A horrible tragedy. Wyatt wouldn't have made it through if it wasn't for his children. Madelyn was the love of his life. He had no choice but to go on."

Such strong words. Oh, to love someone so much that you didn't want to live without them. Yeah, Wyatt would feel that way about Madelyn. Brooke had no delusions about what she was up against. She couldn't fault Wyatt's mother. But she had no idea how hurtful it was hearing her go on about Madelyn. Genevieve couldn't possibly know what Wyatt meant to her.

They walked in silence the rest of the way, the thick-wheeled stroller bumping over rougher terrain, keeping the twins quiet until they reached the stables and a white-fenced corral. Playful horses nudged each other, then raced around the perimeter in an equine game of tag.

"Horsey," Brett called out the second he spotted them.

Brianna followed the direction of his pointed finger and bounced in the seat of the stroller. "Horsey," she squealed, too.

Brooke laughed at how animated they'd become. They lived on a ranch and probably saw the horses every day, but that didn't seem to diminish their enthusiasm.

"Mrs. Brandt, if you'll get Brianna out, I'll get Brett. Henrietta packed carrots. We can show the kidlets how to feed the horses."

Mrs. Brandt chuckled. "The kidlets?"

Brooke shrugged. "I nickname everyone."

"Heavens, don't tell me what name you've picked out for me."

"I promise I won't."

Mrs. Brandt gave her a sideways glance, and then chewed on her lip to keep from smiling. "You have one for me already?"

She was rescued from answering when a tall man in jeans approached. "Is that you, Genevieve?"

Wyatt's mother whipped around and appeared startled. "Oh, uh, hello, James."

James was about the same age as Genevieve, and the hair under his black hat was almost the same silvery-pearl tone. A goatee shaped his chin and jaw and looked marvelous on him. He stared at Wyatt's mother for almost five full seconds, his green eyes sparkling. "Hello."

Brooke made herself busy taking Brett out of the stroller.

"And who is this young lady?" he asked.

"Hi, I'm Brooke. I'm the twins' nanny." With Brett on her hip, she walked over to shake his hand.

He took her in from top to bottom and nodded. "James. I'm the foreman here on Blue Horizon."

"Nice meeting you."

"'Bout time Wyatt saw fit to hire himself a decent nanny."

"Th-thanks. We were just letting the children get some fresh air and hoped they could feed the horses."

"Sure thing," he said, his gaze going back to Genevieve. She did her best to ignore him.

Brianna made noises, stretching her arms up, and James bypassed Genevieve to lift Brianna out of her confinement. "There, there, now, Brianna. Uncle James has you now." He bounced the toddler in his arms and Brianna reached up to pull at the hairs of his goatee, as if she'd done it a dozen times.

Rich, deep baritone laughter poured out of him, the sound amazingly sensual, and Wyatt's mother began fidgeting with the collar of her blouse.

"Don't you have work to do?" she asked, her tone ice-cold.

"Well, now, I've done all that needs doing so far." His chest expanded and he dug his heels in where he stood. "Like always." He bounced Brianna again and she cackled.

Oh, wow. He wasn't a man to be put down by the likes of a strong-willed woman. Watching James with her granddaughter, Genevieve looked lost for a moment, her light aqua eyes filled with something…longing or regret? It was sad in a way, but it wasn't any of Brooke's business.

"Here, let me have her," Genevieve said to James, putting her arms out.

"Grammy needs a hug," he whispered to Bri and when he made the transfer, his arm brushed Genevieve's—maybe deliberately, Brooke couldn't be sure. Wyatt's mother sucked in a breath and stiffened her body.

"I get plenty of hugs," she barked at him, cradling the baby to her chest.

"Not enough, I'd bet." He stared into Genevieve's eyes and for a moment, Brooke felt as if she needed to give the two of them some privacy so they could hash out whatever they really needed to say to each other.

"Brooke, you said there were some carrots?" Genevieve

needed an escape from James's intense gaze, and the excuse of feeding the horses came to the rescue.

"Oh, yeah. Let me get them." Brooke reached for the bag under the stroller and by the time she had the carrots sorted out and ready, James had said a quick goodbye. She caught Genevieve watching his retreat, her gaze on his backside as he sauntered into the stable.

Wyatt's mother turned around, her face flushed. It was hard not to notice…or comment.

"I'm a good listener, if you want to talk about it," she said quietly.

"There's nothing to talk about." Genevieve's eyes flashed in cold defiance, a reminder for Brooke to mind her own business. There *was* something to talk about, but just not with the family nanny.

Brooke recovered quickly and handed Genevieve a few carrots, then grabbed a few for herself. "Shall we?" They walked over to the corral fence. The horses had a sixth sense when it came to treats, and they'd wandered over, nudging each other to get to the carrots.

"Here you go, Brett. Hold it out," Brooke said.

Genevieve followed suit, giving little Brianna instructions.

"You know your way around a ranch." Brooke was impressed at Genevieve's ease with the animals.

"I know horses," Genevieve said. "And cattle for that matter. My husband saw to it that I knew everything there was to know about his business. God, I loved him, but ranching wasn't in my blood the way it was with him."

It was obvious Genevieve's tastes were far more refined. She wasn't one for living out on a remote ranch, gorgeous as it was, without people, nightlife and high fashion.

"But I miss these babies. And my son." She stroked the bay's mane gently. "Though I think he'd rather not have me here."

It was a confession that surprised Brooke. "I don't think that's true."

Genevieve shook her head and chewed her lip, most likely regretting letting that nugget of information slip. Maybe Wyatt didn't want his mother here right now, but James sure had his eye on her. From all indications, he'd probably like her to stay on at the ranch indefinitely.

Genevieve reached into her pocket and unfolded a hand filled with sugar cubes. "Watch this, Brett and Bri." She put out her hand and moved from one horse to another feeding them the sugar. Afterward, she graced each horse with a loving pat on the head. "Sugar cubes are like cupcakes to horses," she said. "Who here likes cupcakes?"

Brett and Brianna grinned and shouted, "Me! Me!"

"Well, maybe tonight, Grammy will give you some, if you eat a good dinner."

Brooke smiled at the joy on their faces.

So far, so good.

The twins' accidental nanny hadn't blown her cover.

Brooke's tummy heaved and bile rose in her throat. Henrietta had insisted on cooking liver and onions for dinner, and the steamy aroma filled the entire room. Apparently, it was a Brandt family favorite. Lucky for Brooke, the housekeeper also fried up a plate of chicken fingers for the twins. Okay, so she wouldn't starve; she'd eat with the children. But the pungent smell and onion was doing a number on her. Blood drained from her face, and she imagined she'd turned a pale shade of avocado right then.

She wanted so badly to put her hand on her stomach, to somehow make it feel better. But standing near Henrietta and Genevieve, two women who'd carried a child, she feared that gesture would be like drawing a bull's-eye on her belly.

Instead she rubbed at her forehead.

"Something wrong?" Wyatt asked, coming up from behind. She hadn't seen him enter the kitchen.

She gave him a half smile. "Just a little headache."

Struck by the concern in his eyes, she put her head down. "I'll be all right in a minute."

"Why don't you go lie down?" he said.

"Yes, dear," Henrietta said. "I think between the three of us, we can manage the twins. Dinner will keep."

Darn right it would. If she ate a bite right now, she wouldn't be able to hold it down.

"Are you hungry?" Wyatt asked.

"Not really."

"Then go lie down. There's headache medicine in your bathroom."

He glanced at Henrietta and she nodded.

Wyatt, Henrietta and even Genevieve had sympathetic expressions on their faces.

"Okay, but just for a little while. I'll get the twins their baths and put them to sleep later."

"Take the night off. I can do all that." Genevieve seemed eager to spend precious time with the children.

"Thank you, Mrs. Brandt."

Wyatt's lips went tight. He wasn't a fan of his mother's insistence on formality.

"I'll walk you up," Wyatt said.

"No, no. That's not necessary." She gave Wyatt a solid, don't-argue look, and he relented. "Thank you," she said to everyone.

She made her way up the staircase and entered her room none too soon, flopping on the bed facedown, and closed her eyes. Getting away from the ungodly smell of liver and onions was half the battle. She immediately felt less nauseous and was grateful she hadn't made a spectacle of herself in the kitchen. She gave herself up to rest.

A gnawing ache in her stomach woke her and she

snapped her eyes open to darkness. She waited a second for her eyes to adjust to the barest glimmer of moonlight streaming into her bedroom. Slowly, she sat up in the bed and got her bearings. The bedside clock read midnight, and another grumble of her stomach reminded her she'd gone to bed without dinner.

Now she was famished.

She rose and walked into the bathroom. Under dim light she washed her face and changed out of her wrinkled blouse. She ran a brush through her unruly hair, then wove the strands into one long braid, letting it fall down the middle of her back.

Barefoot, she ambled down the hallway and peeked in on the twins. She smiled at their peaceful sweetness and air-kissed both of them. The rest of the house was equally quiet. Carefully, she tiptoed down the stairs and into the kitchen, bracing herself for the awful scent of liver. Thanking all things holy, she was happy to find that the horrid scent was gone. Instead the kitchen smelled sweet, and she remembered Genevieve had promised to bake cupcakes for the twins. The aroma of chocolate was a much better scent, but she wouldn't dare. She opted for a piece of French bread, no butter.

She sat at the kitchen table with the bread and a glass of milk.

"Want some chicken to go along with that?"

She jumped in her seat, startled by Wyatt's voice. "My God, you scared me half to death."

He grinned. "Sorry."

"Why don't you look sorry?"

"Because I heard a noise and was hoping it was you."

"You mean, you'd rather face me than a burglar?"

"I'd rather face you, period."

Oh, wow.

He grabbed a chair, turned it backward and straddled it.

His feet were bare, his jeans riding low. A T-shirt stretched tight over his arms and chest, exposing his solid strength. He didn't look like a filthy rich billionaire, but a father of twins with a bad case of drop-dead gorgeousness.

"Sorry about the meal tonight. Liver's a staple around here. I'll make sure Henrietta doesn't cook it again while you're here."

"Thank you."

"How's your head?"

"My head?"

"You had a headache."

"Oh, I slept it off and then woke up hungry."

"Well, eat up."

She nodded and chewed for a few seconds, aware of Wyatt's gaze resting on her.

"How was your day with my mother?"

"It went well."

"Really?"

"Really." She wouldn't tell him that Genevieve had been curt at times and seemed out of sorts when James showed up. "We took the babies for a walk and I met some of the crew and your foreman, James." She searched Wyatt's face hoping for a clue about his relationship with Genevieve. "He seems comfortable around the babies. Brianna adores him."

"He's a good man, likes kids. He's been with us for twenty years."

"Hmm." She took a swig of milk.

"I bet my mother wasn't thrilled to see him."

She snorted and milk spewed from her nose and mouth. He chuckled. "That bad?"

She nodded her head and grabbed the napkin Wyatt offered. Dabbing at her mouth, she kept her thoughts to herself.

"Ah, that's what I was afraid of. It's no secret James is

smitten with my mom. They dated once, last year when she was here for a visit. James was over-the-moon happy and then Mom called it off. She didn't want to have anything to do with him after that."

"Do you know what happened between them?" She was dying to know. It was a great diversion from her own problems. And maybe she could help.

"I have my suspicions. Mom likes James, a whole lot. And that's the problem. He's a threat to her life in New York. If she got seriously involved with him, it would mean moving back to Texas."

Brooke mulled it over for a few moments. From what she gathered about Genevieve, it made perfect sense. "Maybe that's exactly what she needs, Wyatt. She misses the babies very much, and being near you."

"Ah, but she made her choice when she pulled Dad away from the ranch as soon as he retired. I think she believes it would be a step backward if she gave in to her feelings now."

"So James, I take it, isn't a pushover. He gave her grief over it, right?"

"That would be my guess."

She nodded. Now she understood Genevieve's reaction to James today.

Wyatt took hold of her hand, lacing their fingers together. It was clear the conversation about Wyatt's mom was over. Tingles ran up her arm, and her mind got a little fuzzy.

"Come into my study with me, Brooke," he whispered, leaning close. She suppressed the urge to run her hands through his thick hair. "I want…us."

God. She squeezed her eyes shut. She wanted "us," too. It was wrong. They'd made an agreement. While she was here as his nanny, they had to keep their distance. And yet, as she glanced at their entwined hands, the power of his simple suggestion was a pull she couldn't resist. She wanted to be with him. He excited her and made her long for more. They shared a child, and whether he knew it or not, the bond was there, nestling inside her.

She nodded.

A gleam sparked in his eyes and he smiled, pushing all her female buttons. He stood to pull the chair out for her. Then he grabbed her hand and gave a squeeze as they ambled down the long hallway that led to his study.

With a *click*, they were locked in.

"The babies?" she whispered.

"We'll hear them if they cry out."

And then his mouth was on hers and his kisses washed away all her worries and doubts. Within minutes, they were naked on a wide comfy leather sofa. Atop her, his body was steel to her softness, his chest rock solid as it grazed her tender nipples, his hands threading through the braid that had come loose. In haste and urgency, they explored and pleasured each other in the near-darkness. Wyatt spoke sweet words, loving her body, offering her anything she wanted. He wanted to please her, to make it good for her. The gesture made her fall deeper under his spell.

She loved him.

It was not a big surprise. She'd been falling steadily. He was the kind of man a woman didn't forget. Wyatt made her see and feel the difference between the superficial kind of love she felt for Royce and the love she had for him. He was a real man. A good, kind, solid man, and she had fallen head over heels in love with him.

She rode the wave of his passion, giving him all she had to give, making it good for him, too. When they were joined, his flesh deep inside her, she felt safe. Protected. The connection was real, and not just physically. They shared something wonderful, a compatibility and understanding that carried over to their day-to-day living. She'd never felt more encouraged than now. The urge to speak the truth and get it all out in the open was never stronger. Tonight was the night she would tell him about the baby she carried. His baby.

The joy in her heart led to a wild, furious release. Wyatt joined her, and they shared the amazing climb together, the grind and arch of their bodies in complete sync with each other. "Let go, sweetheart," he rasped, his voice tight and tense.

"Wyatt," she moaned, and the pressure rose to an extreme high.

Both shuddered. Both cried out. Both were bathed in sweat and heat. And then they both came down, Wyatt cupping her head and bestowing kisses on her face.

She'd never been happier.

And afterward, when they were poking around in the dark, retrieving their clothes and attempting to dress, she whispered, "I can't find my panties."

Wyatt chuckled. "It's all part of my plan."

"Wyatt!"

"Hold on a sec," he said, and scrambled for the light switch. Soon the dark study was awash in dim light. And oh, if only her panties weren't missing. If only she could've walked out of that room blindly and gone on with her plan.

But clarity was a bitch. Clarity brought pain. Clarity made her see what she didn't want to admit. Wyatt's study, his most private place and the room where he relaxed and retreated to whenever he needed an escape, painted a very telling picture. There on all four walls, the fireplace mantel, the massive desk and bookcase, were dozens upon dozens of framed photos. Madelyn smiling into the camera. Madelyn riding a horse. Madelyn pregnant with the twins. Madelyn in her bridal gown. The two of them, the four of them, the entire Brandt family. Everywhere.

Yes, she'd seen photos of Madelyn in some rooms in

the house. Henrietta said Wyatt wanted to make sure the babies never forgot their mother. Brooke got that. It was understandable. She'd worry if there were no pictures around of his wife and the mother of his children.

But *this*? The room Wyatt considered his sanctuary wasn't merely a study, but a cluttered cathedral meant for worshipping at the altar of Madelyn. *This* was a wall-to-wall depiction of their life together. Every photo, every scene, every unabashed smile told the story of their love.

His love. For his late wife.

Brooke's mouth gaped open and every good thing inside her fizzled like the bubbles of stale champagne. Her shoulders slumped in defeat.

"Brooke." Wyatt reached for her.

She jerked away. "Don't, Wyatt," she breathed in a hush. "I've been a fool."

"No," he said. "You're not a fool."

She found her panties and finished dressing. "Oh, yes, I am. I get the picture now. Literally. How could I not? I can't do this anymore." She lifted her chin to Wyatt's baffled expression. What did he think? That she'd be overjoyed seeing his devotion to his dead wife? Did he think she wouldn't be affected by his homage to Madelyn Brandt, the true love of his life? "We need to stick to the original plan. While I'm here acting as nanny, we need to keep our distance. And this time, I mean it. Don't come looking for me, Wyatt. Got that?"

He stood facing her, his hands on his hips and his mouth pulled tight, refusing her an answer.

"Do you understand?" she asked.

"Let me explain."

"This," she said, gesturing around the room, "is all the explanation I need."

She spun on her heels and exited the study.

Nausea kicked in big-time. Her stomach gurgled and ached and there was no holding back.

Once she got to her bathroom, she was going to throw up.

Eight

Two days later, the babies sat in their high chairs, making a game of tossing toys off their trays. "Now, now," Genevieve said. "Patience, little ones, we're going as fast as we can fixing your breakfast."

Brooke stirred the oatmeal to cool it down, tossing in some fresh cut-up strawberries.

"There once was a pair of silly twins," Genevieve began in a singsong voice, a deliberate diversion from the great twin toy drop. And sure enough, the children's heads popped up, smiles emerging. "Who liked to *drop, drop, drop* their toys onto the floor." Her voice was lovely, sweet, engaging.

"With a *mop, mop, mop* of curly blond strands," Brooke chimed in singing. "On the *top, top, top,* of their heads."

Genevieve chuckled. Brooke danced the bowls of oatmeal over to the table and took her seat in front of Brett while Genevieve sat down beside Brianna.

"The food goes *plop, plop, plop* into their mouths," Genevieve harmonized.

Brooke giggled and aimed the spoon into Brett's mouth. "And they couldn't *stop, stop, stop* filling their tummies."

Genevieve speared a spoonful into Bri's waiting mouth.

The babies giggled at the rhyming verses, enjoying the silly song and their meal. Once the bowls were emptied and the twins were sipping milk from their sippy cups, Genevieve looked over to Brooke. "You're not half bad, Brooke."

A compliment? "You're pretty good yourself, Mrs. Brandt."

Genevieve chewed on her lower lip, giving Brooke a thoughtful stare. "You know, I think you were right. We don't want to confuse the babies. Call me Genevieve or Grammy."

"You mean in front of the twins?"

"I mean, always." When she smiled, her eyes lit up. In the last few days, Brooke must have passed some sort of test with her.

"Okay, I will. Thanks."

Genevieve seemed pleased with herself. "Good. Now what are we going to do with these two today?"

The morning sun was at Brooke's back, streaming warmth into the kitchen. "I think it's going to be a beautiful day."

"Fall has arrived. It's a shame to let it go to waste. There's a nice playground in Cahill. And if I'm not mistaken, the diner there is pretty good. We can let the babies play at the park and then God willing, they'll nap while we have a peaceful lunch."

"Sounds wonderful to me." It meant spending the day away from the ranch and away from Wyatt. That was a good thing, because she was hurting. Seeing him day in and day out was difficult. Her heart hadn't stopped aching. She was doing everything in her power to keep her distance. He wasn't making it easy, though. He was always around. He loved his twins and wanted to be Daddy to them at every turn. There were times when she wanted to run into his arms and other times when she wanted to run far and fast in the opposite direction.

His eyes always found hers during meals, and although she kept out of his path she couldn't help seeing him when he popped in to play with the twins, or feed them or help put them to sleep at night. Thankfully, Genevieve unknowingly made a nice buffer. Brooke and Wyatt were rarely alone.

Which was a good thing.

But it also broke her heart.

"Will you tell Wyatt our plans, Brooke? I have some phone calls to make before we leave later this morning. Give me a couple of hours."

"Uh, okay. I'll make sure he knows where we're going today."

Genevieve gave the children each a kiss on the cheek. "I'll see you later, my babies."

Once she exited the room, Brooke rose to help Henrietta with the dishes while the twins were still in a happy mood. The great toy drop began anew, but it kept them occupied in their high chairs while Brooke was busy. At least one good thing had come from Brooke being here: Henrietta wasn't exhausted anymore. The older lady actually had pep in her step.

"Did I miss breakfast?" Wyatt walked in, looking sharp in a blue plaid shirt and faded denim jeans. That particular cobalt color brought out the deep hue in his eyes and Brooke had to force herself to keep from staring. Her heart beat hard in her chest.

"I've got eggs and bacon cooking for you, Wyatt," Henrietta said.

"Thanks, Etta." He approached his babies, giving them

a pat on the head and kissing their cheeks. "Morning, my darlins'. Brooke." He turned to her, his gaze unreadable.

"Good morning, Mr. Brandt."

He winced. He hated the formality but she'd kept it up for appearances. And now she was grateful she had that crutch to fall back on. It was just one more way to keep her distance. Often, over the past few days, she'd wanted to simply tell Wyatt the truth and be done with it. The duplicity was killing her, but she'd made him a promise she would stay until Genevieve was satisfied and left the ranch. She wouldn't go back on her word. Besides, they'd have a lot to work out once he learned about the child she carried, and having his mother here would only hamper the process.

In a very real way, Brooke was trapped here by her lies.

Her stomach grumbled. She hadn't eaten yet, either. But bacon and eggs would only make her sick. Morning smells did a number on her very sensitive tummy lately. Luckily, her stomach wasn't on the fritz all day long. If she made it past breakfast eating bland foods, then she was usually good to go the rest of the day.

"Have you eaten?" he asked.

"I, um, no. Not yet. The babies woke early and seemed hungry. No big deal, I'll have some oatmeal later."

"Have it now. I don't like eating alone."

Henrietta glanced at him. Her brows gathered at his less-than-friendly tone. Wyatt was clearly out of sorts.

"Fine." She gave him a fake smile and Henrietta handed her a bowl of oatmeal, then dished up the bacon and eggs for him. She placed biscuits on the table, too. How did any Texas woman retain her figure with biscuits, breads or muffins being served at every meal? Brooke was tempted to grab a biscuit and slather it with butter, but thought better of it. Her tummy could only hold so much food, and oatmeal was the far better choice.

"Would you like cinnamon or sugar with it?" Henrietta asked.

"I'm good with this. Thanks."

After she served them, Henrietta exited the kitchen mumbling something about getting down the fall decorations.

Great, now they were alone. Well, except for the babies. Brooke put her head down, concentrating on eating her oatmeal.

"When I said I didn't like to eat alone, I didn't mean this."

"What?"

"You're giving me the silent treatment."

"It's for the best," she whispered.

"Depends on who you ask."

"Wyatt, don't."

"I'm sorry, okay. It was really a dumb move on my part bringing you into that room."

She bit her lip and looked away. Taking her in there in the heat of passion was one thing, but that his shrine to Madelyn even *existed* was the heartbreaker. Seeing his private sanctuary put everything into perspective. He had every right to hold on to his love for his late wife. But why did he have to make love to Brooke as if it meant something to him? Maybe he shouldn't have made love to her at all. "I don't want to talk about it. Okay?"

He sucked in a breath and then sighed. "Okay. Listen, I want to spend some time with the twins this morning. I'd like to take them for a ride."

"A ride? Where?"

"On the grounds."

"In your car? That seems silly."

A smile emerged, transforming his sulky face. "Not in the car. On horseback."

"You've got to be kidding."

He glanced at his children, who were beginning to wiggle and squirm in their high chairs. "Nope. I rode my first horse when I was one year old. Got the pictures to prove it. If you ask me, they're overdue."

"Okay, suit yourself."

"I'll need help."

"James or your mother could probably help."

"I need your help. Mom's not much for riding and James is too busy today."

"Wyatt, I can't ride a horse."

"You've never ridden before?"

"I have. That's not what I meant. I'm not exactly an expert." She was pregnant. She shouldn't get atop a horse, should she?

"You don't have to be. Do you think I'd risk my kids' safety? I have all the rigging to keep them and you from any danger."

"Well, we can't do it today. Your mom and I are taking the twins into Cahill."

"When?"

"In a couple of hours."

"That gives us more than enough time."

Holding Brett in his arms, Wyatt motioned for Brooke to climb atop the horse. She came forward tentatively, the hat on her head shading her troubled eyes from morning sunshine. He wasn't being fair to her. As sure as the sun rose in the east every day, he knew it. But once a notion took root inside his brain, he had trouble removing it. He'd dug his heels in insisting on Brooke's being a part of the twins' first ride. Now he couldn't imagine doing it without her.

Since their argument, she was on his mind constantly. She'd sidestepped him every moment of every day since, whenever she possibly could. He'd hurt her without intending to, and if he had a lick of sense, he'd let these next few days pass without interjecting himself more into her life. But he couldn't do it. He had a powerful need to spend as much time with her as possible.

It wasn't a conscious move on his part to include her on the ride this morning. Hell no. But after hearing her singing that silly ditty to his toddlers, something snapped inside him. He'd practically ordered her to share the morning meal with him, and then insisted she ride with him and his babies. When she left the ranch for good, he'd miss her like crazy.

If only he had something to offer her. But he wasn't over Madelyn and he couldn't bear hurting Brooke again.

"Step on up to the mounting block," he said to her, holding the reins. "These two mares are the gentlest in the string."

"I know how to mount a horse, Wyatt."

He ignored her and helped her up into the saddle, his hand on her rear end giving a little push. Brooke lanced him with a look that could cut ice.

He bit back a laugh. "This is Maple. She's five years old and sweet as her name."

"Good to know."

Brooke placed her boots into the stirrups and adjusted her position. "I'll hand Brett up to you. And then I'll put the rigging around both of you. You'll be snug and locked in. Just keep one hand on him at all times."

"Okay, got it."

He handed the baby up and immediately, Brett started kicking up a happy fuss. His smile was worth a zillion bucks. "There you go, boy. You like that, don't you?" Once they were secure, he gave Brett a pat on the head. His kids liked the ranch animals. They had no fear, and Wyatt's chest puffed out seeing Brett take to being in the saddle.

"Horsey, go!"

Brooke cracked a smile. If anyone could get that sour

look off her puss, it was Brett. "Not yet, little guy. We'll go as soon as Daddy says so."

Wyatt lifted Brianna out of the stroller and then holding her tight, mounted his mare with ease. He wrapped the protective rigging around both their bodies and clicked his heels, guiding the horse over to Brooke. "Can you tighten this strap?" he asked her.

Brooke leaned way over, took the strap he offered and gave a tug. "That's perfect," he said. "All set?"

She nodded. "Bri's all smiles, too."

"You both look cute in those hats."

Brooke rolled her eyes. Wyatt was too damn happy to take offense. "I'll lead. Try not to fall too far behind."

"We'll keep up, don't you worry."

"Okay," he said. And off they went.

They left the stables and got as far as the house when Genevieve came running out. "Wyatt! Stop! You can't take the twins without documenting this." She had her cell phone in her hands. "It's their first ride."

God, he hadn't thought of that. "Thanks, Mom. You're right. I wasn't thinking."

"Yeah, that happens a lot with you," he heard Brooke mumble.

He gave her a sideways glance. "Maybe because you make me forgot my own name."

Brooke had no response to that, but he liked the way her face flushed pink.

"Maybe you'd like to take my place, Grammy G?" Brooke called out. "You should be in the pictures, not me."

Grammy G? When had Brooke started calling his mother that? When his mom didn't react to the nickname, he was totally baffled.

"No, no, Brooke. I'm a better photographer than I am a rider. You two go on. I'll get some video of this, too. Bri and Brett, look over here at Grammy."

The children were in awe, being atop their favorite animals. There wasn't a peep out of them as they rode by the stables and corrals. Wyatt's ranch hands stopped what they were doing to wave. The twins giggled and gave a wave back. James had a big smile on his face, too, until he noticed Wyatt's mother standing in front of the house with camera in hand. All joy was wiped clean from James's face and just like that, he marched over to the house.

Whatever was going on between James and his mother, Wyatt was keeping his nose out of it.

"Uh-oh, looks like trouble is brewing," Brooke said.

At least she was talking to him. Lately Brooke had barely given him the time of day, except when it came to something regarding the children. How did he turn out to be the bad guy, while his mother and Brooke were such good buddies now? "Mom can be a lot to handle. James has his work cut out for him."

"I think James is just what Genevieve needs. She just doesn't know it yet. Women need lots of encouragement, especially when their mind is set on the wrong thing."

"Do they now?" Wyatt gave her an intense stare.

"Yeah, uh, never mind. I'm the last one to give advice." She looked straight ahead. "How far are we going?"

He let her comments drop, but logged them into his memory. Brooke was good at giving him a female perspective. "Oh, don't know exactly. The kids are enjoying it. I guess we'll head back when they start to fuss."

They ambled down a path heading away from the grazing cattle toward one of Wyatt's favorite spots on his property. The meadow was a mix of bluebonnets and tall grass. It was pretty scenery. "Here's where my granddaddy came up with the name of the ranch. Sitting on the ground looking out, he said the bluebonnets appeared to meet the sky like a blue horizon."

"Wow, I can picture that. It's lovely here."

"Yep. There's a pond up ahead. We can water the horses."

The twins were amazingly quiet, satisfied and thrilled to be riding. One day, they'd own their own horses, learn how to care for and groom their animals. Learn how to respect them. They had time for that, though. He wouldn't rush them. Hell, he still needed a nanny for them. He had two preliminary interviews scheduled on the day his mother was due to leave the ranch. He didn't hold out much hope; replacing Brooke in any capacity would be hard. She was great with his kids and, well, great overall.

And in two days, his mother and Brooke would be long gone.

He wasn't ready to say goodbye to Brooke, but he couldn't ask her to stay. He didn't want to hurt her any more than he already had. The dilemma plagued his mind, but he had to think of the twins. They needed someone steady and constant in their lives. Someone they could rely on. Henrietta and Brooke weren't an option anymore.

"Lookee, Daddy. Duckies," Brianna said, pointing toward the pond.

Brett got wind of it, too. "Duckies! Duckies!"

Brooke laughed. The joy on her face and the way she squeezed little Brett tight, as if she loved the little guy, tugged at Wyatt's heart.

"I see them. They're swimming and taking a bath."

"They look like the duckies in the book I read to you," Brooke said. "*One, Two, Three Ducks*. You remember, right?"

The twins nodded without taking their eyes off the birds, their smiles brighter than sunshine.

Wyatt hadn't known this much joy since before Madelyn's accident. It was as if they were a family, similar to the ducks swimming in his pond, sticking together, having a fun time. A knot twisted in his gut. He knew better. He wouldn't dwell on what couldn't be. But still…

Fifteen minutes later, they were back at the stables and off the saddles. The twins were pooped and ready for a morning nap.

He carried the heftier Brett over his shoulders, while Brooke carried Bri as they headed for the house. Dust kicked up, stopping them midway on the driveway as a slick midnight blue sports car came to a halt right in front of them.

And Johnny Wilde stepped out of his convertible.

Nine

"So that's Brooke?" Johnny said to Wyatt after they'd put the twins down to nap. Brooke was upstairs getting ready for her outing with his mother and the children. "You finally found someone suitable as a nanny, then?"

Wyatt gave Johnny a thoughtful look here in the privacy of his study. He'd learned his lesson the hard way and removed the shrine of photos he'd had of Madelyn in the room. Now only a few of his favorites graced the wall. "Not exactly."

Johnny was his best friend, someone he trusted, a rancher and part owner of the Dallas-based Wilde Corporation he ran with his brothers. They'd grown up together and once upon a time, Johnny had even had an eye for Madelyn. But Wyatt had won her over.

"What does that mean?" With the twist of his wrist, ice shuffled around in the glass of lemonade Johnny held.

"It means, and I know I can trust you…" He eyed him carefully and Johnny nodded. "Brooke is a woman I picked up on the road. We were both going to the same wedding and her car had broken down and…well, it's a long story."

Johnny leaned forward in his chair. "You got my attention at *Brooke is a woman I picked up on the road.* Trust me, Wyatt, for this, I have the time."

Wyatt took a swig of his drink. "I know, it doesn't sound like me, does it?"

Wyatt spent the next ten minutes explaining the situation to his best friend. Johnny listened, keeping his thoughts to himself and nodding.

"So that's it. Brooke is leaving in two days, right after Mom leaves."

"Weird coincidence that she's Dylan McKay's sister."

"Tell me about it. Are you still working on the set?"

"Yeah, part-time. The show wraps in less than a week."

"That means Brooke will be going back to California."

Johnny's dark brows rose and white lines appeared in his otherwise tan forehead. "And you're letting her go?"

Wyatt nodded. "I have to."

"Why?"

"Because I've already hurt her. And I can't… I can't." He began shaking his head. "Listen, you know how hard I took Madelyn's death. I'm still grieving. There's a hole in my heart that will never fill up again. If I got involved with Brooke and it didn't work out, I… I'm just not ready for that."

"Too bad, pal. If it were me, I'd ask her to stay. You said she's great with the kids, and well, if she's that hot in the sack…"

"Watch it," Wyatt warned, his blood ready to boil over. He'd told Johnny that he and Brooke had a good time together. He hadn't elaborated, but it was true, Brooke was hot in bed. Yet hearing it come out of Johnny's mouth rankled him no end. "Don't make me sorry I confided in you."

"Okay, okay. Mellow out, Brandt."

"It's just that, Brooke is…"

"Special? Amazing? Beautiful? Oh, yeah, I noticed."

"You only spoke with her for two minutes."

"Two of the best minutes of my life."

Wyatt gave a half groan, half laugh. "Johnny, you're hopeless."

"I'm just trying to help. If you've got feelings for her, Wyatt, don't run from them. You may never come across another woman you like as much."

"That's just it, I'm not looking for another woman. I need a nanny for my kids. Preferably someone with warts and knobby knees. Someone who doesn't distract me every second of the day."

Johnny laughed. "Man, you are tortured."

"Tell me about it. Come on," Wyatt said. "Mom's probably downstairs by now. She'll want to see you."

"She's the main reason I came by. I couldn't let your mama leave for home without saying hello."

An hour later, Wyatt and Johnny were in the garage helping Brooke load the kids into their car seats. Johnny gave Brett and Brianna high fives and then kissed them on their cheeks. "I'll see you next time I come by, kids. Love you both," Johnny said. "Brooke, it was very nice meeting you."

"Same here, Johnny."

"What do you mean, *next time*? You're staying for dinner tonight," Genevieve said. "I haven't seen enough of you today and the twins would love to see more of their Uncle Johnny. Wyatt, didn't you invite Johnny for dinner?"

"Yeah, Wyatt," Johnny egged him on. "I didn't hear anything about dinner."

"You're welcome to stay for dinner," Wyatt droned.

Johnny glanced at Brooke and gave her a big smile. "I'd like that very much."

Brooke smiled back, and Wyatt's jealousy radar went crazy.

"There, it's settled." The queen of England herself would stand up and take notice at his mother's tone. "We'll see you later tonight."

"Sounds good. And hey, will James be sitting down with us? I promised him a visit, too."

"No, James doesn't usually dine with us," Genevieve was quick to point out.

"But I'll ask him to join us," Wyatt said. He wasn't about to throw James under the bus because of his mother. James deserved better treatment. He'd been loyal to the ranch for decades.

"Well, that's just great." Johnny glanced at Brooke, then Genevieve. "You two ladies have a fun outing. I'll see you all later."

Deliberately, Wyatt didn't look at his mother. If she was pissed, she'd aim her wrath at him, and he had enough to worry about lately.

Dinner at the Brandt house tonight wasn't going to be dull.

That was for darn sure.

"Genevieve, your mouth is going to stay that way if you don't untwist it. At least that's what I was always told," Brooke said.

As Wyatt's mother slumped on the wrought iron and wood park bench, her face wrinkled even more. The usually strong woman appeared diminutive sitting next to Brooke. "Sorry, I'm lousy company today."

The children were playing in the park, shoveling sand into a variety of sifters, pails and animal molds. They were getting filthy and having the best day ever. Horsey rides, ducks at the pond and now the sandbox. Brooke loved seeing the joy in their eyes. They were the sweetest kids.

"Why?"

"It's complicated."

"Life usually is." And wasn't that the truth. She was keeping secrets from Genevieve and Wyatt. And one of those truths was beginning to show in the form of a tiny baby bump.

Genevieve nodded. "I like my life. It's full and rich and when I'm helping others, I feel better about myself. I work for charities and foundations and pour my heart and soul into the work. It's what I love. I've made friends. I have a beautiful home in New York."

"Why do I feel a *but* coming here?"

"It's just one big fat *but*. James."

Brooke laughed.

Then Genevieve laughed, too. "I didn't mean it that way. James is…"

"Nice? Handsome? Persistent?"

"Yes, all of it. He and I, well, we began seeing each other and it was marvelous. I mean, we really had a good, good time. But he wanted more."

"And you're afraid to give it?"

"He used to work for my husband. He works for Wyatt now. I mean…what would people say? How would it look?"

"Like maybe two lonely, intelligent people found each other?"

Genevieve smiled sadly. "I don't think so."

"Why do you care what anyone says?"

She shrugged and tears entered her eyes. "I don't. Not really. But it's taken me all this time to get what I really wanted in life—to live on the East Coast, to be part of society rather than being tucked away on a remote ranch. To have friends, go to the theater and enjoy all the city has to offer."

"There are pros and cons to every issue, Genevieve. What if you gave James a chance and found that you were happier than you could ever imagine? You'd be close to your grandchildren and your son. And I'm sure James could be persuaded to do some of those things you enjoy so much with you."

Genevieve's gaze rested on the children playing so heartily in the sand. Little Bri was standing, wearing an accomplished expression and ready to dump the contents of her tiny bucket into a pile. Brett was busy playing with another child's red toy truck. Behind them, a group of older kids were tossing a football back and forth, their laughter and country music filling the park. "I know. I know. All that might be true," Wyatt's mother said. "Lord knows, I'll never have any more grandchildren. Wyatt is through having babies, and I'm missing out on the ones I do have. I'm just…so afraid."

The comment about having babies stuck like a knife in Brooke's heart. Genevieve had just reaffirmed the reason Brooke was being so cowardly. Wyatt wouldn't want their child, and it crushed her to face that fact. How could she tell him? How could she possibly confess her pregnancy knowing how he felt about having more children? "Fear is something I understand. It can stifle you and cause you to make bad choices and wrong decisions."

But Genevieve's reply was interrupted when a football sailed over her head. Brooke saw the wild pass heading straight for Brianna and leaped into the sand, tackling her to the ground and then *thump*! The football smacked the side of her head. Hard. Pain slashed through her temple and her eyes crossed. She closed them until Brianna's cries reminded her that she had the little one tucked safely beneath her body.

"Brooke! Are you okay?" Genevieve came rushing over and Brooke slowly gave her a nod.

"I think so. I'm a little dazed."

"Goodness, Brooke. You saved Brianna. That ball would've really hurt her. Can you sit up?"

"Yes, I probably can." Although everything seemed to be going in slow motion at the moment, with Genevieve's help, she sat up.

Brianna was dazed, too. Then startled by Brooke's quick reaction, she started wailing. "It's okay, Bri. I'm sorry if I scared you."

Brett had gone pale. Any minute now, he'd start sobbing, too. Genevieve cradled both children, hugging them to her chest.

"Gosh, lady. I'm sorry." It was one of the football players. "Are you okay?"

"No, she's not okay." Genevieve's voice carried across the playground. "She was hit by your football. But it would've been worse if my granddaughter took that hit. Why are you playing so close to the playground? You boys should know better."

"Yes, ma'am. Sorry again."

The boy, joined by his friends, grabbed up his football and slumped away.

"My goodness, Brooke. You dived in to save Brianna. I, uh…" Genevieve choked up, shaking her head. "Thank you," she managed in a whisper.

"I just reacted," she said. "I couldn't let anything happen to Brianna."

Genevieve gave her an intense stare. "Are you sure you're okay? Maybe I should take you to see a doctor."

"No. I'll be fine." She touched the sore spot on her skull. Luckily, her arm had come up to partially divert the knock she took to the head. "I'm a little shaken up. You'll probably have to drive us home though."

"Not a problem. Let me get the kids into the car and we'll get you some ice."

One of the mothers from the playground came running

over. "Gosh, I saw what happened. I have an ice pack. Here you go." She handed it to Genevieve. "That was really brave of you," she said softly to Brooke. "Nice tackle. The momma bear in you came out, didn't it?"

She was about to correct the woman. Brianna wasn't her child, but Genevieve didn't give her the chance. "It sure did. I'm impressed."

"Me, too," the woman said. "Well, I hope you'll be all right."

"Thank you."

The woman gave her a sympathetic smile and walked off.

Brooke figured she must be dizzy in the head, because her first thought after that was that she'd managed to impress Wyatt's mother. What would he say to that?

"How about joining me in a glass of wine, Brooke?" Johnny Wilde offered after he'd poured his own glass on the side bar of the dining room. "It'll help heal that injury you took in the line of duty." He gave her a smooth smile, the wine bottle tipped and ready to pour. Thanks to Genevieve, everyone around the table had heard about the incident at the park.

"No thanks, Johnny. I'd better not."

Standing beside him, Wyatt held a shot glass to his mouth and downed the liquor in one swallow.

Brooke looked away. The babies were down for the night and without them as a shield, she had to deal with Wyatt on her own. They'd had a wonderful morning together, taking that ride with the twins. Now he studied her face and head, looking for signs of her injury, no doubt. There was a perpetual frown on his face aimed at her. It was a bit intimidating.

"You sure?" Johnny asked, ready to put the bottle down. "Being the hero of the day has its perks."

"I'm sure. My head is clear and I'd like to keep it that way. Thanks anyway."

When they returned home this afternoon, Genevieve had insisted that Brooke take a nap, while she took over tending to the children. The rest had done wonders. Her head no longer ached. And the bump on her head was teeny tiny, hardly noticeable. Still she felt uncomfortable with everyone staring at her as if she'd rushed into a burning building or something. Her save hadn't been that dramatic, but Brianna would surely have been hurt if that football had knocked her down.

Genevieve was already sipping wine at the far end of the dining room and speaking with James. It appeared to be a civil conversation from the smile on James's face. If a man could beam, he was surely doing it, and Genevieve's occasional quiet laughter was sweet to the ears.

Wow.

During the first course of dinner, glazed walnut and pear salad, Johnny entertained them with stories of growing up with Wyatt as his best friend. They'd gone to high school together and were teammates in baseball and football.

"*Rivals* is a better word," Wyatt was saying. "You were always trying to best me."

"Trying? I always did," Johnny added.

"In whose world?"

"In my world, Wyatt. Don't you remember who ran for more touchdowns? Who had more home runs?"

"I do recall. That would be me. The numbers don't lie. Maybe your recollections need a little tune-up. Check out the stats."

"I bet you still have them."

"They're here somewhere. Madelyn saved them for me." Wyatt's voice quieted.

Johnny's smirk didn't falter. He loved the banter, and the

mention of Madelyn didn't stop him from teasing Wyatt. "If you'd told that girl the moon was made of blue cheese, she would've believed you."

Wyatt didn't smile. Instead he glanced at Brooke, his soft gaze penetrating her defenses. That's all it took: one apologetic look from Wyatt to crumble the walls she'd tried so hard to maintain. He cared about her, she understood that, but it wasn't enough. Not nearly enough.

Genevieve and James rose from their seats to help Henrietta serve the entrée. When Brooke stood to lend a hand, both Wyatt and Genevieve stopped her immediately. "Don't you dare," Genevieve said.

Wyatt's stony stare said the same.

"I'm fine," Brooke said to everyone, but she lowered down in her seat.

"That's the way we want to keep it, right, Wyatt?" Genevieve gave Wyatt a glance and he nodded.

"I'll help, too."

"No need. Your mom and I have this," James said.

Genevieve gave James a smile and off the two of them went.

"Well, would you look at that," Johnny said. "And here I thought Genevieve had no use for good ole James."

Good ole James was a silver-haired, intelligent man of the earth. He was no country bumpkin, and maybe Genevieve was finally seeing his merits. If something good had come from this little deception she and Wyatt were engaging in, maybe it would be that those two were finding common ground.

"Did you have anything to do with my mother's change of heart?" Wyatt asked.

"Me?" She thought to refute it, but that wouldn't be totally true. And she needed to tell as much truth as she could to atone for all the lies. "Maybe. We had a nice talk today. She's a little confused about some things."

"Mom? Confused? She seems to know exactly what she wants."

Brooke shrugged. "I noticed a change in her after what almost happened to Brianna. She's got some thinking to do."

Wyatt blinked at the suggestion that he didn't know all there was about his mother after all. "I suppose. Maybe you saved more than one person today, Brooke."

"Deserving of a Purple Heart," Johnny said, giving her a winning smile. "Or at the very least a pat on the back and a kiss on the cheek."

Johnny leaned over, put his hand on her shoulder and then brushed a kiss to her cheek. It was short and quick, a chaste kiss, yet he'd stunned her. Heat climbed up her neck and one glance at Wyatt's murderous stare at Johnny had a bubble of laughter erupting from her lips. Only Johnny Wilde could get away with something like that.

"What the hell?" Wyatt rasped.

"What?" Johnny feigned innocence and chuckled.

Brooke couldn't contain her laughter, either. But Wyatt was not amused.

The conversation halted when James walked into the room with a sizzling platter of Blue Horizon prime rib roast. "Here we go," he said, setting the platter down carefully in the center of the table. "Wyatt, I'll do the slicing, if you don't mind. And Gen can serve the roast up. Is that okay with you, Gen?"

Genevieve gave him a smile and nodded. "I'd love to."

It was almost comical watching Wyatt struggle to keep his mouth from dropping open. Admittedly, from what Brooke gathered, James and Genevieve hadn't been this civil with each other in quite a while.

Henrietta walked in with a side dish casserole and then retrieved a basket of home-baked buttermilk biscuits. The room immediately filled with mouthwatering aromas.

It was time to concentrate on the scrumptious meal that looked and smelled delish.

With her stomach on the fritz and her head a little sore, Brooke only hoped she could hold it down.

The knock on her bedroom door came at precisely nine thirty. From her bed, Brooke stared at the door, fearing who was on the other side. She didn't want to speak to Wyatt tonight. She had two more days here, and she was trying to make the best of them. Wyatt seemed to have other plans.

"It's me, Genevieve. Are you awake?"

Surprised, she set her novel down and tossed off her blanket. "Just a sec, Genevieve. I'm coming."

She slid her arms into her robe and tied it before opening the door. "Hello."

Genevieve had a helpless look on her face. "I'm sorry to bother you. Do you have a minute?"

"Of course I do. Come in."

Genevieve entered her room and Brooke led her to the pair of wing chairs that looked out onto Blue Horizon property. The night was dark but for a sliver of moonlight. "Have a seat."

"Thanks." She sat.

So did Brooke. "What's on your mind?"

Genevieve tilted her head to one side. "James. We took a walk after dinner."

"Yes, I saw the two of you leave after dessert. So how was it?"

Genevieve inhaled a deep breath. "Wonderful. So sickeningly wonderful, I can't describe it. I, uh, well, I hope you don't mind me confiding in you. I can't imagine talking about this with Wyatt. But James kissed me goodnight and it was beyond amazing. It was bells and whistles going off."

"That's wonderful, isn't it?"

"I hope so. We talked at length and decided to take it slow. But I am going to continue seeing him. Do you think that's the right move?"

"I do, Genevieve. I think taking it slow is a good thing. You can spend more time here in Texas, and maybe he'll come to visit you in New York."

"That's what we're going to try to do. Maybe split our time and see how it goes. It'll give me more time with the twins, too." She nibbled on her lip. "Brooke, is it crazy to do this at my age?"

Brooke smiled. "Not at all. My goodness, Genevieve, if you see what I see when James looks at you, I'd say it'd be crazy not to. If you have feelings for each other, why not explore them?"

Wyatt's mother began nodding, taking in her suggestion. "I don't think I would've come to this conclusion without you."

"Me?"

"You're easy to talk to. I know I can be bitchy at times, but I respected how you managed me."

"You're not bitchy, exactly. And I wasn't managing you."

"Saying how calling me Mrs. Brandt might confuse my grandchildren? That was just the right comeback for me. And well, after your quick reaction with Brianna today, it was like a boulder being dropped on my head."

Brooke rubbed her sore skull. "Make that a football and I'd understand."

"Oh, dear, and I haven't even asked you about your head."

"It's fine. I'm fine. Go on," she said.

"Okay, I won't keep you much longer, I promise. But I wanted to thank you for listening and for your advice today. I have been sort of lost, coming here and seeing James again."

"Well, if I helped you in any way, I'm glad."

"You did. I realized today how badly I want more time with my grandchildren. It all seems to fit now. James and me, more visits to the ranch, less city, more country. I think I can do it."

"I'm happy for you, Genevieve."

"I'm sad I have to leave day after tomorrow. I haven't spent any time getting to know you. It's all been about me. Next time I come out I plan to spend time getting better acquainted with you."

"Uh, well, that would be nice." She felt like a heel, letting Genevieve Brandt believe she'd be here when she returned. Not only wasn't she really the twins' nanny, she was carrying Wyatt's baby and couldn't confide in Genevieve. The woman would probably end up hating her once she found out about all the lies Brooke had told.

What a deep hole she'd dug for herself.

Another soft knock came at her door and she froze. Her heart beat like crazy in her chest. Before her new visitor—more than likely Wyatt—could say something, Brooke called out. "Just a minute!"

Genevieve appeared genuinely surprised. "Who could that be?"

"Probably your son. I promised to give Mr. Brandt my... my schedule for next week. I have to take a few days off and he'd wanted to check with Henrietta to make sure she could cover."

"Goodness, I wish I could help out. I'd love to, but I've had this commitment in Dallas on the books for months."

Brooke swept over to the door. "It's going to work out, don't worry," she said, opening the door to Wyatt's somber face. "*Mr. Brandt*, I'm sorry I forgot to give you my schedule."

Wyatt stared at her as if she'd grown bull horns, and then noticed his mother walking toward him. He scratched his chin, buying time, and finally catching on. "No problem, I just wanted to remind you. And see how you're feeling. Hello, Mom."

"Wyatt. It's late for Brooke. Don't keep her up too long. Gosh, you are so much like your dad. He couldn't go to bed until he dotted his *i*'s and crossed his *t*'s."

"Yeah, the hazards of being a Brandt, I guess."

"Good night Brooke, get some rest." Genevieve patted her shoulder gently and then eyed her son for a moment. "Remember, you can discuss business in the morning."

Wyatt nodded and waited until his mother walked down the hallway and closed the door to her room. Then he sighed. "What was that all about?"

"Mostly about James, but I can't discuss it."

Wyatt didn't press the point. "May I come in?"

"If you have to."

He frowned and stepped inside her room.

Ten

Brooke tightened the ties on her robe and hugged herself around the middle. Wyatt was giving her his signature devilish blue-eyed look that threatened to devour her in one huge gulp. She didn't need any more private time with him. She'd told him to stay away, but he didn't listen very well. "Why are you here?" she asked on a sigh.

He frowned at her bluntness. "I'd like to see your bruise, Brooke."

"Why? The last time I checked, you didn't have 'MD' behind your name."

"Are you saying you need a doctor?"

"No, it's just a bump. It hurt like hell before, but the pain's gone now."

"Well, then. Show me. I couldn't see a damn thing at dinner."

"What's the point of having long hair if I can't cover up my wounds?" She was being deliberately obtuse with him tonight. Because…because, darn him, he was standing in her bedroom like her miracle cowboy again, with doggone sympathy and admiration in his eyes. The two didn't at all mesh, but on him, it looked appealing.

He stood with feet planted wide, hands on his hips, his jaw made of granite. "How bad is it?"

"Oh, for heaven's sake, Wyatt." She stepped closer to him and under a halo of lamplight angled her head slightly, pushing her hair to the side. "See, it's not that bad."

He winced and his breath rushed out. "There's definitely a bump there. Dammit. I wish to God you hadn't gotten hurt."

She believed him, because Wyatt was a decent man. That was the good news and the bad news.

"I told you at dinner, I'm fine now."

"What you did for Brianna…" He shook his head as if he couldn't find the words.

"I'm happy she wasn't hurt," Brooke said softly. "There's no need for you to be here worrying about this."

"Thank you for protecting her."

"You're welcome."

"You're making it impossibly hard for me to find a real nanny, you know."

"You're just saying that because your mother likes me."
I even impressed her today.

"You're likeable, but Mom never takes a shine to people this quickly."

"She's not that bad, Wyatt. I feel terrible lying to her about all this."

"Just for another full day. Then she'll be on her way."

Brooke backed up a step and stared into his eyes. "And so will I."

Wyatt cleared his throat and nodded. "I know. Brooke, listen," he said, his voice deep and raspy. He came toward her, all iron-jawed handsome, and she closed her eyes.

"Don't, Wyatt."

"There are things I need to say to you. Things that need explaining."

"Look, you're off the hook, okay?" She smiled, softening her words. "I don't need to hear all about your heartache and your undying love for your wife. I don't need you to say nice things to me. I'll be leaving soon and…and…"

I'm having your baby.

God, it was on the tip of her tongue. But she held back. In less than forty-eight hours, she'd be gone from Blue Horizon. She needed more time before she told him. She needed to gain some perspective. She needed to discuss her situation with Emma and Dylan. Why hadn't she done that yet? Why had she jumped in with both feet without seeing how deep the bottom was? Without knowing how far she would fall?

Her decision made, she walked to the door and opened it. "Wyatt, I'm tired. I really should get to sleep."

"All right," he said, striding to the door. "Good night, Brooke," he said quietly, and then landed the softest kiss on her cheek. "Sleep well."

She gazed into his eyes. "You, too."

He shot her a dubious look, as if the last thing he would do was get a good night's sleep. He left her at the door and sauntered away. She fixed her focus on his retreating form, all cowboyed up, tight-jeaned and hunky.

Then she closed the door and put her hand to her tummy as tears spilled down her cheeks.

Brooke sat cross-legged in the great room among wooden alphabet blocks, dolls and two little people cars, playing with Brianna and Brett. The twins were a lot of work, but they were also adorable and sweet and Brooke's heart broke thinking she'd be leaving them tomorrow. Not only had she fallen for Wyatt, but she'd fallen for his kids, too.

"Here you go, Breezy Peezy." She handed Brianna a red block.

Brianna flung it across the room.

"No, we don't do that."

Brett giggled and it only egged Brianna on. She picked up another block and tossed it as hard as she could. It nearly hit Wyatt's gazillion-inch flat-screen TV. "Bri. No!"

She grabbed Brianna's hand and the little girl's face turned cherry red and she broke down in sobs. "Oh, it's okay, Bri. It's okay. Come here." Brooke cradled her in her arms, absorbing her genuine, honest-to-goodness tears. They soaked her blouse.

She'd been having so much fun playing with them, she didn't realize their nap time had come and gone, and the twins were both on the verge of hysteria.

Wyatt walked into the room, took one look at Brooke with Brianna and then scooped up Brett. "Nap time."

"Yeah, it's overdue. My fault."

His eyes warmed on his daughter and he ruffled her hair. "They're just having too much fun with you. It's hard not to." He kissed the top of Bri's head and she immediately stopped crying. "You're gonna be okay, sweetie." Then he planted a kiss on Brett's head. "Up we go."

They climbed the stairs and entered their nursery, his compliment humming through Brooke's system. "My mom thinks it's time for the babies to have their own rooms."

Brianna had nearly conked out in her arms during the climb up the stairs. Brooke lowered her down gently and the little one curled her body up, nestled down and fell fast asleep. "Well, I've told you before, I don't think there's any rush. You can do it in a year or so when they develop different tastes."

"You mean like blue for boys and pink for girls?"

She chuckled quietly. "Only if it's their choice. Boys

do tend to prefer trucks and tractors over princesses and castles. At least that's how it worked in my family."

He nodded. "So you think I've got some time? They've had so many changes in their young lives, I don't want to make things harder on them."

"Yes, I think there's time."

"Book?" Brett's tiny voice rang in her ears.

"I'm here," she whispered. It was so cute how the babies called to her.

He put out his chubby arms and Wyatt made the transfer. Brett liked the way she rocked him to sleep. She bounced him up and down, to and fro, and slowly his inquisitive blue eyes closed. She laid him down.

"You're good for my kids," Wyatt said, almost as if he was thinking aloud.

Brooke bit down on her lip to keep from crying herself. She'd been weepy lately, and only part of it was due to her pregnancy. She left the nursery and Wyatt followed her into the hall.

"I'm taking Mom out for dinner on her last night here. James is going and I'd love for you to join us," he said.

"Oh, Wyatt…no, I don't think so. I'll stay home and watch the twins so you can have a peaceful meal."

"The babies are coming. It's nothing fancy, but it was my mom and dad's favorite barbecue place."

"Suddenly, I have a craving for barbecue again," Genevieve said, walking up to them. "And I insist you join us, Brooke. It'll be fun."

"Oh, uh?" What could she say; it was two against one. "Okay, sure."

"I'll drive with James and you and Wyatt can bring the twins."

Three hours later, the four of them were seated in a booth at the Brickhouse, James sitting next to Genevieve and Wyatt next to Brooke. She was as close to him as she wanted to get tonight, breathing in his incredibly rich scent of musk and lime. At times, they brushed shoulders. At times, they brushed thighs. It was hard not to react. Hard to pretend there wasn't more between them. Being here with his family, it dawned on her she really didn't fit in. She wasn't part of the love they shared. Even James belonged here more than she did. He'd known the Brandt family for decades.

A pitcher of beer sat on the table, and all three of them had offered at one time or another to pour her a glass. She shook off their attempts, claiming to prefer lemonade to quench her thirst.

But when the ribs were served, with coleslaw, mashed potatoes and corn soufflé, oddly, her stomach didn't rebel. She dug in as heartily as the others. "Mmm, this is good."

"I knew you'd like it," Genevieve said.

"How long have you been coming here?" Brooke asked.

"Since the place opened," Genevieve said.

"I think it's going on forty years, right, Mom?"

Genevieve smiled. "I worked here as a hostess."

"You did?" James seemed to eat up anything he learned about Genevieve. "I didn't know that."

"It was only for a few months. But I got to eat all the free food I wanted. It was my first job."

They shared a sweet glance.

"My first job was mowing lawns in Ohio. Hostessing sounds like more fun," Brooke said.

The babies were indulging in mashed potatoes and cut-up chicken tenders.

Everyone seemed content.

Until Brooke looked across the restaurant and nearly spit out her lemonade. There, seated in a booth in the far corner of the place, sat Dylan and his very pregnant wife, Emma. Dylan's disguise, a cowboy hat and thick glasses,

might fool some, but Brooke would know her brother anywhere. She froze in her seat. She couldn't panic. Thinking fast, she glanced at Wyatt. "Uh, would you excuse me
for a second? I need to use the restroom." She shrugged.
"Too much lemonade, I'm afraid." TMI, too, but it couldn't
be helped.

"Sure thing." Wyatt scooted out of the booth and she
slid out after him.

"Thanks."

She strolled down the aisle and hoped like hell no one
at the Brandt table was watching her. Luckily, she heard
the twins begin to whine and grumble, which usually drew
all attention their way.

Thankful the restaurant was crowded, with not a single
table empty, she made a quick turn to the left, passed two
booths and then scooted in next to her brother. He jumped,
his eyes going wide seeing her suddenly sitting beside him.
"Brooke? What are you doing here?"

"Same thing as you. Having dinner and hoping not to
be recognized." She slid a quick glance at her bestie. "Hi,
Emma. How're you feeling?"

"Hungry. Seems I'm always feeling that way lately. It's
good to see you, Brooke. We miss you."

"Miss you, too."

"What's all the mystery?" Dylan asked, noting how strange
she was acting.

"Shh," she said to both, slinking down in the seat.
"Please don't ask why right now, but I don't want the people I'm with to know I'm your sister. But it's not what you
think. Just trust me, okay? I promise I will explain everything tomorrow when I come back to Zane's place."

"You sure you're okay?" Dylan asked, giving her a good
once-over with his eyes.

"Yes, I swear everything's fine."

"And I would know that, if you called me every day like you promised."

Emma came to her defense. "Dylan, she's called me several times since she's been gone. We know she's doing well. You have to trust her."

Dylan shot his wife a baffled look and then sighed. "Fine, then. I'll see you tomorrow."

"Thanks. Oh, and nice disguise, Dylan."

She slid out of the booth quickly, before he had time for a snarky comeback, and leisurely strolled back to the table. Disaster averted.

As she sat in the kitchen enjoying the morning sunshine, Wyatt came in, surprising Brooke and disturbing her peace. He sauntered inside with that lazy *I'm Texan* way he had of getting her attention. Wyatt's presence always seemed to surround her, even when he was ten feet away. "Mornin'," he drawled.

"Good morning."

He homed in on her sipping hot cocoa and nibbling on a slice of toast. She'd hoped to have a few moments of solitude before the household woke, but instead she found herself gazing into the clearest blue eyes she'd ever seen. So blue it hurt her heart.

"I'm gonna be driving my mother into Dallas today."

"I know." She'd dreaded this conversation.

He slid into the seat facing her and leaned in real close. "I don't know how to thank you for all you've done." He reached across the table and took her hand.

"There's no need." She glanced at the door. Genevieve or Henrietta could walk in any minute.

"There is a need. You've been amazing in so many ways, Brooke. And you've meant something to me."

Would he care to name that something? No, she didn't think so. It wouldn't be what she wanted to hear anyway. She reached for a napkin with the hand he'd held and dabbed at her mouth. It was a way to break the connection without being totally obvious.

"We're all going to miss you."

"I'll… I feel the same," she said, setting both of her hands in her lap. No sense tempting fate. She couldn't bear to have him take her hand again. It was hard enough gazing into his eyes and knowing things would never be the same between them. "I feel bad leaving the twins with Henrietta. She does so much already."

"It won't be for long. I've got two interviews today that look promising. Whoever I hire could never replace you, but we'll make it work."

"I'm glad, Wyatt. Really. And you know, if your mother moved back to Texas, it wouldn't be the worst thing in the world," she said quietly.

"Yeah, I know. That's a long way off still, but I'm going to build her a cottage on the property. It's something she and Dad had always talked about. They drew up the plans and everything. So, if she wants to come back, she'll…" He cleared his throat. "She'll have some privacy."

Brooke smiled. "That could be the best of both worlds."

"If only everything was that easy." He kept staring at her, his voice husky. She would embed that voice in her memory bank.

She didn't feel much like finishing her toast. And this conversation was just about over. They'd said all there was to say to each other. "Well, I've got some packing to do myself," she said, standing. Wyatt immediately stood, too. "I'll say goodbye now. I'll be gone before you get back."

He stood silently and studied her. There was no *stay and give us more time together* or *I don't want you to leave.*

No, Wyatt only sighed, nodded his head and stared at her lips so long she thought they'd catch on fire. And then he leaned in and kissed her. As far as kisses went, this one was subpar. It was a cautious, someone-might-burst-into-the-room kind of kiss that spoke to Wyatt's unending sense of propriety and decency. It was one of the traits she loved most about him. He always did the right thing, no matter what.

Her eyes stung. Tears threatened. She had to make a clean break and get out of here before she confessed all of her sins and told him she loved him. "Goodbye, Wyatt."

And then she marched out of the room, her head held high, her face perfectly masked in a performance worthy of an Academy Award.

Later that afternoon, with a hole in her heart and missing the twins and their father like crazy, Brooke entered Zane's magnificent custom-built home with two pink bakery boxes in hand. She had a lot of explaining to do, and sugar always seemed to help.

"Hello? Anyone home?" she called out. She might as well get this over with, but on the drive from the bakery in Beckon, she suddenly felt lighter, the weight lifted, knowing she was about to unburden herself of the truth.

"We're out here," Dylan called from the backyard.

She found Dylan and Emma stretched out comfortably on chaise longues on Zane's veranda overlooking the countryside. They sipped from tall glasses of iced tea. "Hello, my family," she said.

"Ah, the prodigal sister has returned bearing gifts, I see," Dylan said.

Emma rolled her eyes. "Hi, Brooke. What did you bring us?"

"A peace offering," she squeaked.

"And why do you need a peace offering?" Dylan asked as he sat up on his chair, all jest aside.

"Because I have a confession to make and it's a big one."

Dylan and Emma exchanged glances.

"I've got red velvet cupcakes for you, Em, your favorite. And for Dylan, I brought an assortment of bakery cookies."

It was a throwback to when they were kids. Dylan had an eye for only the best, even then. He longed for the better decorated, fancier cookies he'd see displayed at the local bakery on his way to school every morning. But Mom couldn't afford the luxury, so she brought home the grocery store brand every week. When Dylan finally made it big, he began sending home fresh-baked cookies on a regular basis to their folks.

"Raspberry shortbread?" he asked.

"And chocolate-dipped macaroons. Take a peek," she said, holding open the box.

Not only did he peek, he grabbed two and gave one to Emma. "These are the best," he told her.

Emma chuckled. "You're like a little boy getting his favorite cookie."

"You're my favorite cookie," he said to her with a wink. "Brooke, take a seat, have a cookie and tell us your big confession."

She lifted a shortbread cookie out of the box and sat down. "Hmm. I've been *craving* these." She bit down and the soft cookie crumbled in her mouth.

"Craving?" Emma asked, scooting up in her lounge chair. "As in the way I have cravings?"

There was another exchange of looks between her and Dylan.

Brooke nodded. "Let me start from the beginning. You see, I met my miracle cowboy on the road to Heather's wedding…"

When Brooke was through telling her story, shedding her guilt about hiding the truth from them and begging for their understanding about the baby, Emma wrapped her up in her outstretched arms. Brooke snuggled into her embrace and breathed a sigh of relief. "Brooke, of course we understand. And to think, our babies will be very close in age. They'll be cousins."

The acceptance in Emma's voice did wonders. "Yeah, that part is exciting."

But Dylan sat pensive, staring at her, absorbing all the facts. "This guy's got to be told he's the father of your child, honey. If he's as decent as you say, he'd want to know."

"You're right, Dylan, he should know, but I'm… I'm in love with him. And he's still grieving over his late wife. The love of his life," she said quietly. "I've heard him say half a dozen times his two children were quite enough. He doesn't want any more. I don't think I could take seeing disappointment or fear enter his eyes when he learns the truth. I wanted to tell him the entire time I was staying there, but…it just wasn't the right time."

"You were too busy playing nanny to his kids and deceiving his mother," Dylan replied.

"Dylan, please." Emma rose to her defense. "We both know some things are out of our control. Brooke did what she thought was right at the time."

Her brother ran a hand down his face. "God, I'm sorry, sis. I just wish you would've come to us first."

"You're right. I should have confided in you guys. I know I've handled this whole situation all wrong. I was hoping…"

"Hoping what?" Dylan asked.

"That Wyatt would fall in love with her," Emma answered.

Brooke gave her friend a nod. No more needed to be said. Heartsick, she choked up. Wyatt had said goodbye to her. He hadn't stopped her from leaving. He didn't love her.

Her bestie had her all figured out. It was most likely because a similar thing had happened between her and Dylan. For a time, Dylan thought the baby Emma carried was his, and when he found out the truth he'd been taken by surprise and deeply hurt. But he came to love both Emma and the baby with all his heart. They were one tidy little family unit now and happy as clams.

Dylan came over and pulled Brooke into his arms. She rested her head on his broad shoulder and felt his love surround her. He really was the best brother ever. "We'll work it out, hon. Don't worry." He stroked her hair and kissed her forehead.

"Thanks. I feel better now that you know the truth. But I'm unsure what to do next."

"Give yourself a day or two," Emma said. "You need to be away from the situation for a while. I'm sure you'll figure out what to do."

"I'm gonna tell him, Em. Maybe just not to his face."

"Just don't text him," Dylan said, trying for levity.

"Maybe I'll send him an email."

Dylan tugged on her hair. "You're a goof sometimes. You know that?"

"Yeah, I know that."

Emma took her hand, and Dylan held her around the waist. The three of them were solid. "We're here for you, Brooke," Emma said.

"If you need something, just let us know," Dylan added. "You're feeling well?"

"Yes, just a bit of morning sickness, but it's not terrible."

"Good," Emma said. "It should pass soon."

"My shoot's almost over. Just a few pickup scenes and we're done and headed home. Don't rush into anything," her brother said. "Take Em's advice and think things through."

"I will. I promise. I already feel ten times better now that you guys know. Thanks. Your support means so much to me. Now I think I need a nap. Confessing is exhausting."

"Have at it, sis. We'll be here when you wake up."

"I think I'll take a nap, too," Emma said. "Our baby might grow up to be a soccer player with all the kicking he was doing last night. I didn't get much sleep."

"It's dangerous, you know," Brooke said, starting to feel her old snarky self again.

"What is?" Emma asked.

"Leaving Dylan alone with that entire box of bakery cookies. He might get pudgy around the middle and then the ladies won't buy tickets to see his movies."

"Funny," he said, reaching for the box, but Brooke was too quick for him. She snatched it up, tossed him a sole macaroon and then strolled away with the box under her arm as she headed for her bedroom.

"You're the one who'll be getting pudgy around the middle," Dylan called to her.

She grinned and thanked heaven for normalcy again.

Well, as normal as her life could possibly be from now on.

Without seeing her miracle cowboy every single day.

Wyatt sat atop Josey Wales, his favorite gelding in the string as the sun descended on the horizon. Riding had always been his balm, a way to cool off from a bad day, a way to let off steam. He'd pushed his horse hard this evening, racing against the sunset, going farther and farther out on Brandt land. Now that they'd turned around, Josey was taking his sweet time heading back to the house.

It was a lonely time of night. The babies were already asleep, thanks to the new nanny he'd hired just today, Loretta Martinez. She didn't have warts or knobby knees. Her résumé had been the best of the women he'd interviewed. Loretta was in her midforties, divorced, a little chubby, and her own children were all grown up. At first, the twins called out for "Book" each time Loretta went to pick them up. It broke his heart all over again that Brett and Bri would have to make another adjustment in their lives. They missed Brooke.

So did he.

He pushed his Stetson back from his forehead and sighed. The ride, the night air and cooler temperatures weren't working. He felt lonesome and isolated, cut off from the world. Abandoned by Brooke McKay. Though that made no sense, since the deal he'd made with Brooke was that she'd stay the week until his mother left for Dallas. She'd honored her part of the deal. He was the one having trouble with all of it.

You big dummy, you didn't ask Brooke to stay. Of course you feel abandoned. It's your own damn fault.

By the time he reached Blue Horizon stables, misery had set in. He dismounted and led the horse inside for grooming. When his cell phone rang, he had a mind not to answer, especially when he saw the caller's name pop up. But it could be important. His mother didn't usually call at night, preferring to FaceTime with the twins while they were awake.

"Hi, Mom," he said.

"Wyatt, what's wrong? I can hear it in your voice. Are the babies okay? Bri didn't catch cold. She was sneezing quite a bit when I left the ranch last week."

"Everyone is fine. I'm just in from a ride and the babies and I are all healthy."

"Okay, good. That's a relief. Actually, I'm looking for Brooke. She isn't answering her cell. Is she there by any chance?"

"Uh, no. She's not. Why do you ask?"

"She promised to give me her recipe for almond crusted halibut. She said it was foolproof and you know how appealing that sounds to me. My cooking skills are lacking lately. I'd like to perfect the recipe for the next time I come out. I'll make it for everyone."

"You mean, you'll make it for James, don't you?"

"Well, if he likes fish, he's welcome to come."

Wyatt chuckled. His mom was so transparent. "Maybe you can email her, Mom."

"Oh, right. I guess I could do that. Speaking of Brooke, I've been thinking about her, honey. Does she have someone?"

Wyatt cleared his throat. He hadn't broken the news that Brooke had been replaced yet. "Someone?"

"A boyfriend or anything? She never talked about her private life."

"Maybe because she wants to keep it private."

"She's great with the twins, Wyatt. But I couldn't help noticing for such a thin girl, she had a bump in her belly and well, she never touched a drop of alcohol even when she was off the clock. One morning I saw her take a look at the ham and eggs cooking on the griddle and turn pea green. I thought she was going to lose her lunch, right then and there."

"What exactly are you getting at, Mom?"

"Nothing. I'm being silly."

"Mom," he said more firmly.

"She's the best you're going to find as a nanny, Wyatt. I don't want you to lose her because she's pregnant."

"You think Brooke's pregnant?"

"I, um, it's just a hunch, son."

Wyatt ran a hand down his face. His whole body shook at the possibilities. He'd noticed a little thickening of Brooke's stomach lately, but hadn't thought anything of it. To him, she had the perfect body. But if he recalled correctly, Brooke didn't have any trouble drinking alcohol at Blake and Heather's wedding. Yet a month later, while she was there, she'd never accepted a drink from him. Little things were beginning to add up in his head now. All those little remarks he'd made about the twins being enough for him and Brooke giving him strange, almost pained looks after his comments. "Mom, I've got to go. I'll talk to you soon."

He ended the call quickly and slumped against the stable wall. Could it be true? Was Brooke carrying his child? Suddenly, and out of the blue, he came to the conclusion that he didn't need to know. It wouldn't matter anyway.

He pushed Johnny's speed-dial number. His friend answered on the first ring. "Johnny? Tell me what's going on with the production. Are they through filming yet?"

"Hello to you, too, pal."

"Listen, this is serious. I need to know if Brooke is still in Texas."

"Wow. You are serious. Yeah, she should be. As a matter of fact, I'm getting ready to go to the wrap party tonight. The whole cast is supposed to be there. I'm assuming she'll be there, too."

"Where is it?"

"They've rented out the Applewood. Are you crashing it?"

"Damn right I am."

"This I gotta see. Listen, I'll swing by and pick you up in half an hour. Deal?"

"Deal."

Wyatt showered and dressed fast, then began pacing the floor and glancing at his watch every fifteen seconds. When he heard the roar of an engine in front of his house, he was out the door instantly. "Hey, thanks for this," he said to Johnny. "But is it okay if we take my car?"

"Sure, why?" Then his friend caught a glimpse of what was happening over Wyatt's shoulder. "You're bringing the artillery?"

"Have to. I need all the help I can get."

Johnny smiled. "When you say it's serious, you mean it."

* * *

Wyatt walked into the Applewood Bar and Grill, an iconic honky-tonk that rivaled the famous Gilley's. The place was swarming with the cast and crew of Dylan McKay's Western movie. Wyatt spotted a few people he'd worked with on the day he'd filled in for Johnny.

Country music blared, a classic Zane Williams hit about loves lost and found. Wyatt moved through clusters of people chatting, scanned over the bar area and peeked into a small stadium arena where wannabe cowboys pressed their luck on a mechanical bull. There was no sign of Brooke.

He turned around and collided smack into someone's chest. The guy was built like granite and didn't offer an apology for blocking his way. When his gaze drifted to the man's face, he understood the reason. "McKay."

"What are you doing here, Brandt?"

They were nose to nose. "I didn't come for the food or the company. I'm looking for Brooke."

Dylan's chest puffed up with brotherly concern. "You weren't invited."

They could butt heads all day, but Wyatt was beyond that. If he had to make nice to Brooke's brother, he'd swallow his pride. "I know. I apologize. But this is important. I've got to speak with Brooke. Is she here?"

Dylan looked him up and down, his expression grim. "You plan on hurting her?"

"God no. I'm here to…"

"What?"

"To make things right."

"That means different things to different people," McKay said, still eyeballing him.

"You have my word, I'm not going to hurt her. That's all I can say for now."

They stared at each other for beats of a minute and then Dylan nodded. "Okay. I dragged her here, but she wasn't in the party mood. She's in one of the private offices. Follow me."

"No, it's okay. Just point me in her direction. I'll find her."

Dylan moved through the crowd and down a hallway. Wyatt followed quietly behind. When Dylan stopped and gestured to a room with a paneled door at the far end of the hallway, Wyatt made a move to pass him. And Dylan got in Wyatt's face again. "Remember what I said."

He tipped his hat. "Got it."

As soon as Dylan walked away, Wyatt whipped out his cell phone and called Johnny. Then he strode over to the door and knocked, his heart beating in his chest like crazy.

Brooke's eyes were just closing when a knock on the door broke her peace. She jumped and the phone on her lap fell to the floor. So much for the novel she was reading. Another knock boomed and this time, Brooke shook out the cobwebs in her head. "Hang on a second," she called.

Music filtered in, the lyrics muffled through the closed door, yet the sweet melody of the ballad came through softly. The din of conversation told her the party was in full swing. Too bad. She'd been ready to leave hours ago, which was weird, since parties were her business. Literally. Maybe Dylan and Emma had had enough country twang and porterhouse steaks for one night.

She rose and went to the door. "Ready to leave yet?" she asked just as she turned the knob and opened the door.

"Now that depends on you."

Her breath whooshed out as she took in the length and breadth of the man she loved. "Wyatt, w-what are you doing here?"

"Funny, your brother asked me the same thing. I guess I'm crashing the party."

She blinked. She couldn't believe Wyatt was standing on the threshold, one hip braced against the doorjamb.

He took his Stetson off, held it to his chest in true cowboy form and gave her a killer smile. "May I come in?"

"Oh, uh…yes. I guess so."

He walked in and turned to her, his smile wider and his face…well, how could a man get even more gorgeous in just a week's time? She was filling up on the sight of him, allowing her heartsick soul to take him all in.

"You look beautiful, Brooke."

"Thank you."

"Why don't we sit down?"

"Why?" She eyed him cautiously. Why was he here? Why were his sky blue eyes glowing like that? A girl could get her hopes up if she wasn't too bright.

"Because I've got things to say to you. And you're gonna listen. Now sit down."

She frowned.

"Please."

She sat on the cream sofa and he sat down next to her, as in, so close their thighs touched. She swallowed hard, planted her feet and waited.

Wyatt sighed as he set his hat on the sofa and then reached for her hand. It fit so nicely in his, and she trembled from his touch. "The truth is, when I married Madelyn, it was for life. I mean, I loved her so much, I could hardly breathe sometimes. She was everything to me. And we had this perfect little family. I was happier than I thought a man had a right to be. But you already know all that. What you don't know is that when you came into my life, I thought it was a brief interlude. I was instantly attracted to you and fooled myself into believing that it was lust. A simple case of lack of sex and female contact."

She gasped. "Are you insulting me, Wyatt?"

"Not at all, sweetheart. I'm trying to explain. And maybe I'm not doing the best job of it. You'll have to forgive me for that. But the honest truth is, I wasn't afraid to be myself around you, because I never thought I could have feelings for another woman. I never thought I would ever find love again. Certainly not so soon after Madelyn's death. She's been gone less than a year and my mind-set was that I'd be alone for a long, long time. Deeply caring for anyone before that time wasn't an option. But then you became the twins' nanny. Granted, it wasn't real, but it was. Wasn't it? I mean, you care for my kids, don't you?"

"Now I'm the one not able to breathe, Wyatt. Yes, I love those kids. They're amazing and sweet and…"

"They've been asking for Book."

A tear slipped down her cheek. "Really?"

He nodded.

"Are you trying to win me back as your nanny, Wyatt?"

"No. Don't cry, sweetheart. I'm trying to tell you I love you. I mean it. I've fallen crazy in love with you. And it took you leaving and a phone call from my mother to make me realize it."

Her heart bubbled up. "You love me?"

"I love you."

She caught her next tear with her finger and wiped it away. "I love you, too."

He squeezed her hand and then leaned in to give her the best kiss in the entire world. A sweet, simple brush of the lips that sewed her heart up good and tight.

"I want you to marry me, Brooke. I want you to come live with me at Blue Horizon. I want you to be my wife and help me raise my twins. But before you answer me, I want you know that my mother thinks you're carrying a child. She may be all wrong but after hearing what she had to say, I realized that yes, I'd want a child I'd conceived with you, but I'd want you to marry me, regardless. I missed you so much, I could hardly stand it."

He got down on one knee. "So I'm going to ask you again. Whether you are or aren't carrying my child, will you marry me? Oh, and wait one darn second."

He pulled out his cell phone and texted someone.

Really? In the middle of his proposal?

Johnny Wilde entered the room, holding two sleepy-eyed babies in his arms. He set them down and once they spotted her, they waddled right into her arms. "Book, Book."

"Oh!" The babies were here! Her eyes watered again. She scooped them up and kissed each one on the cheek. "I've missed you two."

"Mission accomplished," Johnny said, giving a salute and backing out of the room.

Brooke chuckled between her tears.

"They want you for their mommy, Brooke," Wyatt said. "And I just plain want you."

Brooke couldn't believe her ears. She was hopelessly and fully in love with Wyatt Brandt. And yes, she'd have to make some changes in her life, give up her business or run it long distance, but right now, all that mattered, all she wanted, was Wyatt Brandt and his two adorable children.

"You can answer me anytime now," Wyatt said, still on bended knee.

"Yes, I'll marry you," she said, snuggling the twins. "And yes, I'm carrying your child. I was going to tell you before I left Texas. I truly was. I just didn't know how to tell you to your face. I was afraid you wouldn't want me or the baby."

"It's okay, Brooke. I get it. I didn't make things easy on you. I was stuck in my grief and almost lost you because of it."

"I was wrong not to tell you sooner. I'm sorry, Wyatt. I just couldn't find a way."

"You would've told me, Brooke. I have faith in that. I only wish you would've trusted me more. But I get it. We were both raw and cautious from past hurts."

He took her hand and kissed her fingertips. "You have to know, I'm glad about the baby. *Our* baby. It'll be a fresh start for both of us." Wyatt grinned wide, and Brooke's fears were put to rest with that one gesture, that one affirmation of his true love for her.

"I'm so happy."

"So am I." Then he turned to the twins. "Did you hear that, kids? You're going to have a brother or sister one day soon. There's gonna be more little Brandts running around the house."

"It's going to be a madhouse," Brooke said, grinning and picturing it in her mind.

"I can't wait," Wyatt said.

"Really?"

"Really. I'm good with all of it, sweetheart."

Of course he was.

He wouldn't be her miracle cowboy otherwise.

And Wyatt Brandt was that, and so very much more.

* * * * *

If you liked this tale of romance and family,
pick up these other stories from USA TODAY
bestselling author Charlene Sands

HER FORBIDDEN COWBOY
THE BILLIONAIRE'S DADDY TEST
ONE SECRET NIGHT, ONE SECRET BABY
REDEEMING THE CEO COWBOY

Available now from Harlequin Desire!

***

And don't miss the next
BILLIONAIRES AND BABIES *story*
REDEEMING THE BILLIONAIRE SEAL
by Golden Heart award winner Lauren Canan
Available June 2016!

***

If you're on Twitter, tell us what you think
of Harlequin Desire! #harlequindesire

COMING NEXT MONTH FROM

HARLEQUIN *Desire*

Available June 7, 2016

#2449 REDEEMING THE BILLIONAIRE SEAL
Billionaires and Babies • by Lauren Canan
Navy SEAL Chance Masters is only back on the family ranch until his next deployment, but can the all-grown-up girl next door struggling to raise her infant niece convince him his rightful place is at home?

#2450 A BRIDE FOR THE BOSS
Texas Cattleman's Club: Lies and Lullabies
by Maureen Child
When Mac's overworked assistant quits, he's left floundering. But when she challenges the wealthy rancher to spend two weeks not working—with *her*—he soon realizes all the pleasures he's been missing...

#2451 A PREGNANCY SCANDAL
Love and Lipstick • by Kat Cantrell
One broken rule. One night of passion. Now...one accidental pregnancy! A marriage of convenience is the only way to prevent a scandal for the popular senator and his no-frills CFO lover—until their union becomes so much more...

#2452 THE BOSS AND HIS COWGIRL
Red Dirt Royalty • by Silver James
Clay Barron is an oil magnate bred for great things. Nothing can stop his ambition—except the beautiful assistant from his hometown. Will his craving for the former cowgirl mean a choice between love and success?

#2453 ARRANGED MARRIAGE, BEDROOM SECRETS
Courtesan Brides • by Yvonne Lindsay
To prepare for his arranged marriage, Prince Thierry hires a mysterious beauty to tutor him in romance. His betrothed, Mila, mischievously takes the woman's place. But as the prince falls for his "forbidden" lover, Mila's revelations will threaten all they hold dear...

#2454 TRAPPED WITH THE MAVERICK MILLIONAIRE
From Mavericks to Married • by Joss Wood
Years ago, one kiss from a hockey superstar rocked Rory's world. Now Mac needs her—as his live-in physical therapist! Despite their explosive chemistry, she keeps her hands off—until one hot island night as a storm rages...

YOU CAN FIND MORE INFORMATION ON UPCOMING HARLEQUIN® TITLES, FREE EXCERPTS AND MORE AT WWW.HARLEQUIN.COM.

HDCNM0516

REQUEST YOUR FREE BOOKS!
2 FREE NOVELS PLUS 2 FREE GIFTS!

H HARLEQUIN®

Desire

ALWAYS POWERFUL, PASSIONATE AND PROVOCATIVE

YES! Please send me 2 FREE Harlequin® Desire novels and my 2 FREE gifts (gifts are worth about $10). After receiving them, if I don't wish to receive any more books, I can return the shipping statement marked "cancel." If I don't cancel, I will receive 6 brand-new novels every month and be billed just $4.55 per book in the U.S. or $5.24 per book in Canada. That's a savings of at least 13% off the cover price! It's quite a bargain! Shipping and handling is just 50¢ per book in the U.S. and 75¢ per book in Canada.* I understand that accepting the 2 free books and gifts places me under no obligation to buy anything. I can always return a shipment and cancel at any time. Even if I never buy another book, the two free books and gifts are mine to keep forever.

225/326 HDN GH2P

Name	(PLEASE PRINT)
Address	Apt. #
City	State/Prov.	Zip/Postal Code

Signature (if under 18, a parent or guardian must sign)

Mail to the **Reader Service:**
IN U.S.A.: P.O. Box 1867, Buffalo, NY 14240-1867
IN CANADA: P.O. Box 609, Fort Erie, Ontario L2A 5X3

Want to try two free books from another line?
Call 1-800-873-8635 or visit www.ReaderService.com.

* Terms and prices subject to change without notice. Prices do not include applicable taxes. Sales tax applicable in N.Y. Canadian residents will be charged applicable taxes. Offer not valid in Quebec. This offer is limited to one order per household. Not valid for current subscribers to Harlequin Desire books. All orders subject to credit approval. Credit or debit balances in a customer's account(s) may be offset by any other outstanding balance owed by or to the customer. Please allow 4 to 6 weeks for delivery. Offer available while quantities last.

Your Privacy—The Reader Service is committed to protecting your privacy. Our Privacy Policy is available online at www.ReaderService.com or upon request from the Reader Service.

We make a portion of our mailing list available to reputable third parties that offer products we believe may interest you. If you prefer that we not exchange your name with third parties, or if you wish to clarify or modify your communication preferences, please visit us at www.ReaderService.com/consumerschoice or write to us at Reader Service Preference Service, P.O. Box 9062, Buffalo, NY 14240-9062. Include your complete name and address.

HD15

SPECIAL EXCERPT FROM

HARLEQUIN®

Desire

*Mac needs Andi. For work, that is. And when his
assistant quits on the spot to take a much-needed
break, he decides the only way to get her back is to do
whatever it takes to help her out.*

Read on for a sneak peek at
A BRIDE FOR THE BOSS
by USA TODAY bestselling author
Maureen Child, *part of the bestselling*
TEXAS CATTLEMAN'S CLUB *series!*

It had been a long day, but a good one.

Andi was feeling pretty smug about her decision to
quit her job and deliberately ignoring the occasional
twinges of regret. She should have done it three years
ago. As soon as she realized she was in love with a man
who would never see her as more than a piece of office
equipment.

Her heart ached a little, but she took another sip of
wine and purposefully drowned that pain. Once she was
free of her idle daydreams of Mac, she'd be able to look
around, find a man to be with. To help her build the life
she wanted so badly.

Her arms ached from wielding a paint roller, but
working on her home felt good. So good, in fact, she didn't
even grumble when someone knocked on the front door.

Wineglass in hand, she answered the door and jolted when Mac smiled at her.

"Mac? What're you doing here?"

"Hello to you, too," he said and stepped past her, unasked, into the house.

All she could do was close the door and follow him into the living room.

He turned around and gave her a quick smile that had her stomach jittering in response before she could quash her automatic response. "The color's good."

"Thanks. Mac, why are you here?"

"I'm here because I wanted to get a look at what you left me for." His gaze fixed on her and for the first time, he noticed that she wore a tiny tank top and a silky pair of drawstring pants. Her feet were bare and her toenails were painted a soft blush pink. Her hair was long and loose over her shoulders, just skimming the tops of her breasts.

Mac took a breath and wondered where that flash of heat had come from. He'd been with Andi nearly every day for the past six years and he'd never reacted to her like this before.

Now it seemed to be all he could notice.

Don't miss
A BRIDE FOR THE BOSS
by USA TODAY *bestselling author Maureen Child,*
available June 2016 wherever
Harlequin® Desire books and ebooks are sold.

www.Harlequin.com

Copyright © 2016 by Harlequin Books S.A.

HDEXP0516

Whatever You're Into... Passionate Reads

Looking for more passionate reads from Harlequin®?
Fear not! Harlequin® Presents, Harlequin® Desire and
Harlequin® Blaze offer you irresistible romance stories
featuring powerful heroes.

✦HARLEQUIN® *Presents*

Do you want alpha males, decadent glamour and jet-set
lifestyles? Step into the sensational, sophisticated world of
Harlequin® Presents, where sinfully tempting heroes ignite a
fierce and wickedly irresistible passion!

✦HARLEQUIN® *Desire*

Harlequin® Desire novels are powerful, passionate and
provocative contemporary romances set against a backdrop of
wealth, privilege and sweeping family saga. Alpha heroes with
a soft side meet strong-willed but vulnerable heroines amid a
dramatic world of divided loyalties, high-stakes conflict and
intense emotion.

✦HARLEQUIN® *Blaze*

Harlequin® Blaze stories sizzle with strong heroines and
irresistible heroes playing the game of modern love and lust.
They're fun, sexy and always steamy.

Be sure to check out our full selection of books
within each series every month!

www.Harlequin.com

HPASSION2016

Turn your love of reading into
rewards you'll love with

Harlequin My Rewards

**Join for FREE today at
www.HarlequinMyRewards.com**

Earn **FREE BOOKS** of your choice.

Experience **EXCLUSIVE OFFERS** and contests.

Enjoy **BOOK RECOMMENDATIONS**
selected just for you.

PLUS! Sign up now
and get **500** points
right away!

Earn
FREE
REWARDS
Join
Today!
HarlequinMyRewards.com

MYR16R

HARLEQUIN®
A *Romance* FOR EVERY MOOD™

Love the Harlequin book you just read?

Your opinion matters.

Review this book on your favorite book site, review site, blog or your own social media properties and share your opinion with other readers!

Be sure to connect with us at:
Harlequin.com/Newsletters
Facebook.com/HarlequinBooks
Twitter.com/HarlequinBooks